the INGREDIENTS of GOD'S STORY

how cultural context
shapes the way we understand
God, the Bible, and ourselves

John Farwell

The Ingredients of God's Story © 2025 John Farwell

ISBN: 978-1-959544-25-8

The Ingredients of God's Story is a publication of

Phial Press
Austin, TX

This edition printed & distributed through KDP.

Cover image is a composite combining free stock image(s) from Pixabay and other sources, as well as the author's personal image collection. Cover design by Kent Swecker | A New Machine & John Farwell

Publisher's Note: This book's primary ethnographic and geographic focus is on the historic nation of ancient Israel during the 1st century AD and prior. This book does not contain endorsement, criticism, or other commentary concerning the political policies or military actions of the present-day Israeli government.

The views expressed in this book are the author's, and do not necessarily reflect the opinions held by its publisher or editors.

Phial Press is an imprint of Wootton Major Publishing, LLC

www.woottonmajorpublishing.com

To Janie, Tate, Kenslow, and Sadie,

My co-adventurers, who inspire me
& fill my heart with joy... I love you.

the INGREDIENTS of GOD'S STORY

*how cultural context
shapes the way we understand
God, the Bible, and ourselves*

John Farwell

Contents

Resources Available Throughout the Book

My intention is to make this book as interactive as possible. Sparking your curiosity is my goal. I want to encourage you to go exploring, and to help you do so, I've provided additional resources at the end of each chapter for investigating the topic more thoroughly. To assist in this process of exploration, each chapter has prompts and questions for group discussion as well as personal reflection. In the back of the book you will also find a glossary of key terms and a full list of all the cited sources.

Throughout the book, you will find QR codes for various videos. As with other references to supplemental material, these videos are not here due to the endorsement of the videos' producers; I include them because I appreciate the points presented and could not have communicated the concepts any better myself; so why reinvent the wheel? To access them, use your smartphone to scan the code, which should cause the link to the video to appear on your phone. If you do not have a smartphone, the links to the videos are also available in the "Additional Resources" section at the end of each chapter.

Acknowledgements

I would like to acknowledge that I have been blessed to have an amazing, loving and supportive wife. Janie is filled with a heart for adventure, enabling us to live as a family for several extended periods of time in Israel, allowing for this book to be written. I would like to acknowledge my children who have not always been as excited about these adventures as their parents. They have sacrificed much to be a part of this journey. I pray that someday God will weave all those experiences we have shared together into beautiful and meaningful memories. Thank you, Janie, Tate, Kenslow, and Sadie for your love and support. I pray our lives and others are touched by the love of Jesus because of all of our time together living in Israel.

I would like to thank all my professors at Reformed Theological Seminary, Gordon Conwell Seminary, and Jerusalem University College. Especially Dr. Paul Wright for the immense knowledge and wisdom he imparted to all his students while walking the dusty trails in Israel. He made the Bible's geography and poetry tactile, allowing me to *feel along* with those whose stories are contained within.

I would like to thank my editors, Thomas Womack, Sorina Higgins, and Fawn Ellerbrook, who encouraged the completion of this project. Thank you to Jason Smith for publishing this book, and for using your insightful curiosity and grasp of literature to improve it along the way.

I would like to thank the board of Walk the Story for their encouragement: Margaret Head, Bobby Elder, Oday Helal and Craig Sladek. Thank you to faithful friends Will Clark, Eric Wallach, Mike Sigfrids, Cydney Cunningham, Warren Culwell, Daniel Alexander, and Brooke Rychener for being willing to read through many drafts, providing invaluable encouragement and feedback; along with my weekly *Haverims* who are always so encouraging: Brent Glossinger, David Sawyer, Zakk Revelle, Jennifer Huggins, Aaron Fears, Amanda Smith Wiggins, Kyle (Bapo) Roque, Amy Dodd, Ryan Matthews, and Jonathan Van Horn.

Thank you to all our family, friends, Church of the Apostles in Raleigh, Narkis Congregation in Jerusalem, and our faithful ministry partners who have journeyed with us in our ministry endeavors. And thank you to all my fellow Athletes In Action staff whom I've had the privilege of serving alongside over the past 25 years. With their support and encouragement, they have helped me become the person I am today by demonstrating to me the love of Jesus. Thank you to Nicole Ottavi, David & Vicki Daniels, Judy Kirkpatrick, Dave Lower, Shannon Kaney, Eric & April Nelson, Jessica Northenscold, Shane & Coley Kuyper, Jeff Allen, Jim Rumelhart, Doug Pollock, Jason Stankus, Jeff Krieger, and so many more. And to all the players and friends who've join me on adventures in Israel over the past 20 years, this book is a product of many of the stories and lessons experienced with you.

Finally, I thank Jesus for allowing me to experience an incredible life filled with inexplicable grace. I pray others come to experience this same transformational grace, now and forever, by coming to know the reality of His love for the whole world.

Preface

A swirl of snow whipped past my window; it was Christmas time in Michigan. Christmas was always a magical time for me. I loved the scent of my mother's raisin bread coming from the kitchen. On this Christmas, my teenage thoughts began to shift away from the delicious holiday foods, the excitement of Christmas morning, and the anticipation of gifts to more theological ones about the historical and cultural background of Jesus' birth. Most of the images and songs depicting the Nativity present a world very similar to my own climate in winter: cold, snowy, and dark. However, this story's setting is Israel in the Middle East, which for me evokes images of sandy deserts, scorching sun, and camels. As I watched the snowfall, hoping enough would accumulate for a snow day off school, I wondered: What was the first Christmas really like? I was curious about the details of the actual event.

How old was Mary?

Where was Jesus born—in a cave or a stable?

When was he born?

Who were the Wise Men?

These questions about the first Christmas led me on an adventure that ultimately caused me and my family to move to Israel and live there for extend periods of time.

Before moving to Israel, I was delighted to begin my studies at a traditional seminary, which teaches doctrine and theology. The word *theology* means the study of God, with the end goal of acquiring knowledge about him. I enjoyed wrestling through weighty theological issues, but seldom did the topics of the cultural background or historical realities become part of our discussions. Those details and their contexts matter. Theologians mine the Bible for knowledge about God, digging to discover theological gems. Those gems given to us in the Bible crystallized within a unique historical context and culture. The setting and circumstances in which those theological gems formed provide vital information as to the issue God was addressing in real time. Theology is not as straightforward as we'd like it to be.

Scholars debate how those stories in the Bible made their way to us: When, where, and why were they written? Were they edited along the way, and, if so, by whom and why? I admit, I had not anticipated those academic discussions before I began my theological education. I simply wanted to know Jesus better. Unfortunately for me, my seminary studies seldom addressed the original questions that started my journey: I still desired to know more about the historical realities of the Bible and how our understanding of its context impacts theology.

More concerning for me, discovering satisfactory theological answers did not always help me love Jesus and others more. Why? Wouldn't more knowledge deepen my appreciation for Jesus? To answer that, I first have to answer another question: What is the end goal of Biblical scholarship? I believe the ultimate goal of our theological endeavors is to help us become more like Jesus. I know that is a loaded statement, but I believe most of our theological questions, masquerade the emotional needs behind our inquires. By disguising our genuine heartfelt needs in theological language, we attempt to shield ourselves from being vulnerable. What if God doesn't answer? Or what if we receive an answer that is not what we hoped for? How do we process that disappointment? Our theological language provides a buffer to argue with God, the Bible and ourselves. In an act of self-protection, our head and hearts can become disconnected, leaving us emotionally unchanged. Acknowledging what is at stake, to ask honest and vulnerable questions takes courage.

The people in the Bible asked similar questions, as when Job wails, "Why didn't I die at birth?" (Job 3:11) Psalms 42:3 asks plainly, "Where is your God?"

When I discovered reading the Bible in its cultural and historical context, I realized that being human has not changed in four thousand years. God relationally met the people in the Bible's emotional and physical needs within their context. Reading the Bible from this perspective enables me to see I have much more in common with those Biblical characters and their circumstances than I might want to admit. Seeing how God worked in their lives provides me comfort and alleviates some of my anxiety, allowing me to ask more *relational* questions in addition to *theological* ones.

Systematically pursuing knowledge about the Bible academically has a significant role to play in living out a life of faith. The Rabbis around the time of Jesus defined the highest form of worship as *study*, since we have to know who we are worshiping. And the more we know about God, the more we want to worship God—when worship is defined as a whole-life experience—because study ideally begins a cycle of transformation. As I began my studies, I took to heart seeking information about God through the academic process, but that was where I stopped. I became stuck in academic-only mode. A rabbinical statement says: "If you capture the head, the heart may follow, but if you capture the heart, the head always follows." My academic studies of the Bible captured my head, but they did not naturally lead to changing my heart. I was missing the relational heart of God demonstrated throughout the pages of the Bible, calling me to walk with and be like him as a form of worship rather than just knowing about him. Undeterred, I continued to search. I eventually discovered a teacher who approached the Bible academically as well as a historical book about God engaging with real people, in a real time and a real place. He became a mentor and introduced me to Jerusalem University College in Israel, which offers a degree in Biblical History & Geography. Following in his guidance, my family and I moved to Israel. At JUC, I learned to ask different types of questions:

How would the intended audience have understood these stories?

Why are these stories included in the Bible?

What would God want *me* to know and understand, today?

Those were the questions to which I really wanted answers. My focus shifted from mining the Bible for facts and data, to formulating theological conclusions, to seeing all those details as part of God's pursuit of relationship with people. In other words, my persistence paid off.

Understanding the Four Moving Targets

During my studies, I came to realize that the Bible is a dynamic book read differently throughout the ages. Reading the Bible well today requires us to engage with four moving targets. The first moving target is seeking to understand how the original audience would have read and understood what was being communicated within their historical context.

3

How did people read the Bible—or the parts that were available to them—within their own timeframes? The second moving target examines how the New Testament authors connected their writings to the Old Testament to explain and place Jesus within the larger framework of God's redemption plan for the world. The third moving target acknowledges the evolving scholarly process of our understanding of the first two moving targets. Opinions of scholars change over time as we gain new insights through rigorous academic studies and new discoveries through archaeology and textual research.

And the fourth and final moving target? That's *us*.

Let's take, for example, the book of Isaiah. Written to an 8th-century-BC audience in Jerusalem, Isaiah's writings reflect God's communications to those people then, through his prophet. The book of Isaiah is not a time capsule meant only for us today. First, how would Isaiah's words have challenged or encouraged God's people living amid those uncertain times in the 8th century BC? Second, how did the New Testament writers incorporate Isaiah's writings to frame the life and teachings of Jesus within their first-century-AD circumstances? Third, what is our scholarly understanding today of the first two moving targets? Have there been any recent changes in scholarship that impact our answers to the first two questions? Fourth, we are the final moving target. Each day impacts us and changes us in large and small ways; none of us are exactly the same people we were yesterday, nor will we be tomorrow. Therefore, we read the Bible differently each day we wake up and apply our newly acquired information from the previous day.

The place to engage with these four moving targets is what I call the theological kitchen. All Christians work in their own theological kitchens: it's the places where they decide what utensils to use and what information to ingest. Think of your favorite Bible teachers or authors; they all have access to most of the same ingredients, yet each carefully chooses which to include, which to omit, and what proportions to use in their theological delicacies. They are master theological chefs, who understand the ingredients and how they interact with one another and therefore can create exciting new dishes—in this case, new perspectives and insights on the Bible and its application. In contrast, a cook is someone who merely follows a recipe. Many people simply use the recipes of other theological chefs without knowing the purpose of each ingredient or why it was chosen. Depending on the chefs you follow, that can work out well... or not so well. Paul was confident and qualified enough to write, "Imitate me, just as I also imitate Christ." (1 Corinthians 11:1 NKJV) Unfortunately, not every chef putting out recipes is as imitation-worthy as Paul.

This book invites you into the kitchen so you can learn about the ingredients, tools, and methods necessary to become a masterful theological chef. Gaining competence in your theological kitchen is about learning to ask questions and rekindling a curiosity for God, the Bible, and how you fit into the story.

What are the main ingredients that go into these theological recipes? In *Walking the Text*, Brad Gray identifies six major categories (Figure 1).

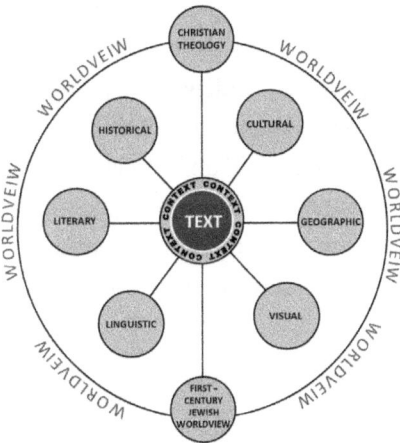

Some are subtle, like literary design, and they are easy to miss unless you are specifically looking for them. Others are more obvious, as with the visual references, but can be obscured because we do not live in the same cultural and geographic environment. Some can be impactful but are left unspoken in the text, as is often the case with historical context. These six elements are examples of ingredients theologians use to create their insights and perspectives.

You might be thinking: How does knowing details (the ingredients) of Biblical geography, archaeology, linguistics, and history help me live a vibrant life of faith in Jesus? In many ways! Understanding the nuance of these details helps provide plausible explanations for what motivations might lie behind the Biblical characters' decisions. It helps to explain cultural interactions and customs. How we read and understand these stories informs our theology and shapes our worldview. The Bible is a collection of stories, recording the history of real people, engaging with a real God, as told to us within

Figure 1: Major Categories of Ingredients in Theological Recipes. Inspired by Brad Gray.

their cultural language, which uses word pictures and other communication methods typical of worldviews very different from our own. My sincere desire for you is that you would begin to read the Bible, from Genesis to Revelation, as a relational book about how God pursues people. My hope is that this book will help you to understand stories that haven't made sense to you before, provide some explanations as models for interpretation, and equip you with tools you can use to decipher Biblical conundrums for yourself.

And who am I, your guide on this culinary journey? Currently, I serve as a country director for Athletes in Action, adjunct professor at Jerusalem Seminary, and executive director of Walk the Story. When I'm not traveling, Raleigh, North Carolina, is my home, where I live with my wife Janie; our three children Tate, Kenslow, and Sadie; and our dog Wrigley (go Cubs!). I earned my undergraduate degree from Purdue University and continued my studies with a Master's degree in Biblical History & Geography from Jerusalem University College. Part of the inspiration for this book comes from the years my family and I have lived in Israel, which brought the Bible to life for me in vivid and life-changing ways. Over the past twenty years, I have had the privilege to walk with people through the land of Israel to experience the Bible in its context. With this book, I extend to you a written version of many of those adventures. Let's step into the kitchen!

Introduction

The past is a foreign country; they do things differently there.

L.P. HARTLEY

It's a dangerous business, Frodo, going out your door. You step onto the road, and if you don't keep your feet, there's no knowing where you might be swept off to.

GANDALF IN *THE LORD OF THE RINGS*

Be Curious

On my first trip to Warsaw's old city, I stumbled upon a quaint restaurant located in a basement on the main square. The smells wafting up the stairs enticed me to investigate. As I entered, the aroma of savory spices filled the air, mesmerizing my senses. Like a cartoon character in a trance following a trail of smoke, my nose led me through a maze of rooms until I eventually found myself standing in the middle of the kitchen. Snapping out of my trance, I suddenly realized I was standing in a place I did not belong. I froze awkwardly, trying to figure out what to do. The chef's eyes caught mine, and he smiled and waved me over to the stove. There, he generously fed me samples of everything he was cooking. That was an amazing moment! I now know how good sauerkraut can taste, thanks to an authentic Polish chef and my ravenous curiosity.

This same hungry curiosity led me to pursue a seminary education. I felt equally out of place there, but I had questions, and it was time to seek some answers. However, attending several different seminaries, earning two master's degrees, and learning a bit about Biblical languages and exegesis did not quell my questions. The most unsettling question was this: *Why am I not experiencing the life the New Testament promises believers?*

I'd hoped more information would lead to deeper intimacy with the Lord; well, it did, and it didn't. Gleaning tremendous amounts of information about God and Jesus helped me to know about him, but I didn't feel like I *knew* him. This led me to pray with heartfelt sincerity: "Lord, I know you, but I want to *know* you." How could I both know him and not know him? My education taught me to appreciate how words carry a cultural weightiness that does not always translate well into English, and one of those words is the Hebrew יָדַע , *yada*, which translates "to know." This nuanced word conveys a much deeper sense of knowing than mere factual head knowledge. *Yada* embodies an experience of someone or something that leads to deep, lived, relational knowledge.[1] When I gained a fuller appreciation of the Hebrew word *yada*, I realized it described my heart's desire: I wanted to *yada* Jesus.

Prescribing more Bible reading to resolve my issue did not feel helpful. I did not need more theological training. I thought: *If Jesus is not actively engaged in the here and now, then all our Christian theology is at best wisdom literature until the eternal life insurance policy kicks in when we die.* The Bible was not the problem. I needed to read it differently, which required me to venture out like Frodo and leave the emotional and intellectual safety of the seminary library. What awaited me to explore was the world of cultural context.

Then it Happened…

No, sorry… probably not what you are thinking. No angelic visitations, voices from heaven, or spiritual epiphanies; however, a specific moment did propel me out of the door of my *Hobbit* hole, onto the road to a journey with Jesus. I was introduced to a video series called *That the World May Know* by Ray Vander Laan. He filmed his lessons on location in Israel. The first lecture, at a place called Tel Gezer, explored that ancient city's Biblical, historical, and geographical context. Ray answered a question I've wrestled with since I was a teenager: "Why did God put his people geographically in the land of Israel?" The answer he offered layered the text with geography, archaeology, ancient Near-eastern global economics, demographics, cultural insights, and more. His explanation was deeply rooted in the realities of the lives of people in the times in which the Bible was written. *This* was what I'd hoped to learn in seminary! *This* was what I desired to understand! You know that satisfying feeling when you have an itch that finally gets scratched? That's what watching that lesson was like for me. My questioning brain finally experienced some relief. I also felt a jolt of hope. Energized and encouraged, I began to read the Bible very differently. Instead of judging and distancing myself from the Biblical characters, I saw myself in them and experienced compassion and empathy towards them. Their struggle to hear, listen, obey, and be faithful became my own struggle—and vice versa. Scratching that agonizing, decades-long itch led to a different way of reading the Bible.

Those who have a similar itch often join me for a few weeks in Israel. Having led groups for twenty years in Israel, I'm often asked if I ever tire of hiking the same locations over and over, teaching the same lessons. I never do, because most people do not realize Hebrew is a concrete language, words imbued with meaning drawn from images in the land of Israel itself, and I see those pictures from new angles every time. The Bible is a word-picture book from Genesis to Revelation. Seeing the actual image associated with a Hebrew word brings that word to life along with the concept it is meant to convey. It is a privilege to be able to lead people through the Land, share these word pictures which connect lingering dots many have had for years, and make the Bible come alive. I feel like a spiritual Santa Claus each day, giving the gift of context that leads to "Aha!" moments. Recognizing context and looking for word pictures are important tools for interpreting the Bible.

I've learned many lessons over the years while walking the dusty trails of Israel, and they have encouraged me to read the Bible with my heart and my head. I'm inviting you to join me as we travel together to a foreign country that may seem quite familiar and bring with you all your lingering questions about the Bible—the ones we don't even ask anymore because we never felt we'd find a satisfactory answer. Let's re-ask those questions and get a little uncomfortable, walking in the sandals of the people of the Bible to *yada* how they experienced God in their life circumstances.

Reading the Bible well, like mastering any craft, requires becoming aware of several different disciplines of Biblical research, each contributing to help create a fuller understanding. In the first half of the book, I hope to awaken in you a renewed sense of self-awareness and wonder about who you are, when you are (your time in history), and how your philosophical understanding of history and communication impacts your ability to read, understand, and thus apply the Bible. This self-awareness begins by acknowledging that you are already in your own theological kitchen (so is everyone else). How well are you cooking?

After the first half helps you gain a general understanding, the second half of the book digs deeply into familiar stories, re-reading them to discover the relational heart of God that can be sometimes buried under our theology. I chose specific stories in which applying these principles greatly deepened my faith while living in Israel. In this second half, we'll see how combining all the ingredients adds flavor to create our conclusions.

Every chef begins their time in the kitchen as a cook, following the recipes of faithful chefs who've gone before them. But if you've ever tried following a recipe precisely, only to have your dish come out not quite as you'd hoped, then you know there is more to cooking than simply following the recipe. The same is true for everyone who picks up the Bible. Great diversity of thought can come from the same passage. The Bible is the recipe for our lives. Not only do we need to read it well, but we also must gain the skills to know how to combine all the ingredients in a meaningful and faithful way. At various times in our lives, we realize that we need to own what we believe for ourselves rather than merely parroting the thoughts and opinions of others with whom we agree. This is the process of becoming a chef who knows what they believe and why they believe it. When we reach this inflection point, that is when our thoughts turn into action—our heads and our hearts begin to sync.

Let's get into the kitchen and start making a mess. I promise it'll be worth it.

SECTION ONE:
The Ingredients

Scholar Krister Stendahl describes how to approach Bible reading in this way: "The task of biblical studies, even of biblical theology, is to describe, relive, and relate, in terms of presuppositions of the period of the texts, what they meant to their authors and their contemporaries."[1] Translation: The best way to understand God's actions, the words of the prophets, and Jesus' life is to put ourselves in their historical and theological context. The Bible covers almost four thousand years of history, recording how God's people adapted over time to meet ever changing circumstances; Jesus' theological understanding and worldview weren't the same as those of Moses, Elijah, or Daniel, nor even of Jews today. God has not changed, but our circumstances have, which impacts how we read and understand the Bible today.

Priming the Pump

"Priming the pump" refers to an old crank handle pump used to draw water out of a well. Often a can of water would be found next to an old pump. Drawing water from the well efficiently required first pouring water from the can into the pump, before one started to crank the handle. In doing so, the water removed all the air pockets which may have formed inside the pump's casing and suction lines. Without taking this necessary step, all your efforts to crank the handle could be in vain. So, let's prime our mental pumps before we begin by asking some questions:

- *What do you believe about the Bible? Is it true? Is it just a story? Is it still relevant today?*
- *Would you say you know God personally or know stuff about Him?*
- *How does studying Scripture help you connect with God?*
- *What do you hope to gain from reading this book?*

1. The Ingredient of Time: Feel the Context

God's story happens within history. If you divorce God from the historical circumstances in which He moved and acted, then you take His words and make them mean whatever you want.

PAUL WRIGHT, PRESIDENT EMERITUS, JERUSALEM UNIVERSITY COLLEGE

For I know the plans I have for you, declares the LORD, plans to prosper you and not harm you, to give you hope and a future.

JEREMIAH 29:11 NIV

The Context of Time

The Bible can be a source of comfort amid difficult circumstances. Jeremiah's famous words prophesied in 588 BC offered hope to the people of Judah: "For I know the plans I have for you, declares the Lord, plans for prosper you and not harm you, to give you hope and a future." Today, this inspiring verse finds itself framed on the walls of homes and inked on bodies as a visual reminder of God's loving heart, transcending momentary struggles, and forging a deeper relationship. Misreading this verse potentially sets us up for tremendous disappointment. If we take this verse out of its larger context and timeline, then we can place unhealthy expectations upon God, misunderstand his intentions, and question his motives. We create the potential to miss seeing how we've created our own discomfort by neglecting our relationship with Him. The context of timing is an important ingredient because of how it flavors our understanding of God and ourselves as we read the Bible.

Let's Go Back to the 6th Century BC

We all interpret history through the lenses of the present, because it is the only set of lenses we own. But how we read and understand the Bible shapes our perception of reality, God, ourselves, and others. Let's go back for a moment to the circumstances surrounding the time of the prophet Jeremiah.

Throughout Israel's history, God sent prophets to call his people to return to a right relationship with him. The Hebrew word for prophet, נָבִיא , *nabi*, comes from the verb to bubble up like a fountain, pouring forth God's word.[1] When we hear the word *prophet*, we often think of someone who predicts the future. However, a Biblical prophet was someone who *poured forth* God's word to cause his people to acknowledge the incongruence between how they were living unfaithfully and the faithfulness called for in God's word. The hope is God's people would repent. If the prophet's efforts failed, then he would predict God would seek to get their attention through unpleasant means.

Let me offer a modern-day example. I am often a "prophet" as a basketball coach, saying things to my players like: "If we don't start playing defense, we're going to lose." No special revelation or insight is required to make this prediction, because the future outcome is easily discernible. Like coaches bawling out unwelcome realities, true prophets of God are often despised for pointing out the people's unfaithfulness. They often lived a solitary, thankless, and even life-threatening existence. According to Jewish tradition, Jeremiah's predecessor Isaiah was sawn in two.[2] Unsurprisingly, the Bible mentions many false prophets who told the people what they wanted to hear, not what they needed to hear.[3]

Scan Here to Watch The Bible Project's Summary of Jeremiah

For years, the leaders and elite of Jerusalem and Judah worshiped the gods of the surrounding nations, took advantage of the poor, and cared only for their personal comfort and security (not the first nor the last time this has happened). For twenty years, Jeremiah poured forth God's pronouncements, attempting to call God's people to repent—no one listened. God then instructed Jeremiah and the scribe Baruch to write down a summary of Jeremiah's message and deliver it to King Jehoiakim, who responded by cutting their scroll into pieces, section by section, and burning them in a fire. (Jeremiah 36) God's message was delivered but not received.

To get Judah's attention, God sent the powerful nation of Babylon to subdue Jerusalem and its leaders. A close reading of the text reveals that the deportation of Jews to Babylon began in 597 BC and would eventually include King Jehoiakim himself. (2 Kings 24) Judah's final rebellion in 586 BC against Babylon resulted in a siege of Jerusalem. Death, starvation, and uncertainty followed, leading to the ruin of Jerusalem, destruction of the temple, and exile of the elite of Judah to Babylon. Jeremiah prophesied that the exile would last seventy years because of their unfaithfulness in their covenant relationship with the Lord. (Jeremiah 25)

Put yourself in the sandals of a person walking the streets of 6th-century-BC Jerusalem, facing starvation due to the Babylonian siege, grieving loved ones who starved to death or were killed, then marching to Babylon as a captive and settling in a foreign land. How painfully disorienting! This person's choices may have contributed to these horrific circumstances because they ignored Jeremiah's warnings, or they could be an innocent bystander suffering along with those responsible. When you gain a sense of the geopolitical realities in which Biblical stories take place, you realize that many of the events that transpire are natural consequences of the choices made by the people involved.

The time horizon of Jeremiah's promise is crucial to having proper expectations of God. Imagine reading Jeremiah's letter after twelve years of living in exile, knowing there would be fifty-eight more. How would you respond? Depending on your age, you might not even live to see his promise come to fruition. Your life of faithfulness would be lived for your children and grandchildren, so they could return to the promised land.

If you are familiar with the story of the Bible, that familiarity can erase any emotional tension you might otherwise feel for these individuals, because you know how the story ends. Maybe you are one of those who likes to read the last page of a mystery novel before you begin. Knowing whodunit lessens the emotional tension as you read. You also clue into details associated with the guilty character that might have otherwise gone unnoticed. Similarly, when reading the Bible, you can be critical of a character's actions, judgmentally thinking, "That would never be me." Or you can escape to the safe haven of theological explanations to justify why the people of Judah deserved what happened to them. Knowing the larger historical timeline, you can see how this horrible moment fits into God's larger redemptive plan. But none of that erases the individual pain of someone who lived through at that time. I wonder what kind of questions might they have been asking of God? When you face painful difficulties, what kinds of questions do you ask of him?

Sometime during those twenty years between the start of the siege and the exile to Babylon, Jeremiah wrote a letter to his fellow Jews already in exile containing those often-misapplied verses of hope: "For I know the plans I have for you, declares the Lord, plans to prosper you and not harm you, to give you hope and a future." God gave this promise to his people as they headed into seventy years of captivity because of their unfaithfulness in their covenant with him. God allowed these events and the seventy years in exile to draw them back to himself, reaffirming his love and faithfulness to his people. The world would see their repentance and restoration back to their promised land, displaying how to live faithfully with God, ultimately leading to the future messiah. Keeping this verse within its cultural and historical timeline leads to a fuller understanding of hope: It is truly defined as *being in right relationship with God, through repentance, leading to restoration.* And it might take seventy years.

God is a relational God. His story is told through his relationship with people, specifically the Hebrews; they were real people, like you and me, who lived in unique times and a set of circumstances in which God engaged them. These real people were not fictional characters contrived to be used as theological props to convey a moral message to us today. When you gain a sense of the geopolitical realities of the times in which Biblical stories take place, you realize the events that transpire are natural consequences of the choices made by the characters involved. To take a verse or their story out of its context could cause us to misunderstand and misapply what God would like us to know about himself and our relationship with him.

God's purposes manifest themselves in his people individually and collectively so that the world can know who God is. This verse offers us hope of relational restoration, after neglecting our relationship with God, so that we can once again participate in God's purposes. The prosperity, hope, and future God promises us is a deeper connection to him, not necessarily a quick fix to our problems that we've created and exacerbated over years. The circumstances leading up to and surrounding the Hebrews' exile and return highlight both where their relationship with God went sideways and the process of their restoration.

Today, God is speaking to us through the specific circumstances in which Jeremiah delivered God's promises. If we take Jeremiah's words out of this larger context or timeline, then we can make his words mean whatever we would like them to mean. In a sense, we can become like a false prophet, telling ourselves what we want to hear. Our wishful thinking may not line up with the actual circumstances we experience later. The disconnect between what we mistakenly understood God's promise to mean and what it really means can be disorienting, even devastating to our spiritual, mental, and emotional wellbeing.

Imagine the alternative: suppose that one day, we experience an exile because of neglecting our relationship with God. The self-inflicted damage we've done to our lives by living unfaithfully might take years to restore. But if we understand Jeremiah 29 in context, we'll realize that the hope and future Jeremiah promises offer us reconciliation to God so that the whole world can see his love displayed through our lives. Knowing that God is playing a long game, hasn't rejected us, and is working patiently to turn our repentance into restoration, puts a whole different perspective on the hardships we go through.

The Ingredient of Humility

Taking one verse out of its historical timeline can have drastic implications. We can misinterpret God's call to repentance and restoration, remaining unchanged. Unfortunately, we are vulnerable to more than taking a single verse out of context; if we are not careful, we can take a whole people group out of context and miss out on all that we could learn from them. But with a little humility, we can even learn from the enemies of God's people. Humility is an essential ingredient for seeing ourselves in the lives of those we read about and learn from their relationship with God in a way that produces genuine transformation.

For example, a people group often cast as antagonists in the Bible are the Canaanites. They are labeled as "pagan" for worshiping Baal, the god of rain and storm—but let's take a moment to seek to understand why the Canaanites worshiped Baal before we pass judgment. Life in the Middle East, then and now, is challenging on its best day and downright impossible on its worst. In biblical times, it didn't take much to tip the scales from life to death. An obvious essential is rain, which in Israel only falls during the late autumn through the winter months and into early spring. These four or five months of rain provide the water necessary to grow barley and wheat. Without it, people will die. End of story. If a drought occurs, few if any places will have excess food to purchase.[4]

Humans worship what we need. The Canaanites worshiped Baal—the god of rain and storm, often depicted holding a lightning bolt—seeking to guarantee rain for their crops and herds. Their worship of Baal sought to make their life more predictable in a very unpredictable environment. We can think this is silly, seeing no correlation between worshiping a god we don't believe exists and his ability to provide rain. However, we do similar things. Do you know anyone who, while watching their beloved team play, crosses their fingers, puts their baseball cap inside out and calls it a rally cap, wears their lucky socks or jersey, and sits in their lucky lounge chair? Intellectually, we know our rituals have no effect on the outcome, yet we do them anyway. We lack any ability to produce our desired outcomes, and yet we want to do *something*—anything!—to give us a sense of control and hope. Behind our self-acknowledged silly superstitions, our hearts seem awfully like those of the Canaanites. Yet we label the Canaanites as unsophisticated pagans. Being human hasn't changed in four thousand years. What *has* changed is only what we think we need to survive and what we think we need to do to get it.

Our lives are equally unpredictable today as we pursue our essentials. What are your deepest needs? Your hopes? Take a moment to consider them and write them down. Our physical needs are easily identified: a job, car, home. Identifying our hopes and desires can be more elusive. What makes you happy or sad? When was the last time you felt deeply disappointed? What would you have liked to see happen? These are helpful cues for getting beneath the surface.

Looking at that list, we'd love to be able to do something to guarantee our desired future outcomes, thus taking away our anxiety and lessening the unknowns of tomorrow. Even as a follower of Jesus, we can unintentionally pursue God like the Canaanites sought rain from Baal. With a greater degree of sophistication, those who believe in God and the Bible can fashion our theology into a tool to make life more predictable and, in a sense, controllable. We think that if we can understand God's rules of how the world works, then we can make choices based on those rules, thus obligating him to respond in a more predictable manner of our choosing. This seeking of controlled outcomes is just repackaged superstition. Inherent in this behavior is a presupposition that we know what is best. However, if we're emotionally honest, we'll admit we are out of control just as much as anyone who has ever walked this planet, including all the people we read about in the Bible.

Emotions are powerful engines that propel us to act. Feeling along with the characters of the Bible, during their timeline, encourages us to learn from their situation and respond appropriately. If you've read through the Bible and are familiar with the stories, your challenge is to set aside the known ending, keeping the characters in their historical timeline amidst their unresolved tensions.

As for the exiles Jeremiah wrote to in Babylon: We know they eventually return to the land. Similarly, we know David eventually becomes king even while reading about him hiding from Saul in a cave. But can we sympathize with them in their times of uncertainty and waiting? Can we feel the pain and confusion with the disciples the day Jesus died on the cross, or do we judge them for not understanding what seems so obvious to us now? We know how those stories end—but at that moment, none of these characters knew it would all work out. Often, their uncertainty didn't resolve the next day. After being anointed king by the prophet Samuel, David was chased by Saul for years before he eventually sat on the throne. Twenty-five years passed between when God promised Abraham a son and Isaac's birth. What is missing from the text of the Bible is *feeling* the time elapse. In one page, an issue can be resolved, but in their lived experience it took years. Focusing on how the stories end, we can miss appreciating the Biblical characters' faithful perseverance (or their lack thereof) in how they responded to living with uncertainty.

Reading the Bible with humility releases grace and compassion to those we read about, but it also allows us to seek and receive grace as well when we recognize we are just like them.

Hope in Things Unseen

It is hard to be patient. Go back and reread the list you wrote of your needs and hopes. Now ask yourself: Are you able to confidently trust God as you wait for him to move in your life? You could be tempted to act like a Christian Canaanite, feeling like you should *do* something to entice God to act on your behalf (read your Bible, go to church, put money in the offering, help someone, etc.). Or you may struggle to believe God will respond, feeling like he's let you down in the past. These are honest feelings, and there are no simple solutions. Keep in mind that one of God's attributes is *mystery*. We are unable to fully know or comprehend his character. This reality is actually a blessing; I do not wish to worship a God I can completely understand, because that would mean he is on my level. I need God to be smarter and more compassionate, loving, and forgiving than I. Knowing (*yada*) that he is a God who loves perfectly allows me to trust him even when I don't understand. This fuels my ability to persevere while trusting in his timing. I learned this from so many Biblical characters who responded similarly, and I would have missed the lesson if I'd taken the Bible out of its historical, cultural, and literary context.

Questions

- How can you see these ingredients shifting your perspective of others and yourself?
- Where in your life are you struggling to trust God? Where might you be holding on to control when God is asking you to let go?
- How might God be using that situation to reconcile you to Himself?
- What is your greatest fear in pursuing God?
- How might your response to God affect not only your life but the lives of others you care about?
- What is a Bible story you'd like to go back and reread now?
- Have you ever wondered if there's more to your relationship with God or your Christian lifestyle? Do you ask yourself the same question I did: why am I not experiencing the life the New Testament promises believers?
- Throughout Scripture, God meets practical needs by stepping into the lives of people right where they are. Take out that list of needs you wrote down one more time, and in humility, ask God to care for you where you need it.

Additional Resources

Gray, Brad: *The #1 Mistake Most Everyone Makes When Reading the Bible*

Rainey, Anson F., and R. Steven Notley: *The Sacred Bridge: Carta's Atlas of the Biblical World*

Richards, E. Randolph, and Brandon J. O'Brien: *Misreading Scripture with Western Eyes: Removing Cultural Blinders to Better Understand the Bible*

Spangler, Ann, and Lois Tverberg: *Sitting at the Feet of Rabbi Jesus: How the Jewishness of Jesus Can Transform Your Faith*

The Bible Project: "Old Testament Overviews > Jeremiah"
https://bibleproject.com/videos/jeremiah

2. The Ingredient of First-Century Culture: *Torah*, *Rabbis*, *Synagogues*, and a Jewish Jesus

> *No one should live without a rabbi,*
> *nor die without making a disciple.*

RABBINICAL ADMONITION

> *On three things the world stands:*
> *on the Torah; on the [temple] cult;*
> *and on demonstrations of piety.*

M. 'AVOT 1:2

Hitting the Reset Button on Jesus

When I travel in a foreign country, the sights, sounds, smells, and tastes provide a constant reminder that I'm not in a familiar place. But over the years of reading and study, I've become so familiar with the Bible that I can forget I'm traveling in a foreign place when I read. I wish the Bible was a scratch-and-sniff book, able to provide supplemental sensory input to remind me that I'm not in North Carolina anymore.

Modern depictions of Jesus can actively hinder our ability to see him in his context. A picture of Jesus hung on the wall of my childhood church. He looked very European: He had pale skin, blue eyes, and the haircut of a kid who plays in a California garage band.

However, Jesus was neither European nor American. The God of the universe entered human history as a Jewish man, living in Judea in the first century AD. Jewish men native to the Middle East then and now typically have olive skin, dark hair, and brown eyes. If I picture Jesus looking like me, I lose one of the sensory inputs that help me keep the story in its context. Seeing Jesus as a Jewish *Rabbi* in Judea during the first century is an essential ingredient.

23

Let's Start at the Beginning

The New Testament reminds me of the first installment of the *Star Wars* saga from 1977, titled *Episode IV: A New Hope*—letting us know that this story starts in the middle of a larger one. Picking up the Bible for the first time, many begin with the New Testament and the story of Jesus. However, God's story told in the Old Testament records more than two thousand years of history leading up to the time of Jesus, so reading the New Testament disconnected from its historical timeline can cause us to miss how Jesus fit within his cultural context. His life, death, and resurrection only make sense when viewing him within the larger chronological story of God's people.

The *Old Testament* is a Christian term for what Jewish people call the *Tanakh*, which is a Hebrew acronym. The *T* is from the word *Torah* תּוֹרָה, the law or first five books; the *N* is from the word *Navi'im* נְבִיאִים, the prophets; and the *K* is from the word *Ketuvim* כְּתוּבִים, the writings, which includes Psalms, Proverbs, Ecclesiastes, and more. Combined, they form the three main sections of the *Tanakh*. I will often use the Hebrew term *Tanakh* to refer to the Old Testament throughout this book as a visual aid to remind us that we are reading a familiar book in its original context.

In addition to the *Tanakh*, two other texts are of great importance, both then and to us today. The *Mishnah*, meaning "study by repetition," also called the Oral Law, records debates between the sages about the *Tanakh*, preserved in writing from about 100 years BC until about 200 AD. The *Talmud*, meaning "study" or "learning", includes both the *Mishnah* and the *Gemara*, the rabbis' commentary on the Oral Law, which was added to up till about 500 AD. These are the primary sources for interpreting Jewish religious law (*halakha*).

Understanding the *Tanakh* is essential to reading the New Testament well. The writers of the New Testament identify Jesus as the promised Messiah by connecting him to Messianic identification markers scattered throughout the pages of *Tanakh*. The New Testament employs over 1600 direct quotations from or allusions to the Old Testament to explain who Jesus was and is.[1] Although it's obvious when I think about it, I still sometimes forget there was no New Testament yet at the time of Jesus. Jesus taught exclusively from the *Tanakh*.

What can be overlooked even more than the *Tanakh* and its role in helping us understand Jesus are the centuries of history leading up to his arrival in the first century AD that are not recorded in the Bible. The quote from the *Mishnah* 'Avot 1:2 summaries well the focus of the devout Jewish practitioners during the life of Jesus: "On three things the world stands: on the *Torah*; on the [temple] cult; and on demonstrations of piety." The four hundred years between the testaments sees a growing emphasis on following *Torah* as cornerstone of Jewish identity. Synagogues begin to be founded and itinerant teachers called *rabbis* emerge as spiritual leaders within the community. The events and circumstances that led to these three elements becoming central to the life of Jesus are often not studied in our churches, because they are outside the history recorded in the Bible. Let's look at a few historical highlights from the four hundred years before Jesus to help us understand his context.

Historical Sweet Spot

When talking about events after the second century AD, a professor of mine used to say, "That is post-interesting." Our focus of studies was the history of the Bible, which ends in the first century AD. Within the larger history of the Bible, the historical sweet spot we are seeking to understand in this chapter is roughly a couple hundred years before and after Jesus. God's relationship with his people begins at Mt. Sinai when they enter a covenant relationship according to the terms outlined in *Torah*. How God's people understand and apply the particulars of *Torah* evolves over time. God never changes, but the circumstances of his people do. For example, the specifics of how God's people worship him adapt: What begins with a portable Tabernacle in the wilderness ends with a permanent Temple in Jerusalem. The Jews living in the first century have fifteen hundred years of history of God engaging with Moses, Joshua, David, the kings of Judah and Israel, the prophets, and the exile and return to the land, to draw upon as they adapt to living under Roman occupation. It makes sense, then, that how a Jewish person in the first century sees the world differs greatly from the way their ancestors saw it while standing at the foot of Mt. Sinai. However, after the Temple is destroyed in 70 AD, the priestly class lose their prominence, and Judaism undergoes a massive restructuring under the leadership of the Pharisees. Judaism moving forward, maintains echoes of its past, but this begins the "post-interesting" era as far as my professor was concerned, and also in terms of understanding the era or version of Judaism that Jesus engaged.

Our historical sweet spot surrounding the first century AD includes some surprising new developments within the life of God's people. During the four hundred years between the end of the *Tanakh*'s recorded history and the writing of the New Testament, *synagogues* came into existence. These were local spiritual hubs for studying *Torah* communally, apart from the temple in Jerusalem.[2] In villages and towns, the *synagogue* (meaning *place of assembly)* was usually the largest building, designed to hold as many people as possible. Serving as a gathering place, they became central to the lives of faithful Jews. The *Torah* scrolls housed there lent these buildings significance, and it is here discussions and debates took place, often led by rabbi*s*, over how to specifically apply *Torah* to people's day-to-day lives.

Synagogues began as what some of us today might call a Bible study. Some scholars regard the book of Ezekiel as the point at which the Jewish faith community began to critically examine the Scriptures while exiled in Babylon. (Ezekiel 33:30-33) There were also Jews in Egypt, particularly in Alexandria, who followed the Greek model of museums and gymnasiums (the forerunners of universities) to maintain their Jewish identity.[3] In Egypt they studied the *Tanakh* in its Greek form, called the *Septuagint*. Scholars suggest that in Israel, these houses of Scripture became central in the lives of Jewish communities towards the end of the third century BC.[4] Today, their ancient ruins dot the countryside of Israel. Scholars assume that most if not every town had a *synagogue*, and possibly more than one. In 2009, a first-century *synagogue* was discovered in the ancient town thought to be the Biblical city of Magdala, home of Mary Magdalene from the New Testament.[5] In 2021, another *synagogue* was unearthed only several hundred feet away. This discovery of a second *synagogue* in such proximity further encourages us to believe that they were essential to Jewish communal life.

Studying *Torah* was so important that even "[w]hen people assembled for joyous occasions such as circumcision or a wedding, a group might withdraw to engage in study of Torah."[6] During his earthly ministry,

Jesus often joined in or initiated these conversations of *Torah* with people in *synagogues*, because people's presence there displayed their desire to learn *Torah* in order to live it out. Addressing this desire, Jesus engaged them in his role as a rabbi, over time becoming one of the most respected rabbis who have ever lived.

None of these elements, which were commonplace in Jewish life by the first century AD, had existed four hundred years earlier. Therefore, our ability to understand Jesus begins with recognizing that he fits perfectly into his cultural context as a rabbi engaging his fellow Jews in and around the *synagogue*, teaching them his perspective on what it means to observe *Torah*.

Jesus stepped into a well-established and sophisticated Jewish worldview culturally, religiously, and politically. The circumstances and history that shaped this worldview are not recorded in the *Tanakh* nor given to us in the New Testament. To understand how the *synagogue* and role of the rabbi developed, let's begin by unpacking key moments of history, beginning with where the *Tanakh* ends. Without understanding this history, it is challenging to fully appreciate Jesus as a rabbi.

The Focus on *Torah*

In Chapter 1, we left off when the Jews of Judah were taken into captivity and brought to Babylon in 597-586 BC. Now, we pick up the story again when the Jews return to their homeland around 538-520 BC. You can read about this specific period in the books of Ezra and Nehemiah. When Jeremiah's prophesied seventy years are complete, thousands of Jews return to Jerusalem, immediately restart daily sacrifices, and begin rebuilding the temple. A little over sixty years later, Ezra arrives and gathers the people so he can read them the entire *Torah*. (Nehemiah 8) This is our first post-exilic reference to a public reading of *Torah*. Ezra calls the people to reclaim their distinctiveness as God's people by obeying his word. Then, thirteen years after that, Nehemiah returns to rebuild the walls of Jerusalem and organize the people.[7] The book of Nehemiah concludes with initiating reforms, purifying the priests, and encouraging the people to keep the *Sabbath*. It almost feels like Nehemiah is herding cats, trying to get the people to keep even the most basic of God's commands like not working on the *Sabbath*. But during this time, Ezra and Nehemiah are planting seeds of individual responsibility for obedience.

To our modern ears, the word *obedience* conveys restriction, confinement, or forced compliance—as in "Obey me or face the consequences." But *relationship* might be a better modern-day translation. Boundaries exist in any relationship: clearly-defined expectations that enable relationships to thrive and be enjoyed. God communicated this kind of expectation to the Hebrews when he said: "If you obey the commandments of the LORD your God that I command you today, by loving the LORD your God, by walking in his ways, and by keeping his commandments and his statutes and his rules, then you shall live and multiply, and the LORD your God will bless you in the land that you are entering to take possession of it." (Deuteronomy 30:16) This is relational language requiring a response, as seen in verses 17-18: "But if your heart turns away, and you will not hear, but are drawn away to worship other gods and serve them, I declare to you today, that you shall surely perish."

The last leaders of God's people recorded in the *Tanakh*, Ezra and Nehemiah, challenge the exiles returning from Babylon to take personal responsibility for their relationship with God by obeying *Torah*. Looking back at the causes of the exile, it would be easy to blame the elites of Judah. However, Ezra and Nehemiah reaffirm each person's responsibility to obey *Torah*, teaching them that individual faithfulness to obey God's covenant impacts the whole community.

At this moment in Jewish history, there is no Davidic king of Judah sitting on the throne. Essentially, these two prophets place the responsibility for spiritual leadership into the hands of individuals. This is where the story of recorded history ends in the *Tanakh* in the land of Judah.[8] Four hundred years later, when the story picks back up in the New Testament, individuals have begun to decide for themselves what it means to obey God in their day-to-day lives. The religious landscape evolved during those four hundred years.

One possible explanation for this development in Jewish society during this time period was individuals' ability to read the *Tanakh* for themselves. Up until the time of the return from exile, people like you and me would not have had direct access to written copies of *Torah*. We don't read in the *Tanakh* about common people having access to these scrolls. The people may have heard it recited or read aloud to them, but direct access seems to have been limited to prophets, priests, and kings. At some point between the return from exile and the second century BC, the *Tanakh* became more accessible. However, the exorbitant cost of owning a complete set of *Torah* scrolls necessitated that a community share one copy. The scrolls were held in local *synagogues*, allowing most people to have direct access to God's word. It was also during this era that the role of a *rabbi*, teacher, began to emerge within Jewish society.

Question of Identity

We do not know exactly how the role of rabbi came into existence or developed over the hundreds of years leading up to the first century. However, we do know that by the time of Jesus, rabbis held an esteemed position in Jewish society. Major developments within a society are usually caused by an event that prompts adaptation. This event for the people of Judah took place a little over one hundred years after Nehemiah, when Alexander the Great conquered Israel in 332 BC, bringing with him *Hellenism*. Hellenism refers to a lifestyle devoted to Greek thought and practices.

Alexander desired to propagate Greek thought and its lifestyle throughout the lands he conquered.[9] He did not force or coerce the local population to adopt his philosophy and lifestyle. Instead, the attraction to Hellenism happened organically over time as Jews lived within Greek-influenced society. To introduce the local populations to Greek philosophy and stories of their gods, Alexander built cities, called in Greek *poleis* (city-states). Designed and constructed with tremendous intentionality, each *Polis* contained four elements: theaters, temples, gymnasia, and arenas. These institutions exposed the local population to their Hellenistic worldview, promoting their virtues and values, many of them counter to those held by the Jews. The Greeks celebrated personal achievement to acquire power and wealth while pursuing sensual pleasure and comfort, with the ultimate end goal of escaping this physical world.

Embracing Hellenism came with economic benefits, because those who learned Greek gained access to greater business opportunities. Judah's neighbors to the north, the Samaritans, embraced the changes Hellenism offered. [10] When they did, Alexander the Great gave them permission to build their own temple on Mt. Gerizim to rival the one in Jerusalem. [11] Their newfound freedoms economically and religiously brought Hellenism to the physical border of Judah.

Although the people of Judah were free to live as they pleased as long as they paid their taxes, the attraction of Hellenism gradually encroached upon Jewish society. We can view the development of the *synagogue* along with the focus on individual obedience to *Torah* and the role of a rabbi as a reaction in resistance to the cultural spread of Hellenism.

This incursion of a polytheistic worldview along with its corresponding morals and ethics necessitated a response by the Jewish community. They debated how to preserve their culture against the attractiveness of Hellenism, asking such questions as: How much of the Greek way of life could and should be adopted? What identifies someone as a faithful follower of *Yahweh*?

Cyndi Parker lists four non-negotiable practices as ethnic identifiers taken from *Torah*: keeping *kosher* dietary laws, performing circumcision, worshiping at one temple in Jerusalem, and observing the *Sabbath* and biblical feasts. [12] *Torah* became the cultural unifier, with the rabbis functioning as one of the main arbitrators of what it meant to be Jewish. Jesus becomes one of those rabbis and is often asked about his opinion on *Torah*.

Rabbis' Interpretations of *Torah*

Every rabbi's goal was the same: to fulfill *Torah* by living it out. Rabbis debated the finer points of interpretation and practice, resulting in the formation of different schools of interpretation, each fiercely defending its position. They functioned as the unofficial spiritual leaders for day-to-day life within the Jewish community, outside of the temple in Jerusalem. In the broadest of categories, rabbis belonged to the very large and diverse group called the *Pharisees*. [13] The *Jerusalem Talmud* identifies seven types of *Pharisee*, referring to the different schools of interpretation. [14]

One is a positive role model, described as a *Pharisee* of love, beloved as a friend of God, like Abraham or Joseph. Other schools possess nicknames reflecting stereotypes about their rigid practices.

Today, if you research the origins of rabbis, the most common understanding you will encounter describes the position formally developing after the destruction of the temple in 70 AD. This period is generally called the beginning of Pharisaical Judaism, referring to the leadership of the Jewish people transitioning from the priesthood of the temple to the religious leaders and teachers known as Pharisees.[15] This account of history is accurate in terms of identifying when the position became official and required ordination. However, teachers of *Torah* who called themselves *sages* or rabbis had a long history leading up to 70 AD. Before *rabbi* became a title of ordination, rabbis were itinerant teachers who traveled with their disciples from village to village, often teaching in local *synagogues* to anyone who cared to come and listen.[16] Revered by their communities for their deep knowledge of *Torah* and the integrity with which they lived out what they believed, rabbis desired to raise up as many disciples as possible to impart their teachings to as many people as possible, even long after their passing.

Two prominent rabbis, Shammai and Hillel, thoroughly influenced the Jewish world of the first century. The next generation of rabbis from these two schools of rabbinical interpretation, such as Gamaliel the grandson of Hillel (Acts 5), held positions of authority within Jewish society during and after the time of Jesus. Their rulings on how to apply Torah were the dominant mainstream opinions by the mid-first century AD.

Shammai lived one generation before the time of Jesus, between 50 BC and AD 30. Conservative in his interpretation, his rigid and stringent application of *Torah* focused on God, not on how his rulings would impact the lives of people. Obedience to *Torah* took priority over practicality. Shammai taught that people will adjust to God's word, not the other way around.[17] Hillel the Elder offered a more practical interpretation. An older contemporary of Shammai, he lived between 110 BC and AD 10. He considered how *Torah* affected people's lives. Brad Young summarizes Hillel's perspective, suggesting he might have said something like: "*Torah* was made for man, not man for the *Torah*." To obey *Torah* meant a life of freedom and joy, not strict observance that became burdensome.[18] Hillel developed principles of interpretation and arrived at conclusions that Jesus often used himself, and these principles are still used today within Jewish theological circles. Hillel was also known to display patience and kindness toward both Jews and Gentiles.

Both men produced large numbers of disciples who became rabbis themselves. Jesus would debate with these disciples, whose teachings often aligned with Hillel and only rarely reflected Shammai's interpretation.[19] The massive influence of these two rabbis is preserved in the *Talmud*, with more than three hundred intense debates recorded between the houses of Hillel and Shammai. The sheer volume of recorded exchanges between these two schools, continuing long after both rabbis had died, provides evidence for the impact of Hillel and Shammai on Jewish life in the first century AD.

Each rabbi strongly believes his interpretation of *Torah* is the only way for a faithful follower of *Yahweh* to fulfill God's command "to love God [...] by walking in his ways, and by keeping his commands and his statutes and his rule." (Deuteronomy 30:16) This mindset of searching for what they believe to be God's desired application of *Torah* led to heated discussion between differing schools of rabbinical thought. Disciples of Hillel and Shammai often confronted Jesus, challenging him on his understanding and application of *Torah*. Many contentious exchanges between them fill the Gospel accounts. Knowing some of the positions of Hillel and Shammai, we have insight into these nuanced debates. These exchanges often conclude with Jesus focusing on the inner motivation and heart intention behind one's actions, rather than on the specific application of *Torah* itself. (Matthew 15:11-20)

Live Like your Rabbi

Jesus lived his earthly life like his rabbinical contemporaries. A section of the *Mishnah* called "Ethics of the Fathers" prioritizes raising up disciples, which requires master teachers.[20] *Talmid* תַּלְמִיד is the Hebrew word for *disciple*—which means "learner"—one who literally repeats the actions of his teacher. No rabbi ever said: "Do what I say and not what I do." A disciple's understanding comes from his lived experience of following his rabbi's example. Raising up disciples was the means to spread their brand of obedience. One could determine a person's beliefs and which rabbi he followed by observing how he kept *Torah*, since different rabbis taught different interpretations and practices. Most often a rabbi's students would begin as teenagers, males in particular, with a passion to learn to live their lives like their rabbi.[21] The goal of a disciple was not to know what the rabbi knew, but to be like their rabbi in his walk with God. This is an example of how Judaism stresses action more than belief, because belief informs actions.[22]

Rabbis viewed their way of observing *Torah* as the only way to fulfill God's command. All other interpretations were deemed to be *abolishing Torah*, which is a rabbinical phrase referring to a wrong interpretation of *Torah* (in their opinion), leading people away from fulfilling God's commands. For example, they debated the definition of work and its implications for *Sabbath* day observance, when and how to wash hands, and many other issues involving ritual purity.

Rabbis vehemently argued with each other, driven by the belief that a wrong application of *Torah* would have drastic consequences. They also built fences around *Torah*: protective buffers between the specifics of a command and its application in practice. Their purpose was to enable people to avoid inadvertently violating *Torah*. The first recorded "fence" comes from Moses himself in Exodus 19. In preparing the people to receive *Torah* as a community, God commanded Moses to tell them to consecrate themselves and wash their clothes in preparation for the coming third day. (Exodus 19:10–13) Moses added to what God commanded, telling the people to refrain from having sex for these three days as well. (Exodus 19:15) When Moses added to what God required, he aimed to protect the literal command by adding more stringent expectations. If someone broke the fence of additional requirements, they hadn't broken God's specific command. Debates between the different rabbinical schools are recorded in *Mishnah* and *Talmud*—what Jewish tradition calls the *Oral Law*. These books are held by Jews to be inspired by God on par with *Torah* itself. Justification of holding the *Mishnah* in such esteem comes from Leviticus 26:46—"These are the decrees, the *laws*, and the regulations that the Lord established on Mount Sinai between himself and the Israelites through Moses." (emphasis added) The plural use of the word *laws* led the rabbis to conclude that God gave both the written and oral *Torahs* to Moses at the same time.[23] The *Mishnah* and *Talmud* also contain *midrash*, a Hebrew word that describes what we would call a sermon or an explanation of Scripture. Jewish *midrash* employs well-defined principles of hermeneutics to unravel a deeper meaning of the sacred text for the purpose of intensifying *Torah*.[24]

Of all the Jewish groups, only *Pharisees* were known to have disciples, which leads us to believe Jesus would have been viewed by his fellow Jews as a *Pharisee* himself. He challenged other rabbis' interpretations of *Torah* as an insider, neither condemning nor commending them for what they taught, but questioning their ability to practice what they preached.[25] To challenge the status quo of accepted interpretations and practices, Jesus offered his own interpretation regarding the heart behind issues such as hand washing, ritual purity, healing, and work on the *Sabbath*.

As an outsider, it's easy for me to dismiss the value of the oral law (which was the socially acceptable understanding at the time of how to apply *Torah* to a given situation); however, Jesus understands the value and importance of the oral traditions. He does not go out of his way to offend and only challenges the oral law when he feels it is too stringent in its application. For example, when he heals on the *Sabbath* day, he follows the oral law requiring healing by word and not touch.[26] Even then, the other *Pharisees* are furious and want to kill him for violating the command against working on the *Sabbath*. (Mark 3, Luke 2, Matthew 12) Undeterred, Jesus remains steadfast in his commitment to live in faithful obedience to the Father and show others how to as well. He wasn't seeking to intentionally offend the *Pharisees* or anyone else. If offense was taken, he taught his disciples to turn the other cheek.

Following a rabbi requires a deep level of commitment and trust in their theology and their practice. Disciples had to be willing to receive insults, verbal abuse, and even physical harm to live out what they truly believed. It was very important to choose your rabbi wisely—just as it is for us today.

The Ingredient of Jesus, the Jewish Rabbi

Seeing Jesus as a first-century rabbi was a major reset for me. Understanding what it meant to be a disciple of a first-century rabbi has massive implications. For instance, it causes me to reconsider what Jesus meant when he invites the disciples to "Come, follow me." As with the disciples then, Jesus is inviting us now to live like him, not just know what he knows.

Growing up, I was taught to believe in what Jesus taught, but if I actually did any of it, that was a bonus. I know now recognize that that perspective was basically Hellenized—it framed Jesus just as we would a Greek philosopher who extolled great ideas. But that understanding is not the Jewish Jesus. To be a disciple of Jesus is to ask this question:

If what we believe doesn't change how we live, do we really believe it?

This question is at the heart of what it means to love God with all your heart, soul, and strength. (Deuteronomy 6:5) Therefore, the ingredient of Jesus being a Jewish rabbi in the first century is the most important flavor of the entire dish.

Questions

- How does seeing Jesus as a Jewish rabbi change your perception of him?
- Knowing the expectations of a first-century disciple, does this challenge and/or enrich your understanding of what it means to be a disciple of Jesus? Would you consider yourself a disciple of Jesus today?
- Are there any stories or interactions you've read between Jesus and others that make more sense now that you know how strongly rabbis held their interpretive positions?
- Why do you think there is a disconnect between what we believe and how we live?
- Have you erected any spiritual "fences" to help you live faithfully? Have they helped you or tempted you more? Who in your life reminds you about God's grace when you break through your "fences"?
- Considering our deepened understanding of what it means to be a disciple, are you being discipled by someone that is pointing you toward the way of Jesus?
- Consider your answers to the questions above, and take time to pray about any adjustments you may need to make.

Additional Resources

Athas, George. *Bridging the Testaments: The History and Theology of God's People in the Second Temple Period.*

Moseley, Ron. *Yeshua: A Guide to the Real Jesus and the Original Church.*

Tverberg, Lois, and Ray Vander Laan. *Walking in the Dust of Rabbi Jesus: How the Jewish Words of Jesus Can Change Your Life.*

Walton, John H., and J. Harvey Walton. *The Lost World of the Torah: Law as Covenant and Wisdom in Ancient Context.*

Young, Brad H. *Meet the Rabbis: Rabbinic Thought and the Teachings of Jesus.*

3. The Ingredient of Responsibility: Our Source Material

You will be the same person in five years as you are today except for the people you meet and the books you read.

CHARLIE "TREMENDOUS" JONES

The Bible was meant to be a conversation.

TIM MACKIE, THE BIBLE PROJECT

Checking the Source

The Bible is the bestselling book of all time, and the most famous. When you hear the word *Bible*, what is your first thought or emotion? Is it reverence, fear, curiosity, boredom, confusion, apathy, invigoration, or possibly disdain? All those feelings are real, and I have felt many of them myself at times. If you grew up in a church environment, the Bible may evoke a deep sense of reverence. Maybe you respect it even if you don't always understand it.

The word *Bible* itself: It comes from the Latin word for *book*, referring to a time when each book of the Bible was written on an individual scroll.[1] These books were collected and bound together in what we now call the Bible. Written over a two-thousand-year span of time, the Bible relays how God's relationship with the Hebrew people became the conduit through which the whole world could come to know and understand who the God Most High is: his nature, character, and purpose.

In academic contexts, scholars debate how and when the Bible was originally written and who edited it along the way. Don't be fearful of these discussions; they are helpful and necessary for us to appreciate how the Bible made its way to us today. Language evolves over time. Just as I'm not writing this book using sixteenth-century Shakespearean *thees* and *thous*, the Bible's composition spanned two millennia in languages (primarily Hebrew) that were continuously changing and developing, all the while maintaining its sacred identity and purpose as God's word.

The Bible's Journey Back to Us

Let's pick up where we left off in the previous chapter, around 70 AD. Understanding this history will provide perspective and help you to appreciate the freedom you have, to read the Bible for yourself today. The first great Jewish revolt against the Romans marked a turning point within the world of Judaism when the second temple was destroyed by the Romans. Without the temple and its priesthood, Jewish identity coalesced around the surviving Pharisees and their interpretation of *Torah* (the five Books of Moses; also called the Law). The Jewish people continued to enjoy favored status within the Roman legal system because they were an ancient religious group. Early on, the first followers of Jesus (who called themselves followers of "The Way" (Acts 9:2; 22:4; 24:14) or *Nazarenes* (Acts 24:5)) fit comfortably into the diverse world of Judaism. Slowly, animosity and resistance grew among the traditional Jews against those Jews who reinterpreted the *Tanakh* (the books that Christians today call the "Old Testament") based on Jesus being the resurrected Messiah. Eventually, the larger Jewish community pestered the Romans to distinguish between ancient Judaism and this new sect, who followed their rabbi Jesus' interpretation of *Torah*, arguing that Messianic Judaism was a new religion and thus should not receive protected status by the Romans. Rome agreed and labeled the followers of Jesus as such, leading to the eventual persecution of the early church.

In its infancy, the early church was thoroughly Jewish in its orientation. Separating from mainstream first-century Judaism into a distinct group later called *Christians* was a slow process that took place over several hundred years. At key moments, clear lines were drawn. In AD 132, a man named Simon bar Kokhba (meaning "son of a star" in Aramaic) claimed to be the Messiah and led a revolt against Rome. The followers of Jesus didn't join their fellow Jews in this fight, for obvious reasons. Rome's Emperor Hadrian quelled the rebellion, utterly dismantled the city of Jerusalem, and expelled the Jews.[2] At this time, the first non-Jewish person assumed leadership of the church of Jerusalem.[3]

Numerous other historical realities that added to this gradual separation between traditional Judaism and the new Christianity. No longer legally tethered to Judaism and its protected status under Roman law, the followers of Jesus were forced to spend the next few centuries as an underground faith community.[4] Not until 313 AD, when Emperor Constantine issued his Edict of Milan declaring Christianity a legal religion, did Christianity emerge as a major player in the public eye. Much later, after their schism in 1053, the Roman Catholic and Eastern Orthodox churches became the two streams of ancient Christianity. Other, smaller groups existed with their own unique theological traditions, but their histories are not as well preserved.

Controlling a narrative is important to any institution. Over time, as the center of Christianity moved westward towards Europe, access to the Bible was eventually controlled by church leaders who supervised the production of hand-copied manuscripts in Latin. The official interpretation of Scripture reverted into the hands of a few, as the general population either lacked direct access to a copy or could not read Latin.

As one would expect, the church emerged as a political player on the world stage. Christianity became a banner to rally under, a tool for shaping public opinion, and a means for motivating the masses to action. Voices of influence were limited to the educated elite in powerful positions within the church. Theological and doctrinal pronouncements were formed by those within these inner circles, then disseminated to the masses. Dissenting views weren't tolerated, and those who dared oppose the church on any issue paid a price. For a thousand years or more, direct access to the Bible was scrupulously mediated by the priesthood.

Opening the Floodgates

The dam holding back the Scriptures from the masses began to fail when one man, Martin Luther, started asking questions. On October 31, 1517, he nailed his ninety-five theses (points for scholarly debate) to the door of All Saints' Church in Wittenberg, Germany. He hoped to spark a healthy discussion reevaluating some of the teachings and practices within the Catholic tradition. Instead, he unintentionally birthed what's called the Protestant Reformation—the word *protest* becoming the basis of the label *Protestant*.

One of Luther's next endeavors was to translate the Bible into German. By translating the Bible into the regional vernacular, it became accessible to anyone who could read their own language, not just Latin. Moreover, the invention of the printing press 150 years earlier allowed for mass distribution of copies of the readable German Bible, opening the floodgates for a diversity of theological thought and practice. As with the Pharisees many centuries before, heated theological debates exploded, especially over issues related to baptism and the eucharist, resulting in deadly confrontations between differing groups of reformers—all because individuals could now decide for themselves what they believed, since they had access to the Bible in their native language.

Now that the Catholic church was no longer the sole arbiter of doctrine, other religious institutions began to disseminate their theological worldviews. But just as the Catholic church had done, these new churches also enacted restrictions and consequences for questioning *their* theological conclusions. Less than a century after Luther's death, groups of religious refugees from Europe came to what is now the Northeastern United States to escape oppression from various churches and church authorities. In this New World, those who risked their lives crossing the Atlantic said, in essence: "No one will tell us how we're to live—not the institutional church, and especially not the head of the Church of England." Later, their descendants rebelled against King George IV and any form of self-appointed leadership, religious or secular, leading to a tremendous diversity of theological thought.

Today, the Christian landscape around the world is filled with countless denominations, new church movements, parachurch organizations, independent churches, etc. Anyone with a Bible can attract a crowd, start a church, gather a following, publish a book, write a blog, or preach on a street corner. Unfortunately, we still kill each other over theological issues—though in the United States we mostly only kill people's reputation when we disagree.

The Bible in the Hands of 19ᵗʰ-Century Scholars

Just as the Reformers sought to break free from the Roman Catholic theological worldview, so some scholars and thinkers desire to be unshackled from the Bible as the primary source by which to interpret and understand our world. The Age of Enlightenment embraced the philosophy of empirical science to pursue what they believed to be our highest virtue—human happiness—without necessarily being tethered to the Bible.

During the centuries leading up to this moment, the church had defined the acceptable positions to hold on every aspect of life: social norms, religious doctrines, and even our understanding and explanation of the natural world. But during the seventeenth century, philosopher Francis Bacon developed *empiricism*. The empirical method of research makes use of observation to come to its conclusions, and this method of research was soon applied to how we know and study the Bible. The nineteenth century provided plenty of newly observable information pertaining to the Bible as a frenzy of archaeological research began across Israel, Greece, and Turkey. This new data, combined with research into language, geography, and history raised many questions, exposing gaps in our understanding of the Bible's historicity. Not all the details lined up perfectly, which led to more questions.

The empirical method seeks a blank slate to allow observation to guide the process of discovery. Applying the empirical method to the Bible necessitates wiping away any assumptions one might have about the Bible and begin by reading and researching it like any other ancient historical document. However, removing one's bias completely is impossible. Naturally, some hoped to reaffirm their long-held beliefs about the Bible, while others researched with a heightened degree of scrutiny, and in some cases overt skepticism. They both sought answers to the same question: "Does the Bible contain accurate factual historic and scientific information?" In our modern language, we would ask: "Is the Bible true?"

One approach to resolving discrepancies found in the Bible was to assume the original text was accurate but then, over time, errors crept into the copies. This question leads to more foundational ones: "How did the Bible get to us, and does it accurately preserve the original documents?" These questions seek to discover whether the gaps we observe are due to transmission, copying errors, or some other cause.

Western application of the empirical method often involves taking things apart to understand them, observing the parts which make up the whole. This same approach when applied to the Bible is called *deconstruction*. I realize this word today can have a negative connotation. Some well-known Christians with large social media influence have publicly "deconstructed" their faith, explaining why they no longer believe in God or the Bible. Their stories are heart-breaking and often complicated, and so is the process of deconstruction. Yet every beautiful renovation begins with a deconstruction, so it is helpful to know the motivation behind someone's decision to deconstruct their faith. Are they deconstructing to renovate or simply to tear down?

Biblical deconstruction begins with the words that make up the Bible itself. Exploring the transmission of the Bible from one generation to the next is called *lower textual criticism*. Such textual research asks: "Is the copy in my hands today the same as the original?"—a basic question that leads to many other, more nuanced ones. Critical scholars suggest that if they could prove the Bible had been edited over the centuries, then this editorial process would open a whole new set of questions, including: "Who did the editing?" and "Why did they feel the need to make these edits?" The answers to these questions become fodder for all kinds of speculation as to the copyist's intentions and motivations.

As I suggested in the beginning of this chapter, editing the Bible over two millennia should be expected. The language alone would need to be updated to communicate effectively over such a large swath of time, as well as specific references such as the names of locations; a copyist might have to update a city's name to reflect their current situation. For example, in Genesis 14:14, Abram travels north to rescue his nephew Lot. The location mentioned where the rescue takes place is called Dan. There's one small problem: At the time when this event took place historically, the location's name was Laish. (Judges 18:27) The city's name changed when the tribe of Dan moved north: they left the land allotted to them by Joshua, captured the city of Laish, and renamed it Dan. (Judges 18) This name change happened at least five hundred years after Abram rescued Lot. Conclusion? A copyist working *after* the time described in Judges 18 probably made this edit to the text of Genesis 14 to help people understand where Abram traveled within their geographic reality.

Other critical scholars question the intentions of the editors, asking: "Were the edits made to make a particular group look better or worse? Is the Bible merely theological propaganda? If so, why and for what purpose?" For those with a more critical view of the church, Christianity, or religion, this line of questioning opens up the possibility to look at every identifiable edit and hypothesize about the motives for making such an edit. Acknowledging the editorial process over the centuries, some conclude we do not have a reliable copy of the Bible reflecting the original in part or whole. They might ask: "How did each edit impact church doctrine at the time of the edit's insertion? Who or what motivated these particular edits? What impact did these edits have on the larger society?"

Lower textual criticism has a counterpart called *higher textual criticism*, which seeks to answer some of the questions raised above. This criticism asks the question: "What did the text mean to the original audience and subsequent generations within their historical context, and how did their understanding at that time influence their worldview?" These are important questions for historians to ask, as well as for us today as we are making history.

Our concern is not when empirical science observes conundrums within the Bible—plenty exist. Instead, we care how one assigns intent and motivation to why they exist in the first place. If you've ever watched a program on the History Channel, then you've probably heard critical scholars openly challenge the historicity of the Bible as unreliable and even going so far as to say the Bible contains myths, in part or whole. For example, when former Catholic priest John Dominic Crossan was interviewed as an expert by the producers of a History Channel documentary exploring Jesus' resurrection, he firmly tells the audience that at Jesus' crucifixion, his body was thrown into a common grave, and he did not resurrect.[5] Before the proliferation of the internet, critical voices like these challenging the historical veracity of the Bible were commonplace on mainstream media. Today, many more voices have joined the conversation—some are experts, and some are not.

Critical scholars presented as historical experts are very smart, well-educated, confident in their opinions, and can be very persuasive at times. They often ask uncomfortable questions. As followers of Jesus who hold the Bible to be God's word, we can't be afraid to ask or explore questions, especially about the Bible. Plenty of intelligent, reasonable, and credible answers exist that affirm the Bible's authenticity and reliability as God's word. When someone raises these kinds of questions, it's helpful to clarify: "Why are you asking?" Are they seeking information or confirmation? In other words, have they already made up their mind, and they are looking only to affirm what they already believe? Or are they honestly looking for information they don't already have? Or maybe the question making you uncomfortable is your own! Why does it make you feel that way? Are you nervous about what you might discover? Are you willing to consider the evidence and accept, even for the sake of argument, the possibility of an answer you don't like or don't want to be true?

Fear of hearing an opinion that challenges a strongly held belief is real. When this happens, the amygdala in our brains can fire, producing a flight-or-fight response as if we were being chased by a bear.[6] Knowing this, it's understandable why we avoid confronting challenging topics and uncomfortable possibilities. But when the issue literally defines the foundation of our reality, such as the Bible, sometimes we've got to face the bear.

An emotional bear attack might be an event or question that causes a crisis of faith, challenging our understanding of God and the Bible, cornering us, forcing us seek answers to questions we've been avoiding. Our pursuit of answers can drill down to asking things like, "do we even have reliable copies of the Bible?"

Deconstructing the Bible to better understand it is not the problem. In fact, deconstructing is often a necessary ingredient for growing in our maturity and owning our beliefs—to "take hold of that for which Christ took hold of us." (Philippians 3:12) What matters is how we put the individual pieces of our understanding back together again.

A chance discovery in the wilderness of Israel helps us understand those pieces and increases our confidence in the Bible we have today.

Why the Dead Sea Scrolls Matter

Remember our historical sweet spot for our understanding of Jesus are the two centuries before and after him. An important question to ask is, "Can we know if the *Tanakh* we have in our hands today resembles the one Jesus would have read?" It's been two thousand years—surely edits took place!

Before 1948, the oldest complete copy of the Old Testament we possessed was the Leningrad Codex, dated to 1008 AD. [7] That's a thousand years removed from Jesus. Was the Bible altered in its transmission from the first century to 1008 AD? This one question contains both higher- and lower-textual-criticism questions. We need to be reading the same words of the *Tanakh* as Jesus to begin to try to understand how people in the first century understood and applied them. I believe we have reason to be confident that reliable transmission took place over the centuries, but it was a messy process.

The debate between those scholars who believe we possess reliable copies and those who don't was rekindled by an amazing discovery in 1947. Around the end of the first century BC, the ancient site of Qumran— an inhospitable, desolate, rocky scarp sandwiched between the foothills of the Judean Mountains and the undrinkable water of the Dead Sea— became home to a group of people identified by the Jewish historian Josephus as the Essenes. [8] Annual rainfall there is scarce to nonexistent. Why choose to live is such a desolate place? The Essenes were priests who left Jerusalem about 130 years before Jesus to protest the corruption, greed, and lack of pure spiritual focus they observed within the priesthood and its leadership. Desiring to live a life dedicated to embodying God's commands, they chose to settle in a place which they believed reflected Isaiah 40:3— "In the desert, prepare the way of the LORD." Living in isolation, they focused on studying Scripture, seeking to live a life of faithfulness to Yahweh as they awaited the arrival of the Messiah, whom they believed would reinstate them in their rightful roles as priests in the temple in Jerusalem. [9] One of their main tasks was copying and preserving *Tanakh*, a painstaking process. The scrolls they produced were eventually buried in caves in the surrounding hills.

Fast forward to 1947, when a shepherd was throwing rocks, attempting to move his flock, and an errant throw produced the sound of something breaking in a hillside cave. Investigating, he discovered a broken, ancient clay vessel containing scrolls written in Hebrew. These scrolls were produced at various times over hundreds of years, dating from the third century BC—copies the Essenes presumably brought with them from Jerusalem—and on into the first century AD—copies the Essenes made themselves. Archaeological excavations eventually revealed eleven more caves with pieces of almost a thousand manuscripts of various kinds, about one-fourth of them being biblical scrolls.[10] Partial or complete copies were found of every book of the Old Testament except Esther.[11] Some were written in Paleo-Hebrew, the Hebrew script from before the First Temple period (1000-586 BC). Scholars compared the texts of the Dead Sea Scrolls to the much later Masoretic texts and found them remarkably similar despite the thousand-year gap between them.[12] As a result, we can say with confidence that the Old Testament in our hands today is very similar to the one Jesus would have read.

Deviations do exist between the Hebrew texts—remember, language is always evolving! Differences in spelling and word order should be expected, given the constant changes in how we use language. Additions and deletions in certain texts have led scholars to conclude that the copyists felt the freedom to make limited modifications to the texts as they copied them, attempting to clarify certain aspects for their contemporary audiences. However, the process of transmission is not as clean as we'd like it to be. For example, you may have noticed that in the book of John, Chapter 5 (the story of Jesus healing the paralytic at the pools of Bethesda), your Bible most likely has brackets or a footnote around verse 4. The brackets denote a section that is not in the oldest known manuscript but is in subsequent ancient copies. The best explanation is that the person who produced the later copy added information, attempting to help the reader understand the motivations for the paralytic to be at the pool. Similar examples are found throughout the Gospel accounts. Such scribal additions have been identified by lower criticism and do not necessarily affect higher criticism.

Furthermore, additional scrolls have been found north of Qumran in caves called the Bar Kokhba caves.[13] Many types of documents were found, including biblical manuscripts. These scrolls provided valuable information for lower textual criticism because these copies also very closely matched the Masoretic copies made nine centuries later.

Scholars Questioning the New Testament

Applying this same scrutiny to the New Testament, how do we know with confidence that what we read today accurately reflects the original texts from two thousand years ago? Bart D. Ehrman sets out to answer this question in his book *Misquoting Jesus*. In the introduction, Ehrman gives us insight into his motivation for pursuing this project. He shares that the New Testament manuscripts "made a real difference to me emotionally and intellectually, to my understanding of myself, the world I live in, my views of God, and the Bible."[14] However, if it could be proven that the original texts of both the Old and New Testament have been significantly altered over the centuries, he says, such textual editing would call into question the Bible's authority, eroding its trustworthiness and undermining its ability to inform us about God.

Ehrman understands the Dead Sea Scrolls infused new confidence in conservative Biblical scholarships to counter the major concerns of lower textual critics, although, as with John 5 and similar New Testament texts, questions remained about scribal editing (whether intentional or unintentional). Ehrman applies the same critical approach to the thousands of ancient New Testament manuscripts in existence. The sheer volume of New Testament manuscripts—thousands more than any other ancient text—aids scholars in identifying scribal anomalies between the various texts to discover their original form. Ehrman cites scholarship identifying almost 400,000 variations; however, these include mere misspellings, updated spellings, and inverted word order. [15] He acknowledges that most of the differences between the texts are immaterial and insignificant, and he knows that his stringent methodology would disqualify any ancient document from being verifiable. His rationale for such a strict methodology is based on his concept of the Bible as God's *inerrant* word. He lays out his argument:

It was the words of Scripture themselves that God had inspired. Surely, we have to know what those words were if we want to know how he had communicated to us, since the very words were his words, and having some other words (those inadvertently or intentionally created by scribes) didn't help us much if we wanted to know His words.[16]

Ehrman's logic makes sense, given what's at stake. For him, *inerrancy* not only refers to the factual information contained in the Bible but also to the transmission of the words themselves.

Similarly, renowned theologian and scholar Wayne Grudem states: "Inerrancy simply means that *the Bible is without error*. It's a belief in the total truthfulness and reliability of God's words."[17] Thus, any error found in the Bible would reflect poorly on God's character. In this view, potential errors would include both textual cohesion and historical and scientific information contained within the Bible. Because God knows all, for all time, any mention of history or the natural world must match our current scientific understanding (setting aside for a moment the reality that scientific knowledge is continuously being updated as our understanding of the natural world increases). If we claim the Bible is inerrant according to Ehrman and Grudem's way of thinking, and if any aspect of the Bible can be proven to be false in its presentation of facts, then that error would call the whole Bible into question.

We are keenly aware how our understanding of our world has grown over time. When a discrepancy is discovered between the Bible and our current understanding, fault is often levied against the Bible. However, one possibility is that our current scientific interpretation could be off and not the Bible. Or again, when trying to verify some historical aspect of the Bible, such as locating a particular town that has yet to be discovered archaeologically—a refrain I heard often during my studies in Israel was: "The absence of evidence doesn't mean the evidence is absent." The evidence could be waiting to be discovered.

What Ehrman wants are the words of God: not copies of copies, but the original autographs, to ensure accuracy. Without them, the conclusions drawn by higher criticism are called into question. Any scholar would say this is an unfair expectation for any historical document. But this is God's word, not just any document.

We will examine more closely in the next chapter what led Ehrman to follow his line of reasoning as I'm sure he is not alone in his thinking. I've had some of the same thoughts myself.

The Ingredient of Responsibility

The Bible is a dangerous book. People's interpretation of the Bible has been used to justify all kinds of horrific behavior: wars, slavery, and many other forms of injustice. However, without the Bible, we also would be severely limited in our ability to know God, who defines love, joy, peace, patience, kindness, goodness, gentleness, and self-control. Our moral standard would be driven by our human intuition alone and defined by those with the power to impose their values upon others. The weak would inevitably be crushed by the strong. What stands in the way of this becoming our reality 24/7 is people who know and love God and choose to live like him based on how they read the Bible. God and his word stand in opposition to the unjust ways of the world. That's clear when we read the Bible as I believe God intended.

For me, the issue of lower criticism has been settled to my satisfaction, but you might have more questions. That's great! Keep digging into the evidence. Once you're satisfied that we have reliable copies of the Bible, to read and interpret it well begins by engaging with higher criticism—understanding the Jewish mindset and theological worldview of the first century, not sixteenth-century Enlightenment Europe, not the economically convenient views of the Industrial Era, not our post-truth perspective of today. Understanding the higher criticism of each of those eras is important, because they influenced subsequent generations and still influence worldviews today. I've found it to be immensely helpful to go back to the beginning of this historical chain, starting with the person of Jesus and how his followers understood the *Tanakh* as they composed the New Testament.

The Bible has made it into our hands. Now we have the responsibility to determine how, if at all, we will allow God's word to guide our lives. In the next chapter, we'll explore the importance of reading the Bible as a first-century Jewish person did and how this ingredient helps us understand what God might be communicating to us.

Questions

- What is the Bible to you? What value do you place on Scripture?
- How do you feel when you pick up a Bible?
- How important is the Bible in guiding your life?
- What is your biggest concern, apprehension, or even fear when engaging with Scripture?
- Is there an issue with the Bible that you've struggled with?
- Is there a position the church holds (theologically or in practice) with which you disagree? Why?
- Why do you believe what you believe about the Bible? Can you articulate it to someone else?
- How will you go about researching your questions about the Bible from here? Will you make the time to do it? If you don't already have a plan or an established habit, consider making one for the next month. What question will you explore, and what resources will you seek?

Additional Resources

Lightfoot, Neil R., *How We Got the Bible.*

Mackie, Tim, and Jon Collins. "What Is the Bible?" BibleProject, 15 Feb. 2017. https://bibleproject.com/explore/video/what-is-bible/

Walton, John H., and Brent Sandy. *The Lost World of Scripture: Ancient Literary Culture and Biblical Authority.*

Tverborg, Lois. *Reading the Bible with Rabbi Jesus: How a Jewish Perspective can Transform your Understanding.*

Huff, Wesely. "Can I Trust the Bible?" https://www.wesleyhuff.com/can-i-trust-the-bible

4. The Ingredient of Reading like the Original Audience: Reading While Jewish

Reading While Black

—TITLE OF A BOOK BY ESAU MCCAULLEY

The proper worldview context for interpreting the Bible is not evangelicalism, Catholicism, the Protestant Reformation, the Puritans, or even the modern world.

—MICHAEL HEISER

The book *Reading While Black* offers a perspective on how the author's African American experience imprints itself upon his reading and understanding of the Biblical narrative. For each of us, our past informs us of our present and touches every aspect of our lives. We are complex individuals, and the variables that shape how we interpret our lives are incalculable. Not everyone within the same country, culture, ethnicity, or even household experiences and interprets shared experiences the same way.

We can all read the same Bible and quickly become offended, since many of its cultural norms and social constructs violate our modern sensibilities. Yet what triggers a twenty-year-old when reading the Bible might not offend a fifty-year-old, or what bothers an American from Los Angeles might not upset someone from rural Kazakhstan. Keeping this in mind, let me suggest that a healthy curiosity can guard against making unfair and judgmental assumptions about others, even those we read about in the Bible. Curiosity is a helpful ingredient, encouraging us to ask questions and seek to understand before drawing conclusions.

Higher textual criticism is about being curious when reading the Bible. It asks questions like: *How would the original audience of the Bible have* understood what was being communicated to them? How did they respond? This approach seeks to understand the Biblical characters on their terms.

A Case Study

The world of Biblical scholarship is diverse and can be just as contentious as first-century rabbis arguing with each other over an issue of *Torah*. Biblical scholars have their own personal biases along with their academic ones. They're trained to look for certain elements in the text. For example, I've been trained to be sensitive to the geographical significance of locations mentioned in the Bible. Others have different priorities, and it is helpful to know the presuppositions and backgrounds of any scholars we read.

Awareness of a person's background helps us to ask deeper questions, like appreciating their past, time in history, and challenges they faced may help us put their writings into a larger context. Being curious about these details is immensely helpful when exploring the history of the church. Whether reading Augustine, Aquinas, Luther, Edwards, or Graham, it's helpful to learn about their individual life circumstances emmeshed within their larger historical context. These esteemed theologians wrote to address burning issues of their day, including what it meant to be a follower of Jesus given their specific circumstances. The same holds true today: it is helpful to be curious about the background of scholars we read, especially the ones who may have a more skeptical approach to reading the Bible.

Bart Ehrman, the author mentioned in my previous chapter, is a great example. His *New York Times* bestseller *Misquoting Jesus* argues that the New Testament has no claim to being called God's word because we do not have the original autographs. A fair claim to consider. In his preface, he shares a bit of his life story, providing us with some insight into the personal history that led him to eventually write his book. During his teenage years, he became a born-again believer, holding to the inspiration of Scripture as God's divine word as a core tenet of his Christian faith. He attended Moody Bible Institute, which teaches that Scripture is God's inerrant and inspired word, valid for explaining our reality and guiding how we live. After earning an MDiv and PhD from Princeton Theological Seminary, he changed his position. He reasoned that if we don't have the original autographs, then we don't possess the actual inspired words of God. He concluded: "I came to realize that it would have been no more difficult for God to preserve the words of Scripture than it would have been for him to inspire them in the first place."[1] Without the original words of God, he ultimately concludes that the Bible offers little to no valid information to help us know who God is or how to live today. His opinions match the popular sentiments of many skeptical scholars. What happened at Princeton that led him to change his mind?

Maybe Mark Made a Mistake?

The pursuit of knowledge involves being honest, open, and willing to ask hard questions. Ehrman poses a challenging and legitimate question: if we don't possess the exact words of God as written by the original authors, then it's reasonable to ask: "What if God did not say it?" Essentially, he is suggesting that people have put words into God's mouth. However, many other scholars confidently affirm that we have enough high-fidelity copies of the New Testament to connect these writings to their original autographs. But Ehrman's issues with the Bible do not end with the transmission of the New Testament itself: He cites numerous incongruities between the Gospels as evidence against their authenticity and credibility. Countless books and articles by peer-reviewed scholars have addressed all these issues and offered plausible explanations for these supposed incongruities; nevertheless, Ehrman and others like him take a house-of-cards approach, saying that only one piece of data needs to be slightly misaligned to cause the whole Bible's authenticity to collapse.

If we throw out the entire Bible based on some apparent variants in textual transmission, then logically, we can no longer use it as a basis for faith and practice. Untethering ourselves from the Bible as a plausible explanation of our reality also has devastating emotional consequences: It can only take a moment for everything to change. I've experienced such tragedies myself. In 1993, my niece passed away from a congenital kidney disease after living only three amazing months. Her picture is still near my desk decades later. I had just recently returned home from my first mission trip when I held her for the first time and then heard the prognosis for her future. Our whole family was devastated, but we trusted the Lord even when we didn't understand.

Faith can be fragile. A moment like this can derail everything, causing some to doubt or even lose their ability to believe in God. Others respond by leaning in even more closely to Jesus. God never promises we will escape suffering in this world, but he does promise he will be with us in our pain. (Deuteronomy 31:8) But it isn't always physical or emotional suffering that causes moments like these. A crisis of faith can start with a simple question.

Ehrman explains that his crisis-of-faith moment came while he was pursuing his PhD at Princeton. While writing a paper attempting to reconcile Mark's account of Jesus' words in Mark 2:23-28 with their source story in 1 Samuel 21, he went to great lengths to form an argument affirming the inerrancy of Scripture. On his paper, his professor wrote: "Maybe Mark made a mistake?" This simple one-liner matched his growing

Scan Here to Watch Scholars Responding to Erhman's Work

questions regarding the inerrancy of Scripture and gave him permission to openly question the New Testament's textual origins. From that moment on, he no longer assumed that a plausible explanation existed to defend any perceived incongruity found in the text.

Well—did Mark make a mistake? Rather than answer that directly, I would like to walk us through a process of asking other questions to see if an answer can be found—one that befits the context of Jesus' audience and might resolve the perceived error in transmission. "Reading the Bible while Jewish" is a helpful ingredient here.

Higher Textual Criticism Can Help

Reading the passage below, let's be curious and ask questions, applying some of the tools we've acquired so far:

One Sabbath Jesus was going through the grain fields, and as his disciples walked along, they began to pick some heads of grain. The Pharisees said to him, "Look, why are they doing what is unlawful on the Sabbath?" He answered, "Have you never read what David did when he and his companions were hungry and in need? In the days of Abiathar the high priest, he entered the house of God and ate the consecrated bread, which is lawful only for priests to eat. And he also gave some to his companions." Then he said to them, "The Sabbath was made for man, not man for the Sabbath. So the Son of Man is Lord even of the Sabbath." (Mark 2:23-28)

In the story just before (in Mark 2:18-22), Jesus addresses fasting, which was a customary practice twice a week among some *Torah*-observant Jews, especially the Pharisees. (Luke 18:12)[2] In this passage I've quoted, Jesus discusses observing the Sabbath in response to the Pharisees' complaint about his disciples' supposed Sabbath violation when they rub grain in their hands. By the first century, Sabbath observance (in some form) had become a universally accepted practice among Jews across Israel and the diaspora, regardless of their level of religious observance. The first-century-AD Pharisees had created strict guidelines of what constituted work on the Sabbath day.[3]

In the story that follows (Mark 3:1-6), Jesus heals a man with a crippled hand in a synagogue on the Sabbath. Traditions at this time considered healing to be work, and thus healing was forbidden on the Sabbath unless done by word only. This interpretation came from the *Talmud*, rabbinical commentary on *Torah*, preserved and transmitted in Jesus' day through oral tradition. *Talmud* states that one could heal on the Sabbath day, but only with words—there was to be no touching the sick person or putting on salve.[4] In this instance, Jesus observes the oral law by using only words to heal, yet the Pharisees still became disgruntled. The Pharisees of the first century knew the *Tanakh* and used this knowledge to define what it meant to live as a faithful Jew, and Jesus' numerous interactions with them often involve disputes over the application of *Torah*. In Mark 2:23-28, Jesus leans into the Pharisees' deep knowledge of *Tanakh* to subtly challenge them on whose interpretation of *Torah* they are following.

Ask Questions of the Text

Here's a practical suggestion: Get out a piece of paper and have it with you the next time you read your Bible. Write down questions as you read, then look at your list. You probably will not have the time to hunt down every rabbit trail, but pick one you find most interesting and dig a little to see what you unearth.

I would like you to put this into practice now. Stop and reread Mark 2:23-28 for yourself. What questions do you have?—No, seriously: take a moment to write down your questions before you keep reading. Here are some I came up with about this short passage:

1. Why were they walking in a grain field on the Sabbath?
2. What is the Sabbath?
3. Wasn't there a rule at the time that people could walk only so far on a Sabbath day?
4. What towns were near where the disciples were?
5. Were they stealing someone's grain?[5]
6. Who were the Pharisees?
7. Who set the rules for the Sabbath day?
8. What was the context of the story about David that Jesus mentions?
9. Why does Jesus bring this up here?
10. Who was Abiathar?
11. Where was this exchange between David and the priest taking place?
12. Why could only priests eat the bread?
13. Why did Abiathar give bread to David and his companions?
14. Jesus says: "The Sabbath was made for man, not man for the Sabbath"; this sounds important, but I don't understand. What does he mean?
15. How does this story tie into the one before (in 2:18-22) and the one after (in 3:1-6)?

These are just a few questions; I'm sure you thought of many more. So, where do we begin to answer them?

Let's start with the Old Testament reference to David. It can be found in 1 Samuel 21:1-9, with the background unfolding in the previous chapter. At the end of chapter 20, Jonathan confirms for David that his father Saul intends to kill David and urges him to flee to save his life. Chapter 21 opens with David on the run and in search of food. He goes to a place called Nob. Its exact location remains unknown, but it's thought to be southeast of Gibeah, near the location of Saul's capital on the eastern side of the ridge that today makes up the Mount of Olives.[6] There, David meets a priest named Ahimelech. Here's our supposed inerrancy problem, because Jesus gives the priest's name as Abiathar, who was Ahimelech's son. As we saw earlier with Ehrman, for some critical scholars, if one piece of evidence is proven false, the whole becomes invalid. However, I believe Jesus' insertion of Abiathar was intentional and not a mistake by Jesus, Mark, or the scribal copyist.

Jesus naming the wrong high priest in Mark 2 does create a conundrum. The traditional way to address this issue and protect the inerrancy of Scripture is to say that this incident in 1 Samuel 21 took place during the lifetime of Abiathar but not necessarily while he served officially as high priest. Not satisfied with that answer, some scholars suggest that the loaves of bread belonged to Abiathar (who was a priest at the time), and he himself gave them to David or persuaded his father to give them. This provides a succinct answer that maintains the integrity of Scripture and the cultural understanding of how priests functioned, but this answer still doesn't get it done for me.

There's another way to read this. Let's get our ingredients and get cookin'.

Ahimelech and Abiathar

Who are these two priests, and why do they matter? Doing a simple Bible search, you can quickly find their references. Ahimelech, a descendant of Eli, served as the high priest during the reign of Saul at a temple at Nob. Saul accuses Ahimelech and his fellow priests of helping David, whom Saul perceives as a rival to the throne, and he orders his men to put the priests to death. Ahimelech's son Abiathar escapes execution and flees with the ephod, the breastplate vestment of the high priest. Abiathar finds David and his men, and David offers him protection. He eventually serves them as their priest. (1 Samuel 22:20-23, 23:6) In the meantime, Saul names Zadok, from the house of Eleazar, high priest to replace Ahimelech. After Saul's death, David officially ascends to the throne, and Abiathar becomes the high priest and king's companion. So now there are two high priests serving at the same time: Zadok and Abiathar. Only one high priest at a time is supposed to serve until his death, but David allows both men to continue to serve as dual high priests. This situation will cause problems in the future, after David's death.

Ancient Near-eastern kings produced lots of children through their many wives, which sometimes meant chaos of succession upon the king's death. David never publicly names his successor; he privately promises Bathsheba that their son Solomon will become king but makes no formal announcement. As David nears death, Bathsheba reminds him of his promise. (1 Kings 1:13) Keeping his word, he gives her instructions for Solomon to ride his donkey to the springs of Gihon and be anointed as king by the high priest. (1 Kings 1:38-40) As the only water source for the city of Jerusalem, the spring of Gihon is a gathering place. Choosing such a public location for the ceremony guarantees that word will quickly spread throughout the city about Solomon being named king by David.

But David's other sons, anticipating an impending power vacuum, jockey to seize the throne. One way to gain credibility would be to have the high priest as a political ally. But there are two high priests. Adonijah, David's oldest surviving son, convinces Abiathar to support him, while Zadok supports David's choice, Solomon.[7]

As David nears death, he offers Solomon guidance, encouragement, and instructions. Read 1 Kings 2: David essentially gives Solomon a detailed hit list, telling him who he should kill and who he should honor and trust. Solomon eventually orders his older brother and rival to the throne killed. (2 Kings 25) But now, what to do with the two high priests? One followed his father's wishes; the other did not. Solomon doesn't want to put Abiathar to death, so banishes him to his home in Anathoth. (1 Kings 2:26-27) Zadok becomes the lone high priest.

This event not only figures into Jesus' words in Mark 2, but also affects the priestly line after the Jews' return from exile in 516 BC. When the first temple was destroyed, the priesthood was decimated along with all genealogical records. Upon returning to Jerusalem, the leadership needed to choose which line of Aaron would be the family line from whom the high priest would be chosen. The line of Zadok was selected. The Hebrew plural of *Zadok* is *Zadokim*; when translated into Greek, it becomes *Sadducees*—the line of high priests in Jesus' day.

The Days of Abiathar the High Priest

When reading the Gospels, we can't forget Jesus' primary audience. Here, the Pharisees call out Jesus' disciples for plucking grain and rubbing it on the Sabbath. Based on their interpretation of *Torah*, rubbing is a clear violation of the command against working on the Sabbath. However, the sages made provisions to allow *Torah* to be broken to save a life, especially on the Sabbath.[8] Jesus' disciples are hungry; I won't go so far as to say they are in danger of starvation, but Jesus desires to make a bigger point to the Pharisees about himself. He responds to the Pharisees by using the rabbinical principle of hinting to the text, a technique that by the medieval period would be called *remez*.[9] With much of Scripture memorized, rabbis taught in biblical shorthand, quoting a small line of Scripture while assuming their audience knew the rest of the passage and its context. Today, if I said to you, "For God so loved the world—" and stopped, you could probably finish the verse and tell me that it's from John 3:16. You might also recall the context of Jesus and Nicodemus in their nighttime discussion about what it means to be born again.

Jesus uses this technique often when teaching, because his audience has a high degree of biblical literacy. Therefore, when Jesus says the wrong name of the high priest, it's a safe assumption his audience notices and presumes it's intentional. Why would Jesus change the high priest in this story? Well, this story begins with a dispute about how to keep the Sabbath. By Jesus retelling of the story of David eating bread only the priests were allowed to have, he highlights Ahimelech violating *Torah* to save a life, thus faithfully serving Yahweh and his anointed, David. Ahimelech pays a heavy price for his faithfulness and is killed by the wicked king Saul, the epitome of someone who displays unfaithfulness to obey Yahweh and listen to his anointed servant. Fast forward to the end of David's life: Ahimelech's son Abiathar is presented with a similar choice, and like Saul, who chooses to oppose God's anointed, he opposes Solomon. All these historical details would come flooding back into the minds of the Pharisees. Then, Jesus identifies himself as the Son of Man, who "is Lord even of the Sabbath". The Messiah, God in the flesh, is now standing in their presence interpreting *Torah*, explaining how he desires them to observe Sabbath. Like Abiathar, they are presented with a choice. Will they make the same mistake and oppose the man God chose to ascend to David's throne, who will rightly interpret *Torah*? Or will they learn from Scripture and choose the Son of Man whom God has sent? By purposefully misquoting the *Tanakh*, Jesus challenges their interpretation of how to keep the Sabbath while identifying himself as the Messiah who has come to show them how to rightly live out *Torah*. Will they listen? Will we listen?

This exchange perfectly captures how a rabbi would teach, making his point indirectly by subtle use of the text. It also displays Jesus' genius. Several reasonable explanations exist to resolve the issue of Mark 2, but my presupposition is to first look at how a first-century rabbi would read the text and craft an argument for his Biblically literate audience. I believe reading the Bible while Jewish is an open and honest approach to answering some of these hard questions, as well as to healing our hearts.

The ingredients of curiosity and higher criticism can be beneficial to us in every aspect of our lives, not just in studying the Bible. Seeking to understand something or someone requires asking questions, which starts a conversation. During the conversation we might discover together what we think and believe. What I'm looking for when studying the Bible is a good conversation, because we are the main ingredient in reading the Bible well. Let me explain what I mean in the next chapter.

Questions

- How curious are you when you read your Bible? Why or why not?
- How do you discern who is a trustworthy source when you're studying the Bible?
- How do you respond when you hear opposing points of view on the same issue?
- Is there a passage of Scripture that causes you to have serious questions or doubts?
- How do you feel about scholars whose approach is more critical and skeptical? Do they have a place in our discussions as people who believe in the Bible?
- How does your understanding of higher criticism change how you read the Bible and engage with others?
- Have you experienced a "crisis of faith" moment? Did it cause you to lean into God or pull away?
- Where do you need to adjust your perspective to engage with Scripture through the lens of context?

Additional Resources

Beitzel, Barry J. *The New Moody Atlas of the Bible*

Beitzel, Barry J., Jessica Parks, Douglas Mangum, and Kristopher A. Lyle. *Lexham Geographic Commentaries*

Brown, Michael L. *Why So Many Christians Have Left the Faith: Responding to the Deconstructionist Movement With Unshakable, Timeless Truth*

Coursey, Chris M. *The Joy Switch: How Your Brain's Secret Circuit Affects Your Relationships—And How You Can Activate It.*

Georges, Jayson. *The 3D Gospel: Ministry in Guilt, Shame, and Fear Cultures*

Nisbett, Richard E. *The Geography of Thought: How Asians and Westerners Think Differently… and Why*

The Erhman Project: https://ehrmanproject.com/

5. The Ingredient of Knowing Yourself: What Is Your *Skopos*?

Man is the measure of all things.

—PLATO, PROTAGORAS

Without geography, you are nowhere.

—ATTRIBUTED TO JIMMY BUFFET

Studying Biblical History & Geography at Jerusalem University College involves hiking to the top of many a dusty hill around the country of Israel. When reaching a summit, our esteemed teacher Paul Wright would politely ask us to get oriented. Months before our class began, we'd spent hours and hours marking maps, identifying key towns and roads, highlighting the movements of Biblical characters. Now, standing on one of those remote locations marked on our maps, we'd lay our maps on the ground and orient them to the north with the help of a compass. As they aligned with the landscape around us, our maps became three dimensional, and we'd gain tangible geographic awareness and new perspective on what St. Jerome is said to have called "the Fifth Gospel"— the land of Israel.[1] Jim Monson called the land of Israel a chessboard, because the topography remains unchanged, causing people throughout the millennia to move in similar patterns regardless of the time period in which they live.[2] Studying the geography of Israel offers insight as to how/why people traveled through the land and the significance of where they chose to live.

The distinct physical features of Israel makes the land a character in the Biblical story. However, its influence often goes unnoticed. The same can be said for our life maps. The total sum of our past experiences informs us of our present, but we often are unaware of the connection. Our personal history becomes our emotional geography, which influences how we see and understand the world around us. How elusive is this map!

Before any journey begins, we must get oriented by identifying our desired destination; equally important is knowing our starting location. In terms of reading the Bible, we are the starting point. Important questions that we need to ask include:

- Who are you?
- When are you?
- Where are you?
- Where do you want to go?

The Greek philosopher Protagoras observed thousands of years ago the importance of individual perspectives when he said, "Man is the measure of all things."3 Each of us possesses our own unique perception of reality. From the moment we're conceived, our senses absorb, record, collate, and store our past experiences to be used later to understand the present and predict the future. This processing of information-gathering happens subconsciously and in the blink of an eye.

Have you ever overreacted to a situation? In a millisecond, you went from being calm to being in fight-or-flight mode. Your response was not a conscious decision: It just happened. Your past informed your present, and your self-protection instincts kicked in. You can have a similar reaction when reading the Bible. Have you ever felt anger, contempt, or even fear when reading a particular story from the Bible? If so, you are no different than scholars like Ehrman, whose past informs their theological views. You may not know Greek and Hebrew or hold degrees in theological studies, but your response is just as sophisticated as theirs— in that moment, your past became the measure of all things as far as how you perceive the Bible. *You may not see yourself as a theologian—but you are.*

When it comes to reading the Bible, YOU are the main ingredient. Switching metaphors for a moment back to the map illustration: As we read our life maps, we navigate the best course of action. But are we reading it accurately? Do we have the map oriented in the right direction? It only takes being a few degrees off at the start to end up hundreds of miles away from our desired destination. We can view the Bible as God's map, explaining the world from his perspective, helping us navigate through life. The challenge is to read the Bible in an unbiased way, which is literally impossible because we are human. God's reality is reality. I must orient myself to his reality, or I risk doing harm to myself and others while having little chance of arriving at my desired destination.

Who Are You?

While I was taking a class on the early church fathers, our professor, Petra Heldt, often asked: "What is the *skopos* of the author?" *Skopos* is an academic word, drawn from the field of translation theory, meaning *purpose*.[4] She wanted us to research the background of the author: where they came from, when they wrote, who they studied under, and what questions fueled their writings. For example, many of the second-century AD authors we read were labeled heretics by Eusebius and others in the 4th century; to see if these claims of heresy held true, we read them in their own words. A helpful tool in our evaluation was having a grasp of the questions they were commenting on and understanding the language they were using to write their theological perspectives. Having this information changed how we understood their arguments, leading us to better understand or perhaps reevaluate the label placed upon them. Knowing their story, history, language, philosophical principles, and cultural context was integral to understanding what they were trying to communicate.

What is your *skopos*? Why do you think the way you do? How do your thoughts influence your actions? What if others knew your history? How would that help them understand who you are? These are great questions, for sure, but we have one small problem: The person who knows us the least is often ourselves. We may not realize how much we take knowing ourselves for granted. We often live life on autopilot, seldom slowing down to consider why we do what we do; everything we do just makes sense to us. A missing piece of our self-awareness is the *why* behind our actions. Sometimes, conflict with others compels us to stop and explain our *whys* to someone else and seek to understand theirs. They are probably as unaware of their *whys* as we are of ours. The Bible can also create conflict when we wrestle with *why* questions as we read. When we are offended by the Bible, who will explain the Bible's *why* to us?

Lots of things can trigger us. We can easily take offense in a nanosecond when our brain's powerful search engine, scanning our database of the past, informs our sympathetic nervous system to respond. Feelings of fear, anger, and anxiety begin to rise in us. Switching from our subconscious, we become aware that something is wrong. Our database identified a correlation to an event from our past, triggering our need to respond to protect ourselves or others.

We can also experience our sympathetic nervous system's reaction when reading the Bible. We have no choice but to read the Bible through our past experiences. Will our intense feelings cause us to draw closer, seeking to understand, or pull back? If we judge the Bible based on our personal experiences, then we're at risk of making the same shallow pronouncements as Eusebius, labeling others heretics even though we lack awareness of their context, their *why*. Our personal lens colors how we see everything.

Consider a single mom I know who raised four children in the 1970s while receiving less pay for the same job as her male counterparts. She worked hard to provide for her family, embodying the motivation for the women's liberation movement. While reading the story of Jesus healing Peter's mother-in-law in Matthew 8, her lens tinted her interpretation of Jesus' motives through her current circumstances, which led her to perceive Jesus to be a stereotypical male from the 1970s. She concluded that Jesus healed Peter's mother-in-law to ensure a woman was available to serve him. Given her experience, that's a reasonable guess at Jesus' motivation. But what she didn't know was that in the hospitality-rich culture of first-century Israel, it would have been shameful for a host not to be able to serve her guests—sick or not. Jesus restored her to full health to take away any potential shame she might have felt from herself or her neighbors, not because he needed anything from her or wanted a woman to serve him. This shows how two people can read this same story and reach quite different emotional conclusions. My friend's personal set of lenses quite naturally caused her to misinterpret Jesus' intentions and motivations.

We can easily misinterpret anyone's intentions, whether it's a stranger walking down the street, a spouse, coworker, etc. I've come to realize I've often misunderstood the intentions of my own children. The relational costs of these misunderstandings can be high—at times painfully high. We are also vulnerable to misperceiving God's intentions and motivations. Our past—good, hurtful, and indifferent—can cause us to read our life maps inaccurately, leading us to hit roadblocks, stumble into pitfalls, and go astray from our desired destination.[5] We end up hurting ourselves and those we love by not orienting ourselves to God's reality as presented in the Bible. When we acknowledge that being "the measure of all things" is very personal and subjective, this realization can slow us down and encourage us to become curious. Asking questions of ourselves, seeking to understand others, and doing our best to see the world as God does is the beginning of the journey. In that process, our sympathetic nervous system, operating from past experiences, can get in the way of progress.

When Are You?

Reading the Bible as cultural outsiders, we may often feel unsettled and even shocked by the stories we read. Imagine Jacob waking up the morning after his wedding to discover Leah next to him, the older sister of Rachel, whom he thought he was marrying—only to then marry Rachel a week later! That story still bothers me. What about polygamy? What about slavery? What about David sleeping with Bathsheba, not hiding his actions? What about Jephthah sacrificing his only child because he made a vow to God? The characters at times don't blink an eye at behaviors we would never accept today.

Lacking any plausible explanation for these hard-to-read passages, we can easily pass judgment and impugn the character of the people whose stories we consider sacred. Revisionist history, judging the past by the norms of today, can cause us to speed-read through culturally uncomfortable moments without seeking to understand why God wants us to wrestle with them.

I'm not excusing behaviors we would find reprehensible today. Unfortunately, the Bible seldom offers explanations or commentary on its cultural context to aid the reader's understanding. For the original audience those social norms mostly made sense, so why waste the ink? The most powerful values are those that go without being said—and are also the hardest to decode and understand.

An example of this is how we understand marriage in Biblical times. The intent of creating a union was to strengthen both families, attempting to secure a better future for generations to come. Falling in love was not a determining factor in who one married. With the match arranged by the parents, the couple most likely knew little or next to nothing about their future spouse before they were betrothed. Although arranged marriages still happen in many parts of the world, this concept is very foreign to most westerners. The thought of an arranged marriage strikes at the heart of our desire to be in control of our lives.

Our modern views of marriage can cause us to misinterpret how the Biblical characters might have felt about marriage. One such example is the betrothal of Mary and Joseph. The Gospels of Matthew and Luke provide details, telling us they were pledged to be married. (Luke 1:27; Matthew 1:18) Young girls often became betrothed soon after they began their menstrual cycles, so Mary was probably around thirteen years old and Joseph was probably four or five years older.[6] If Mary and Joseph's betrothal followed the cultural norms of their times, then their parents arranged the marriage. Not much of a love story.

Today, feeling in love ranks as the number one determining factor when choosing a mate, possibly with some input from one's parents. Other more pragmatic considerations make the list, but love has the final say. When ranking attributes of importance when choosing a spouse, love moving to the top of the list marks a shift even from 1939, when women ranked love fifth on a list of factors in choosing a spouse.[7]

A modern proposal can be elaborate and carefully planned, creating a very romantic moment. In contrast, a betrothal ceremony in the first century was meaningful, but not romantic. After the fathers agreed to the match and negotiated the dowery, they would bring the young people together for the ceremony. The 2006 film *The Nativity Story* depicts Mary's response to her betrothal as less than enthusiastic. The decision to portray Mary this way came from the director, guiding the actor to portray this moment with disappointment and apprehension. However, this interpretation comes from our modern sensibilities. Replaying this scene as if it's set in the present, we'd ask, "How would you feel if

Scan Here to Watch a Scene from *The Nativity Story*

someone told you whom you were going to marry, and you had little or no say in the matter?" Two thousand years removed from this culture's values and expectations, we can easily be offended, feeling Mary was forced into a marriage against her will. Some young women—and young men!—in the first century may well have felt that way, but their expectations of life and marriage were vastly different from ours today. Honestly, we have no idea how Mary received the news; she might have been excited to be betrothed.

It is natural to read a story in the Bible and wonder how we would feel in that situation. We could easily take offense because we operate with a different set of expectations. I experienced this while sharing the details of the first Christmas with a group of recent college graduates. As I was explaining the significance of Mary and Joseph being pledged in marriage, I noticed one young woman's body language shift. When I described the ceremony in detail, this young woman expressed her frustration, feeling as most of us would about someone today being forced into a marriage not of their own choosing. Although I tried to give her some historical context, she could not move past feeling Mary was a victim of an oppressive cultural system. Her time in history and perspective on marriage impacted how she read this story, and probably ruined her Christmas.

The times in which we live define our expectations for many aspects of life, including marriage, and they will probably shift and change with the next generation. Culture is always shifting, but whether for better or worse is a constant debate. Our challenge is to withhold judging interactions in the Bible prematurely until we know what the norms and expectations were for that time. Injustice is injustice, but not every event we read about in the Bible that makes us feel uncomfortable falls into the category of injustice against a person within their historical context.

The Bible contains many stories that challenge our modern sensibilities, leading some to put the Bible down, never to pick it up again. Of course, it's possible that these biblical stories, so jarring to us, could have offended even the people to whom they were written! The Bible pulls no punches, recording stories which expose us to historical realities that include injustice, selfishness, greed, and malice. Picking our Bibles back up, how then should we relate to these stories? What commentary does the Bible offer about the culture back then as well as our culture today?

Remember, I said at the beginning that getting into the kitchen will be messy. Accepting the mess of the Bible helps see that we have more in common with the characters of God's story than we'd like to admit. Once I come to this realization, I'm in a place to receive from God, ready to read my map as he wants me to, so I can live as he would have me live.

Where Are You?

Where you come from influences the kind of questions you ask of the Bible. Physical and social environments shape cultures, eventually forming a unified way of thinking within a people group: how they collectively see the world and their place in it. Individual decisions are made within a shared worldview; people know what social norms are expected of them in their day-to-day lives, and they respond accordingly. Conflict occurs when those norms are violated. Learning the core values of a culture can help us decode their decision-making process, which can differ vastly from culture to culture.

The Bible is an equal-opportunity offender. Everyone on the planet will probably be triggered at some point by something they read in it. The only possibility of avoiding this discomfort is if we happened to be raised within a culture very similar to those of the Bible's. Even then, there still exists the real possibility of being offended, because values change within a culture over time. What do we do when we read stories within Scripture that bother us, violating our cultural sensibilities? Hopefully, you've learned to ask questions. Interestingly, the theological and Biblical questions someone from the United States is asking will most likely differ greatly from someone who lives in another country because of the differences in their culture's core values.

Here's a prime example of a possible cultural clash with the Bible. For those who grew up in the U.S., we may have inherited a sense of self-reliance from those Europeans who settled in the Americas and brought with them the desire to live a life of self-determination. Eventually, they put this ideal into words. The *Declaration of Independence* captures the colonists' longing for the right to pursue their own life, liberty, and happiness. Yet the focus on individual rights and the desire to protect one's personal freedoms created a theological conundrum. In a culture that values freedom of choice, some bristle at the doctrine of *predestination*.

In the simplest terms, this doctrine describes God as all-knowing of past, present, and future. If God knows the future, then we are not free to choose a choice other than the one God knows will be selected. Applying this logic, predestination holds that God determined from the moment he created the world who would follow him and who would not.[8] We can't determine our own fate, because God alone decides our destiny, spiritual and otherwise. This notion can cause many people to find fault with God and not themselves, seeing themselves as victims of fate—God's predetermination.

Westerners value individualism, but what about someone who was raised in an honor/shame culture? They may value supporting the community more than carving out an individual path. Respect for elders and hierarchy may lead them to trust in and yield to those in authority over them; to do otherwise would be shocking, unthinkable even.[9] I didn't grow up in that kind of culture, so I struggle to imagine what they would find offensive or challenging to their cultural sensitivities in the Bible. What kind of questions would they ask God?

In their book *Misreading Scripture through Western Eyes*, Randolph Richards and Brandon O'Brien explore how western culture misinterprets events in the Bible because of differing cultural values. An example they give is King David's affair with Bathsheba. As a westerner, I read this story and lay all the blame for the sexual assault of Bathsheba and murder of Uriah completely on David. He created the whole mess from beginning to end. However, someone from an honor/shame society could read this story and come to a completely different conclusion. Possessing a high respect for those in authority, they could conclude that Uriah is at fault, reasoning that if he had followed David's urging to go home to be with his wife, David's tracks would have been covered, both men's honor would have been protected, and everything would have gone on as before. But Uriah refuses to obey the king's requests and ultimately ends up taking his death certificate back with him to the front lines of the battle, where David's commander allows him to be killed by the enemy. I'm so predisposed to my cultural values, it's hard for me to consider this interpretation. But in some cultures, respect and honor for those in positions of leadership is unquestioned—not how a typical person from the United States thinks about those in authority!

If we westerners view the Bible as emanating out of a completely foreign culture, we can be quick to divorce ourselves from uncomfortable stories and details as if we have nothing in common with those characters and their choices. Unfortunately, human nature transcends cultures and I too can be like David, selfishly imposing my will upon others and trying to cover my tracks—maybe not to the same degree or in the same manner as David did, but selfishly all the same. God's king is supposed to protect the weak, yet he acted like all the heathen kings around him, who took whatever they wanted, whoever they wanted, whenever they wanted.

The prophet Nathan seeks to get David's attention by telling him a story of a man whose only lamb was taken from him, which stirs up David's righteous indignation and leads him to repentance. (2 Samuel 12) We all need a Nathan in our lives to confront us when we selfishly wield our power over another. We can easily point to David's sin and say, "I would never act like that," but Jesus challenges this notion by teaching us that the root of sin (not being like God) is in our hearts. For example, if I look at a woman lustfully, that's as if I've committed adultery. (Matthew 5:28) Perhaps by focusing on our heart (our thoughts and desires), Jesus was bridging cross-cultural gaps that might exist in how we read the Bible.

None of us read and understand the Bible perfectly. Each of us has personal and cultural biases to overcome. We can easily misjudge people's intentions and motives or, comparing our values and norms to theirs, we conclude our values are better. Jesus desires that we compare ourselves to him, and to his values alone. We need to see Jesus clearly for who he is and not who we've made him to be in our minds. Let's look at a Biblical example of how God broadened someone's understanding of himself.

When God Gives a New Lens

Zechariah's story is found in Luke's Gospel; he is introduced to us as a priest serving in the temple. There were two kinds of priests, both from the tribe of Levi, but only those specifically from the line of Aaron could perform the daily rituals and sacrifices in the temple. God chose Aaron to be the first high priest with his sons to assist him. (Exodus 28) Successive generations from the line of Aaron fulfilled these duties until the destruction of the first temple. Upon returning from exile in Babylon, a specific family line within the ever-growing lineage of Aaron had to be identified as the line of succession to serve in the Temple and from which to select the high priest. Going back to a story we've already discussed, the post-exilic leadership chose the line from the family of Zadok, the last high priest of David's reign and the one who anointed Solomon king. (2 Samuel 8:17; 1 Kings 1:39) The Hebrew name for Zadok's descendants, the *Zadokim*, was translated into Greek as *Sadducees*. As the priestly class of the first century AD, the Sadducees developed some very specific theological beliefs. Traditional scholarship holds that the Sadducees believed *Torah* was the only authority, discarding the rest of the *Tanakh* (this assertion is debated by scholars today). They also did not believe in a resurrection from the dead, nor did they believe in angels.[10] Because Zechariah is serving in the temple when we meet him, we can assume he is a Sadducee, since they were the only ones allowed to serve there.

From the time of 1 Chronicles 24, the priests were divided into twenty-four divisions, each serving two weeks a year.[11] The layout of the temple was divided into two sections. The first section is where the priests entered twice a day. Passing through the temple doors, they would enter the holy space where the menorah, table of showbread, and altar of incense stood.[12] There, in front of this curtain, a priest would offer his prayers and burn incense twice a day. A curtain separated the holy space from the Holy of Holies, where the ark was placed before it was lost to history after the destruction of the first temple. The high priest alone would enter Holy of Holies one day a year, during the feast of Yom Kippur. In the time of Zechariah, this space was assumed to be empty.

Each morning and evening, a priest was chosen by lot (random selection) to enter the holy place of the temple, offer prayers, and burn incense while the daily sacrifices took place outside upon the altar.[13] On the day of our story, Zechariah is chosen by lot to offer the prayers during the daily sacrifices. (Luke 1:9) To fulfill his duties, he enters the holy space and is offering his prayers—when he is interrupted by the angel Gabriel! Zechariah, naturally, is startled. It is one thing to be shocked by an angel when you believe in their existence; it is quite another if you don't believe in them at all. God interrupts Zechariah's life and, in a moment, challenges what he previously believed about God and the Bible. The theological recipe Zechariah had been taught was missing some key ingredients. Gabriel's appearance confronts Zechariah's and the Sadducees' beliefs about how God can communicate with his people using angels as messengers.

Like Zechariah, none of us possess perfect theology, and we all need some correction in how we see God, ourselves, and others. I believe God desires for all of us to see him more clearly for who he is and not how we've fashioned him in our minds. On rare occasions, God may orchestrate an event like Zechariah's encounter with Gabriel to get our attention. In my experience, I've more often seen him use times of conflict, struggle, or seasons where I become disoriented and feel lost, to cause me to stop and reexamine my map.

We all need God to interrupt our lives to help us see him for who he is and guide us to read Word more clearly. Like Zachariah, our preconceived beliefs may not match God's understanding of reality. In our dynamic and flavorful experience of studying Scripture, we are the key ingredient. And each of us can read the Bible differently. Some recipes include the line, "add salt to taste"—meaning it's up to you how much to add, according to how your tastes have developed over time. If the impact of our stories, bias, and understanding is underestimated, we can add too much flavor and overpower the intent of the text. Growing an awareness of how our past influences our perception and understanding of the present provides us a valuable foundation for healthy Biblical study. We need to slow our brains down and ask ourselves lots of why questions, seeking to dig a little deeper into how we arrived at our conclusions about God in the first place.

Questions

- What past experiences have significantly shaped how you see yourself, God, and others?
- If you could ask God any question, what would it be? How would having an answer to that question help you in your relationship with God?
- Think of a time when you overreacted to a situation. What were the thought processes that led you to respond the way you did?
- Have you encountered a story in the Bible that makes you uncomfortable, that challenges or offends your modern beliefs? If so, did this lead you to disengage with or lean into Scripture? Why?
- Since we often have blindspots when evaluating our strengths and weaknesses or overall health, consider asking your spouse or a trusted friend to provide feedback and insight. You may also consider answering the questions yourself to see if there are any differences!
  - What is your favorite thing about me?
  - Where would you say I excel or thrive?
  - What's one thing you see me struggle with regularly?
  - What's one area you think I could grow in?
- Have you ever asked God for help when taking inventory of yourself and experiences? Psalm 139:23-24 provides a prayerful framework to invite God into the process.

**Digging into our past and origins can be difficult. Seeking professional support from a counselor or therapist may be a wise and fruitful pursuit.

Additional Resources

Allender, Dan B. *To Be Told: Know Your Story, Shape Your Future*

Benner, David G. "The Spiritual Journey" Trilogy: *Desiring God's Will: Aligning Our Hearts with the Heart of God*; *Surrender to Love: Discovering the Heart of Christian Spirituality*; and *The Gift of Being Yourself: The Sacred Call to Self-Discovery*

Friesen, James G., E. James Wilder, Anne M. Bierling, Rick Koepcke, and Maribeth Poole. *The Life Model: Living From the Heart Jesus Gave You*

Warner, Marcus. *A Deeper Walk: A Proven Path for Developing a More Vibrant Faith*

New Line Cinema: *The Nativity Story* (film clip)
https://youtu.be/_zyt6VLQTC8?si=qcYMRx55yOoRpnbs&t=382

6. The Ingredient of How We Understand History: History Is Messy

Anybody can make history.
Only a great man can write it.

—OSCAR WILDE

History is an agreed upon set of lies.

—ATTRIBUTED TO NAPOLEON BONAPARTE

Everything about [this] find [...]
is so darn difficult to interpret.

—"PUZZLING FINDS" FROM THE BIBLICAL ARCHAEOLOGY SOCIETY

Samuel Gray. Samuel Maverick. Patrick Carr. Crispus Attucks. James Caldwell. Recognize any of these names? These five men lost their lives in a heated exchange between British soldiers and American Colonists in the event known as the Boston Massacre. They are remembered today by five stones, in the middle of a busy modern-day intersection, marking the place where they fell. Their tragic deaths became etched into the folklore of the American Revolution by an engraving produced by Paul Revere.

Revere's engraving, first published in 1770, portrayed the British soldiers as the instigators of the bloodshed. His desired effect was to stir up emotions among the Bostonian colonists to fan into flame the sparks of a revolution.[1] Revere's engraving, now commonly found in U.S. history textbooks, reflects the historical sentiments of Bostonians during the early stages of the American revolution.

There's one small problem with this iconic image: It does not reflect the events as they happened that day. A trial was held to determine who was responsible for the deaths of the five men. The British soldiers, represented by the future second president of the United States, John Adams, were acquitted of all charges.[2] The Bloody Massacre image is a perfect example of *propaganda*, presenting a biased narrative to further a political cause.

Many people assume history is merely facts. My educational experience encouraged this view because so many of my history exams used fill-in-the-blank questions, testing my knowledge of specific details. However, history is more than mere facts about who, what, where, and when; it is also why. The *why* of any story transcends time and space, connecting us emotionally with historical figures through shared life experiences. When we're answering the *why* question, history can take on a life of its own as historical events are reevaluated and reinterpreted by subsequent generations and different data points are stressed or downplayed to better suit the new interpretation. *There is no memory without interpretation.*[3]

History can be more of an interpretive art form than a science. We have two main sources of information for understanding history: historical documents and physical artifacts. The latter often come from the field of archeology, especially when investigating ancient history, which began as an auxiliary of biblical studies. The Bible and other ancient documents provided clues, guiding the earliest explorers where to dig. Locating cities mentioned in the Bible became essential, giving rise to the field of Biblical geography. Historical research combines the expertise of archaeologists, anthropologists, and historians, all together evaluating documents and artifacts to draw their conclusions.

Like history, archaeology is an interpretive science. Many factors can make interpreting archaeological finds confoundingly difficult. As we explore the ways ancient documents and artifacts can help provide information, it's important to remain aware of their limitations. We need to understand these two essential ingredients, history and archaeology, both factually and philosophically. Our understanding of the issues raised by these two fields of study will help us to ask good questions when we're reading the Bible. Let's start with history.

When Did History Begin?

I'd never really considered this question: "When did history begin?" I always thought history was self-evident. I was confronted on a cold February night in Jerusalem when I sat in my very first class at Jerusalem University College. "When did history begin?" was literally the opening line of the first lecture by Professor Yigal Levin. His answer to the question was matter-of-fact: "Writing."

The earliest recorded writings date to around 3300 BC, almost 5,400 years ago. Many historians agree with Levin: History begins with writing because writing provides context; without writing, it can be difficult to know anything with much certainty. An archaeologist can dig up artifacts providing evidence of human activity, but can only offer educated opinions as to the purpose and use of those objects unearthed. Written documents from that period could possibly provide an explanation for what archaeologists discover.

Interpretation is Everything

The little mermaid Ariel can help us appreciate the challenges of interpreting artifacts. In the 1989 Disney film *The Little Mermaid*, Ariel creates her own museum of sorts, filled with items familiar to humans, but from a world unfamiliar to her. She labels things in a manner that makes sense to her, calling a fork a *dinglehopper* as she brushes her hair with it. A tobacco pipe becomes a *snarfblatt*, a rare musical instrument. Without writing, archaeologists and anthropologists can be like Ariel, attempting to divine the use and purpose of an object. Even writing is not going to resolve all their issues.

The earliest writings deal mostly with commerce. They provide information regarding the costs of goods over centuries. This information can be used to explain ancient financial systems, because we literally have the receipts. But they only tell us part of the story.

As writing developed, its uses expanded beyond accounting to correspondence between kings and rulers as well as recording the acts and decrees of those leaders. All the writings that survived came from people with financial means who could afford a scribe. The Pharaohs' temples and burial chambers tell their life stories from their perspective, but we have plenty of examples that call into question how accurately those stories reflect the facts.[4] Who doesn't want to make themselves look better, especially for eternity? Written records and physical artifacts, then, might record how someone would *like* to be remembered, rather than what's historically accurate.

What was life like for someone who wasn't royalty? Average people in the ancient world did not keep personal journals—or if they did, those haven't been preserved. The data in our possession comes from a thin layer of ancient society, not representative of the whole. Historians a hundred years from now will experience the opposite—they'll have a treasure trove of information. Every word we text; every email we send; every blog, snapchat, and video we post—all these will be available for study. From a president in the White House to a sixth grader in Alaska, everybody has the potential to leave a digital footprint (except those who lack access to digital technology). As long as electricity continues to run, the data will be preserved and this information will be available for future generations to study.

How we present ourselves to the world now is much like how Pharaoh depicted himself in the wall carvings of his palace or tomb: We all desire to be perceived in a favorable light of our choosing. Staged and photoshopped images capture a perfect moment, but only a moment. Historians of the future could potentially use these pictures to create a timeline of our lives covering the who, what, where, and when questions. But the why questions remain, like: "Why did he get that tattoo in Albuquerque?" "Why was he in New Mexico in the first place?" To answer these questions, future historians or biographers examine all our texts, emails, and videos to try to piece together our motives. Even then, I assume some questions would remain unanswerable. However, if the historian is attempting to explain the *whys* of a larger cultural moment, then all this data would only represent one person's perspective on the issue. History requires putting puzzle pieces together. Sometimes we have a lot of pieces, other times only a few, and each historian must decide how they fit together. This process is part of the art form.

Art Critics Can Have an Agenda

The word *critic* often has a negative connotation, but it simply means someone who provides an evaluation of something, like a piece of art, or someone's thoughts and ideas, and ascribes merit or fault to it. A critic's assessment is meant to be persuasive, positively or negatively, and ultimately can be labeled an opinion. As I mentioned before, we all have a personal bias that informs our opinions. Our biases predispose us to see things a certain way; our evaluation can have an agenda. We already know what we believe to be true, and often we only seek information to confirm our beliefs. When it comes to historical critical research, a question to ask is this: "Is the goal of our research to understand the past, or is our desire to challenge a widely held view that we believe is inaccurate?" Historians are people too, with their own bias and possible agendas. Motives are everything.

The *Jesus Seminar* is an example of historical research, I contend, with an agenda. A group of Biblical scholars gathered in 1985 with the goal to determine which words of Jesus as recorded in the Gospels he actually said, and which were words were put in his mouth later by the authors of the New Testament. [5] Some scholars argued that the New Testament authors later ascribed sayings to Jesus for theological reasons or to suit their personal purposes. Voting in secret, the *Jesus Seminar* scholars couldn't agree amongst themselves to answer the question. "Is the Bible historically reliable to accurately record facts, namely Jesus' precise words?"

I believe that some of these scholars genuinely sought to understand what we can know about the words of Jesus. Others apparently hoped to erode people's confidence in the Bible. Let's pause for a second and critically think about the implications of their premise. I wonder: How could these scholars know with any degree of certainty which of the words recorded were actually spoken by Jesus and which ones were not?

All this theoretical background is important because the Bible does contain history. Eighty percent of the Bible's content is narrative (stories of events), but it seldom provides us with details regarding the characters' motivations and intentions. That's why many sermons or talks given on Biblical topics attempt to answer the *why* question by infusing a story thousands of years old with relevance for us today.

When we're thinking about the Bible's narrative sections, a helpful question is: What is the Bible's primary objective? The Bible first and foremost is a theological book that also contains history.[6] Its purpose is communicating God's relationship with us. The people, locations, and stories included are meant to help us know God better. As a factual document, the Bible is incredibly helpful in identifying and locating specific towns and cities, but not all of them. In describing how to evaluate the facts contained in the Bible, Jordan Ryan says that the best question to ask about a given statement is not "Is this true or false?" but "What does this mean?"[7] I would add: "Why does God want us to know this?"

However, knowing that the Bible's first objective isn't to be a history textbook doesn't dissuade us from seeking hard evidence to prove the Bible's accurate recording of history. Let's get digging.

Looking for Hard Evidence

What tangible evidence is needed to prove the historical validity of the Bible? Believers and skeptics can both ask this question. In the mid-1800s, the desire to find such evidence became a race between England, France, and Germany, and an early photograph was the starting gun. One of the earliest known photos of Jerusalem was taken in 1844 by Joseph-Philibert Girault de Prangey (scan the QR code to see it). His photo made its way through the parlors of Europe's aristocracy as stories of untold riches waiting to be discovered captured their imaginations: Solomon's treasure, the Ark of the Covenant, the Holy Grail. Discovering these coveted trophies would confirm the Bible's historical authenticity.

Scan Here to See the First Photo of Jerusalem

The invention of the steam engine spurred on the race, cutting travel time between Europe and the Holy Land from months to weeks. None of the aforementioned items were found, but many other artifacts were. They now reside in the great museums of Europe and Istanbul. Many could be interpreted as confirmation of the Bible's historical record.

One challenging issue for archaeology is proving the existence of historical figures. King David is an example of an important historical figure whose existence was, for a long time, only attested to by the Bible. How can archaeology prove or disprove his existence? Until about fifty years ago, the consensus of secular scholarship held that King David was a fictional character, created by the ancient Hebrew writers of *Tanakh*. Lacking any archaeological evidence for David, scholars and historians felt confident in their assessment.

But then, in 1993 at Tel Dan in northern Israel, an archaeologist unearthed a *stela* (a stone tablet with writing) mentioning the "house of David."[8] This piece of evidence caused a seismic shift in the scholarly consensus. However, as was to be expected, the ninth-century-BC *stela* sparked many more *why* questions than it answered. The unidentified king who authored the inscription describes slaying the kings of Judah and Israel. Many suggest Hazael of Damascus, who ruled from 843-796 BC, as a strong candidate, since the *stela* chronicles the defeat of Joram of Israel, who reigned in 849-42 BC, and Ahaziah of Judah, who ruled for one year in 842 BC.[9] Both of these kings died in the same year.

One important question is, why was this *stela* at Dan? Dan was one of two cities, along with Bethel, where Jeroboam placed golden calves to mark the northern and southern territorial boundaries of Israel. (1 Kings 12:26-30) Dan also happens to be the last city in Israel as one travels north to Damascus. Another question is: Why mention the house of David nearly a century after King David's death? Hazael possibly wanted to remind everyone, before arriving in Damascus, of his victories over the kings of Israel and Judah, the heritage of the house of David, who had subjugated Damascus in the previous century. Here is a piece of evidence implying King David's existence, but many questions still remain about the details of David's life, his reign, and the extent of his kingdom. The inscription provides an important piece of the puzzle, but only one piece.

What Are You Looking For?

Archaeologists are looking for pieces of the historical past. Their questions guide their research and sometimes lead them to reconsider long-held beliefs. For example, the 2007 film *The Lost Tomb of Jesus* documents an archaeological discovery that, if proven true, would change Christianity forever. James Cameron (director of *Titanic* and the *Terminator* franchise) served as executive producer; Jewish investigative reporter and filmmaker Simcha Jacobovici directed the movie. They claimed that a tomb found in the Jerusalem suburb of Talpiot in 1980 by archaeologist James Tabor contained the bones of Jesus.[10] What led them to believe they had found the tomb of Jesus was the discovery of bone boxes, called ossuaries, etched with the names of Jesus and other family members mentioned in the Biblical account. The docudrama implies they'd found Jesus' bones, thus proving he did not resurrect from the dead, essentially erasing the core tenet of Christianity.

Before asking the obvious, pressing question, "Did they really find Jesus' bones," let's ask a different one:

"What did Cameron and Jacobovici set out to find?"

I had the privilege of spending two weeks on an archaeological dig in Jerusalem with James Tabor and Shimon Gibson. They've been working together for years, including on the Talpiot tomb. I spoke with both of them about the docudrama's production. Gibson gave me the impression that the producers started out with an agenda to discredit Christianity despite evidence which could have easily explained the existence of ossuaries with names matching those of Jesus' family while referring to different people entirely. You can watch a response video produced by SourceFlix in which Gibson explains the problematic issues as he visits the Talpiot tomb.

Scan Here to Watch Shimon Gibson Discuss the Talpiot Tomb

You've Got to Want to Dig

Archaeology requires motivation, money, and determination to be as objective as humanly possible. Each of these factors is worthy of exploration to determine how they influence the end result of archaeological research.

Archaeology is arduous, painstakingly precise, and unglamorous. I experienced this firsthand when I participated in a dig outside the ancient walls of the Old City of Jerusalem. Our days began at five a.m. Much of my time was spent sweeping up dirt before pictures could be taken as we slowly descended, inch by inch, past the garbage of the 1960s to more interesting layers of history. As centuries-old artifacts saw the light of day for the first time in a millennium, they were carefully cataloged, documented, and photographed. All the finds would eventually be stored in a warehouse, waiting for an archaeologist to analyze and then publish the findings, but decades can pass before such findings are eventually made public. No archaeologist wants to stop their more active work to write, unless their findings could dramatically rewrite history. To this day, final reports from digs in the 1960s and 70s remain unpublished.

Now, let's go back and ask: How does a town disappear from human history, then later become so interesting that someone thousands of years later wants to go, find it, and spend lots of money to uncover it? It all starts with the real estate adage: *location, location, location.*

For a location to be habitable, it must have sources of food, water, and means of protection. Once they find these essentials, people establish settlements, that grow into towns, that then become part of strategic trade routes or crossroads. Then, the economic and military value of these locations causes other people to desire them as well. Battles ensue over the real estate. The locals either repel the invaders or get overrun. Because of the city's strategic location, the victors rebuild, often reusing the materials already on site. The process repeats itself, creating layers of civilization called *strata* within a *Tel*, an ancient mound of successive levels of habitation. For example, Tel Gezer consists of more than twenty-five *strata* in an area of thirty-three acres. The repeated destruction and rebuilding raise the elevation of a site over time until these locations take on the look of an extinct volcano. A major battle creates a destruction layer, a thin layer of ash. Matching the historical records with these destruction layers helps sync the different strata to a historical timeline, prompting esteemed archaeologist Gabriel Barkay to say frequently: "Someone's bad day is a good day for an archaeologist." Destruction layers are often very reliable historical markers.

The earliest archaeologists in the late 1800s dug for artifacts. As the process of archaeology developed, the reasons they dug also matured to include seeking answers to questions of historical importance. A more scientific approach produced practices with more precision. Modern archaeological digs now begin with a site survey looking for surface pottery, often followed by taking sonar or radio soundings before a shovel touches the dirt— unimaginable a hundred years ago. But we still need to interpret what is found, and that comes with a host of challenges, including finding someone to pay the bills.[11]

Follow the Money

By the time archaeological findings reach the general population, they're typically either overly sensationalized and/or simplified. For example, a recent article hit the internet titled, "A glimpse into the wardrobe of King David and King Solomon, 3000 years ago."[12] Pure clickbait. The artifacts found have no direct connection to either famous king mentioned—but *made you look*. Anyone who does research needs to get attention, because attention attracts funding.

Archaeologists need patrons and grants if they are going to dig. The motivations of the archaeologists themselves can attract different types of donors who desire specific outcomes, because securing funding often requires notoriety and a good story. In the early 1900s, Montague Parker, with the help of a Christian mystic, claimed to know the location of the ark of the covenant in Israel. Funds were raised and he set off to Israel in 1909. But he failed to find the ark, and he nearly died in the process. More recently, a Christian group from Texas who believed the Lord had given them the precise location of the ark raised funds and traveled to Jerusalem. They enlisted Barkay's assistance as one of the leading and longest-tenured archaeologists in Israel; he also happens to be an expert on Jerusalem. As he recounted the story to me, he shared: "I didn't believe them, but they were willing to pay." The group confidently led him to the place they believed was the ark's exact location within the Church of the Holy Sepulcher. Leading him to a door off the main room, they said, "It's in there." Mystified, Barkay shook his head: The church's bathrooms were in there! Barkay had dug extensively throughout the Holy Sepulcher during his career and knew the place very well. What the group didn't know was that those very bathrooms had recently undergone renovations, requiring archaeological verification work to be conducted as part of the process. Nothing of historical significance existed below those toilets.

Patrons and their money are needed for research to be conducted. Their funds make archaeology possible; we hope it is money well spent.

Slow to Change

Changing long-held beliefs requires conviction and determination; this is as true of archaeologists as anyone. For decades, the location of the Biblical city Bethsaida was identified as Et Tel, a site located on a hill north of the Sea of Galilee. Bethsaida, which means *house of the hunt*—as in fishing—is famous for being the hometown of several disciples, including Peter. Its current site identification is about a mile and a half away from the Sea of Galilee. Why would fishermen live so far away from the water? The explanation offered is that the shoreline must have receded away from the site over the past two thousand years, but we don't have enough evidence to prove this hypothesis. The geographical position of Et Tel led Professor Steven Notley to search for another plausible location for Bethsaida, closer to the water. Scouring ancient travel journals, comparing old maps, and researching city toponyms, he did an initial site survey at a place called El Araj located on the shore. The first several seasons of digging at El Araj found evidence of occupation at the site from the first through the fifth centuries AD. The team also found the remains of the Byzantine era Church of St. Peter, commemorating the apostle Peter's hometown, Bethsaida. [13] (John 1:44) These discoveries indicate that the shoreline of the Sea of Galilee remains relatively unchanged from Jesus' day, and that El Araj is the likely location of the Biblical Bethsaida. [14]

However, Rami Arav, the archaeologist who discovered the waterless Bethsaida, still contends that Et Tel is the location, despite this new information. Knowing this, I asked Dr. Notley why other scholars are reluctant to adjust their long-held views. He politely responded that time would take care of everything: The data will eventually persuade others to change their entrenched positions. (While I waited to ask my question, he and his assistant were discussing the money needed for next year's dig).

Digging continues at El Araj, attempting to further confirm the likelihood of its being the Biblical Bethsaida. But in the future, another ancient town could be discovered nearby that could change our opinion. Archaeology requires being as objective as possible and remaining open to new information.

Becoming a student of history and archaeology requires curiosity and discernment. Before we start applying what we've learned by looking at specific stories in the Bible, we have one last topic to address—the philosophy of language. Understanding the process of communication is just as important as the words that are used to communicate.

Questions

- What is your definition of history? Why?
- Do you believe your understanding of history is subjective? Why or why not?
- How does your perspective on history impact your understanding of the past?
- Viewing the Bible as a theological book that contains history, how would you feel if an aspect of the Bible could not be historically verified?
- What archaeological discovery, if any, would increase your faith in the Bible? Why?
- After reading this chapter, how will you evaluate archaeological information more critically? Why?

Additional Resources

Bolen, Todd. "Photos Illustrating Scripture and the Biblical World" https://www.bibleplaces.com/

ESV Archaeology Study Bible

Hess, Richard S. *Israelite Religions: An Archaeological and Biblical Survey*

Hoffmeier, James K., and Dennis R. Magary, eds. *Do Historical Matters Matter to Faith?*

Kennedy, Titus. *Unearthing the Bible: 101 Archaeological Discoveries That Bring the Bible to Life*

Kramer, Joel P. *Where God Came Down*

Lawler, Andrew. *Under Jerusalem: The Buried History of the World's Most Contested City*

Oswalt, John N. *The Bible Among the Myths: Unique Revelation or Just Ancient Literature?*

Keimer, Kyle and McKinny, Chris. "Archaeology: What It Is and What It Does" https://onscript.study/chris-and-kyle-archaeology-what-it-is-and-what-it-does/

Expedition Bible: "The Jesus Tomb... Unmasked!" https://www.youtube.com/watch?v=N8ki0CAxc6M&t=1153s

7. The Ingredient of How We Communicate: Language Is Messier

Words are the ingredients of communication, but the same word can mean different things to different people. We each use language to explain and define our reality. However, language evolves constantly, and the same word can have different meanings to different people across different time periods.

Here's an example: The common Arabic expression, *Inshallah*, means "If God wills it" but can have very different implications in various contexts. When getting our car fixed in Israel, we asked our Arabic-speaking mechanic if the car would be fixed by tomorrow. He responded with "Inshallah." His use of *inshallah* was his way of saying he didn't know how long it would take to complete the repairs. To say *no* directly in his culture would be rude and even shameful, so he gave us a politely evasive answer that allowed him to save face.

My wife experienced *inshallah* differently. At the conclusion of her language-tutoring sessions, she and her tutor would agree on the next time to meet. Once they'd picked a time, her tutor always said "Inshallah." This expression acknowledged that she wasn't in control of what the future holds. Yet she always showed up for their sessions, which led Janie to understand the word differently. They enjoyed their time together; in addition, the tutor's financial incentive encouraged her *inshallah* to happen. Two speakers using the same word gave it quite different meanings.

Cross-cultural communication is challenging enough between people living today, let alone adding a few millennia to the mix when reading the Bible. If history can be subjective, how much more so the language used to write that history? To grasp what's being communicated at any given time, we need to be aware of the process and philosophy of communication, which dramatically affects how we read the Bible.

Why the Rosetta Stone Matters

Written language uses symbols with shared assigned meanings and those symbols combine to describe our world. Egyptian hieroglyphics are a classic example. They were unreadable before 1800, even though linguists, archaeologists, and anthropologists combined their expertise to attempt to decipher their meaning. The discovery of the Rosetta Stone in 1799, during Napoleon's invasion of Egypt, was the key to unlocking this mystery. The *stela* contained one identical statement in three different languages: ancient Greek, Egyptian hieroglyphics, and Demotic (a cursive form of ancient Egyptian). Of those three, only the Greek was known, so it was used to translate the other two. Egyptologists cracked the code, beginning the process of better understanding how ancient Egyptians viewed their world.

What if an Egyptian from 196 B.C. could double-check the work of the Rosetta Stone's translators? Would they confirm its accuracy? To do so, that ancient Egyptian person would need to know our language fluently, as well. Indeed, they would have to understand our culture, too. Being able to read a piece of writing is one thing; understanding its fullest meaning is another. Cultural translation will always be a messy process because it requires a cultural expert of two different worlds to translate accurately back and forth.

A Little Knowledge Can Be Dangerous

Three semesters of biblical Hebrew allowed me to read Hebrew script, but I don't know what all the words mean, let alone the depth of cultural nuance behind each word or phrase. Becoming truly fluent in a language takes a lifetime of continuous immersion, and linguistic research never ends. Textual experts make use of research from the fields of anthropology and archaeology to glean cultural insights whose meanings are themselves embedded in words. Over time, new discoveries necessitate reevaluating the definition of words. The goal of translation is to accurately convey the basic meaning of a word and its cultural underpinnings, including its connotations—the internalized emotional connections the word could elicit beyond definitions found in a dictionary. Comprehension of words is just the beginning of the process of understanding; truly understanding how someone thinks and feels about the world through the language they use requires a deep understanding of the culture in which the word's meanings are formed. Acquiring this level of sophisticated knowledge of any language takes far more than a mere three semesters of study.

My Hebrew professor taught that students of a language have two moving targets: first, the word itself (with its spelling developing over time); second, its meaning during a specific time period. How, then, can we know with absolute precision what words meant to a group of people in a particular time period? Total certainty is probably out of reach, and studying linguistics requires continuous open-minded research.

English speakers have experienced the development of our own language as the meanings of words change over time. For example, if I said, "I'm gay" two hundred years ago, listeners might have responded: "I'm glad you're happy." Today, I could possibly be communicating something quite different. A word's meanings morph in real time, and new words develop to meet the emotional and physical demands of the moment. Aware of this reality, the Oxford English Dictionary adds new words to its volumes every year. The word *rizz* won word of the year in 2023. (If you don't know what *rizz* means, find a teenager and ask them). The spellings of words also change over time, as well. When my grandparents were in grade school, they were taught to spell *plow* as *plough*; a holdover from American English's British ancestry. Language is not static because we live in a dynamic environment.

Language is ultimately philosophical, because it's the means by which people describe their world and ascribe meaning to it. Often, the words they use are understood fully only by cultural insiders. For example, I have a hard time following the "Who's on First?" comedy routine by Abbott and Costello—that's the point (use the QR code to watch). Imagine an English-language-learner trying to comprehend that skit; they would have little chance. To get the joke, one would have to have a basic knowledge of baseball, the days of the week, and pronouns. The joke is about how hard it is to understand simple words if we take them out of context, even though they mean exactly what they mean at face value.

Scan Here to Watch "Who's On First?" by Abbot & Costello

Communication is Philosophical

There are two main questions that we need answers to, and I'm confident you can handle the truth, because we all too often experience the challenges of communicating well every day. The first question is: How do we know something? The second is: What are the words we use to communicate that knowledge? These are philosophical questions. A composite definition of philosophy is: "The study of the fundamental nature of knowledge and reality as a system of thought."[1] Each of us possess an individual understanding of what we know about the world, and this personal knowledge creates our perception of reality. Our perception of reality becomes a system of thought explaining how we see the world and our place in it—essentially addressing our internal *why* questions. Our *whys*, which we use to assign value, meaning, and purpose, inform our actions and interpret new information that comes into our spheres of experience. We use words to communicate our *whys*, to explain to someone else how we experience and see the world. Moreover, the words we use to communicate our *whys* can be very individualized, because *we each create our own personal dictionaries in our heads.*

How do we share all this deeply personal information with another person? It can be extremely difficult. My wife and I have been married for almost twenty-five years, yet we still experience conflict due to our different definitions of the same word. We now joke over our different words for a common leafy green vegetable. I always call it salad; she calls it lettuce. So, I might ask her, "Would you like salad for the tacos?" and she'd respond, "Do you mean lettuce?" Our length of time together and knowledge of each other certainly helps minimize such misunderstandings, but there is still much we're discovering about each other. Like everyone else in a long-term relationship, my wife and I both use shared and personal dictionaries, have different communication styles, and assume that we think the same, all of which gets in the way of seeking to understand. We assume too much. If this is the case between two people who know each other well and share geography, language, and culture, imagine trying to communicate with a neighbor, someone from another state, or (more challenging) someone from another country. Imagine God trying to communicate with us!

How Does God Communicate with Us?

Language and its meanings form through shared experiences that eventually create a culture of shared understanding. For example, to get a laugh in our house, all you have to do is say *crêpes* in a foreign accent. Everyone remembers the time we tried to order a crepe overseas, but the waiter struggled to understand our accents. A man nearby came to everyone's rescue and said *crêpe* with the appropriately placed syllables. This is an example of insider language within our family, a short-hand reference to a shared experience from our past. Spend time with a group of people long enough, and insider language will emerge, emphasizing shared experiences and collectively agreed-upon words to describe a past event. Nothing like a good one-word joke to make people laugh!

However, we all too often experience the not-so-funny frustration inherent in the process of communication, because we lack shared experiences with other insider groups and their corresponding mutually-agreed upon dictionary. If we could say, hypothetically, that God has one limitation— it's us! *We* limit his ability to communicate his reality to us because of our limited shared experiences. God knows and experiences all; we don't. Our experiences are confined to a tiny fraction of our own world, our moment in space and time. So, for God to communicate with us and be understood, he uses metaphors and shared experiences held in common by both parties to communicate ideas and concepts beyond our experiences. It's like Albert Einstein using toy trucks, bananas, and string to communicate quantum physics to a five-year-old. To share a concept someone has never experienced, we have to use language, "It's like...." We must find common ground to have any chance of communicating something new with someone outside of our culture... and that means that at least one of the two communicators must know the other's cultural background.

It's a good thing God is God. He made our world and knows it better than we do. In the Bible, God communicates who he is, which we would never be able to understand otherwise (Psalms 145:3), by describing his character using images and metaphors embedded within a Middle Eastern culture from thousands of years ago. He's a *shepherd* (first used in Genesis 48:15 and throughout the *Tanakh*). He's a *rock*. (Deuteronomy 32:15) He's *living water*. (Jeremiah 2:13) Those words and their corresponding images come from a time, land, culture, and language much different from our own. We have some cross-cultural work to do to grasp how God is communicating with us. I do believe God communicates with great intentionality, and our job is to figure out what he meant when he spoke to the original audience. We need to ask: What did they hear and how did they hear it?

Communication Is Intentional

Why do we speak? We desire to be known, heard, and seen—basic human needs. We use words to share our inner world with others so that they can understand how we see the outer world. God spoke for the same reasons; without God's initiation, we wouldn't know much about him. The Bible's existence demonstrates God's desire to be known, but it can be challenging to interpret, which leads to misunderstandings. We've all experienced the hurt and frustration that can come from misunderstanding or from being misunderstood.

Due to all these complexities, researchers have long sought to understand the process of communication. In the simplest terms, they've identified two parties involved in communication: the sender/speaker and the receiver/hearer. Miscommunication occurs when the expectations of the sender are not met by the receiver. This perspective has led to some philosophical approaches that focus primarily on what the hearer receives, almost to the point of negating the intent of the speaker. Observationally, this approach makes sense: What the hearer receives is the end result of communication. This approach to understanding communication can be called a *postmodern* perspective.[2] Its predecessor, the *modern* era, can be described as a time when a majority of the population shared a common view of the world (or at least gave the appearance of doing so), with much of Western society seemed to use the same dictionary, crisply defining words and terms. The expression "black or white" is emblematic of this era, since concepts and ideas, like right and wrong, were viewed as wholly distinct. Little to no gray area was acknowledged.

The postmodern era acknowledges the existence of gray areas, as evidenced by, for example, miscommunication.[3] Postmodern theories of language take into account the fact that we all have different shared experiences and means of communicating, which makes it difficult to define words, the foundation of successful communication, to everyone's mutual satisfaction. Postmodernism seeks to understand why sometimes we'll ask for a glass of juice and get water instead; it asks: What did the hearer hear, and why?

Postmodernists observe and acknowledge that we all don't think the same; thus, we can use the same words but have different intended meanings. I think we need to acknowledge that the intentions of the speaker are the reason communication happens in the first place. Overemphasizing the end result of communication (or miscommunication) implies the existence of an original thought by the speaker; otherwise, there would be nothing to be misunderstood. If our emphasis is only on what the hearer receives, then the intentions of the speaker are a moot point. However, acknowledging our frustration in trying to be understood tells us we had an original intent when we spoke. Our words have *intended meaning* and if we want to communicate our intentions, we need to build shared dictionaries.

I once heard a recording of an exchange between the late, now-disgraced, apologist Ravi Zacharias[4] and a college student that exposes the illogical aspects of postmodern thinking when taken too far. During a Q&A, a student took the microphone and said: "Words, words, words—words have no meaning."

Zacharias responded, "What?" Again, the student repeated his rant. Zacharias repeated his response. The student began once again to repeat himself, but as he did, his voice began to fade while the realization came slowly upon him: He was using words to discredit the meaning of words. Words do have inherent meaning to the speaker, spoken for a reason. Having those words received and understood as intended by the receiver takes time and patience. When it comes to the Bible, if we embrace the extreme version of postmodern language theory, then it would not matter what God intended when he spoke; we could make his words mean whatever we wanted them to mean.

The words of the Bible are meant to communicate God's understanding of our world: his definition of reality, described in words. We need a dictionary shared between us and God if we are going to be able to comprehend what he is communicating. Neglecting this effort puts us at great risk of harm, because God's reality is reality. We will experience a great deal of frustration with God and others over matters much more significant than lettuce if we live out of our own definitions of words, crafting our own perspective on reality in the process. Thankfully, we can choose to spend time seeking to understand others and building a common dictionary with those we love, including God. We can start with the words of the Bible: I personally believe these words of the Bible were chosen intentionally and carefully and preserved for us so we can understand the world from God's perspective.

Emotionally Packed Words

In the Introduction, I referred to the Bible as a word-picture book. Not only do many of these words reflect the physical environments of the land of Israel, but they also carry with them an emotional component. One of the unexpected treasures those who travel with me to Israel bring home with them is the emotional connection to many words from the Bible. For example, after someone hikes in the heat through the desert, finding shade provides immediate relief and enables them to feel what the Psalmist meant when he said: "The LORD is the shade at my right hand." (Psalms 121:5) Being physically present in the land brings this verse to life in vivid ways.

Such contextual reading can help interpret confusing passages, too. In Psalms 23:2, we read "He makes me lie down in green pastures." Reading this passage as a farm boy raised in Michigan, I envision a field belly-high with alfalfa as far as the eye can see. But if we were standing in the wilderness on the eastern slopes of the Judah mountains, the area called "the green pastures," we would be bewildered by the phrase, because most of the year, the hills are brown and look barren, giving the impression that there is little for sheep to eat. Yet this is the place the Psalmist probably thought of as "the green pastures." Why? Well, the Psalmist taps into the emotional reality of shepherding sheep. In what appears to us to be a desolate place with little provision, the sheep feel safe to lie down and rest because they trust that their good shepherd will protect and provide for them, giving them what they need when they need it. In Psalm 23, we are the sheep, and God is the good shepherd. The *aha!* moment hits when we realize that God desires to care for us in the same way. Possessing a culturally accurate word-picture changes everything.

Closing the Chronology Gap of Understanding

Words are infused with both literal and emotional meanings, so a single, benign word can trigger one person but not another. For me, it's two words: *Soviet Union.* Hearing that phrase sparks a twinge of anxiety inside me. Growing up towards the end of the Cold War, I heard discussions of nuclear war all over the news, and the Soviet Union was always the proverbial bogeyman. I remember practicing duck-and-cover drills in elementary school in preparation for a nuclear attack, as if being hunched under our school desks was going to provide protection. The fear was real, and the words *Soviet Union* still evoke negative emotions in me decades later.

Forty years does not seem that long ago in comparison to the timeline of the Bible. But our ability to emotionally comprehend the impact of events from forty years ago can be equally lost upon us as those from two thousand years ago. Let me illustrate. Ronald Regan spoke to the National Association of Evangelicals in 1983. In his speech, he famously called the Soviet Union "the evil empire," citing the Soviets' tyranny over and control of their own people.5 When speaking or lecturing, I often play this clip of Reagan's speech and then ask someone under the age of thirty: "What did President Reagan mean by those words?" Some can remember the former Soviet Union and that it is now called Russia. But seldom is anyone able to put President Reagan's words into the context of the cold war and explain how his words emotionally resonated with the Baby Boomer generation. If Reagan's words, spoken four decades ago, have lost their cultural and emotional context for Millennials and Gen Z, then how much more have the words spoken in a different culture and language by Jesus two millennia ago been lost on all of us? Or the words of Moses some fifteen centuries before Jesus? Illustrations like this can help us to consider the challenges we face when reading the Bible.

In the first half of this book, we've explored helpful ingredients that will assist us in understanding ourselves and the Bible. The Bible was written to real people in a real time and place; God sought to engage them, and he desires to do the same for us today. These ingredients will be sprinkled throughout the second half of the book. See if you can spot them as we unpack some familiar stories with an eye towards cultural contextualization. Reading the Bible as God intended is about knowing we belong, walking alongside Jesus, wanting to be like him, and internalizing our theological conclusions. How we choose to live depends in part on how we read the Bible, so let's continue to learn how to read it better together.

Questions

- Do you have an inside joke or phrase shared between friends or family?
- When was the last time you felt misunderstood? What role did language play in creating confusion? How did you seek to be understood?
- Are there phrases or expressions that are hard to understand in the Bible? If so, what are they? How would knowing what they meant to the original audience help you?
- How do you interpret/misinterpret the Bible because of your own language bias?
- Have you read a passage of Scripture that stirred your emotions? If so, what was the passage, and why did it connect with your heart?
- How will you apply your new knowledge of these key ingredients to read the Bible as well as you possibly can?

Additional Resources

Schaeffer, Francis A. *How Should We Then Live? The Rise and Decline of Western Thought and Culture*

Tverberg, Lois. "Welcome to En-Gedi...."
https://engediresourcecenter.com/

Veith, Gene Edward. *Postmodern Times: A Christian Guide to Contemporary Thought and Culture*

Abbot & Costello: "Who's On First?"
https://youtu.be/sYOUFGfK4bU?si=5sF3sNKktEOZ3EHr&t=64

SECTION TWO:
Reading with Different Eyes

Have you ever held an opinion on a topic or issue with seemingly unshakeable conviction, only to discard that position entirely when something more compelling or convincing comes along? I think we've all done that a time or two. When it comes to Biblical studies, I've found adopting a "file cabinet" mentality is helpful. Like many people, I'm often inclined to discard ideas that have been supplanted by ones I find more convincing. But when it comes to the Bible, storing away different opinions on the same subject adds to my depth of understanding. Sometimes this creates some mild cognitive dissonance, but acknowledging various perspectives on a particular issue helps me to be intellectually flexible and curious rather than just seeking the one right answer, especially when multiple reasonable answers are available and the evidence isn't sufficient to favor one over the others.

8. Speed Bumps

*Our understanding of Scripture must always be open to
refinement. All interpretations of Scripture need to be
tentatively final. They have to be final in the sense that
obedience cannot wait for the disciple to read yet one more
technical article in biblical studies. At the same time, all efforts
in biblical interpretation are flawed. Our interpretation of
Scripture, therefore, must never be closed to correction and
revision.*

—KENNETH BAILEY, *JESUS THROUGH MIDDLE-EASTERN EYES*

*Your Bible was written for you,
but not to you.*

—JOHN WALTON, *THE LOST WORLD*

My family and I have been privileged to live in Israel for long periods
over the past twelve years. Each time we transition from the U.S. to Israel,
we need to do some mental adjusting. One adjustment involves unmarked
speed bumps: They lurk everywhere in the Holy Land. Six speed bumps
lie between the main road and the turnoff to our home outside of
Jerusalem—six opportunities to jostle my kids in the back seat. My
familiarity with the road works against me; deep in thought or
conversation, I often forget their existence (the speed bumps, not the
kids), and then my car and its passengers experience startling bounces.
In my defense, the speed bumps are perfectly camouflaged, matching the
black asphalt of the road. In an act of self-preservation, my children count
the bumps as we drive to help me be aware. "One.... That's two.... Hey,
Daddy, here comes number three!" When catching unintended air with
our little Honda, I feel embarrassed, frustrated by my lack of attention.
Why do I forget they exist? My familiarity encourages my mind to wander,
to my detriment and to others'.

The same thing can happen when we read our Bibles. We're familiar with the stories, so our minds wander while we read. Instead of paying attention to what the text actually says, we often replay in our heads what we've been previously taught about that particular passage. Our over-familiarity is as if we are reading on autopilot, our minds not fully present.

But then we hit a speed bump: something in the story that seems strange, jarring, or inexplicable. We're snapped back into a sudden awareness that this story wasn't written to us, but to people who lived thousands of years ago. What we're reading probably made much more sense to them, but we've lost some cultural context that would help us readily grasp its meaning and application.

It is tempting to want to move on, but we can't keep skipping over stuff that doesn't make sense. We need to slow down and exercise some courage to ask questions, such as: How do these messy bits fit into the larger story? Why does God want me to know them? Courage and persistence are needed, because I don't know if I will find a satisfying answer, and I can be tempted to ignore confusing parts. But also, if I'm honest, sometimes catching air while hitting a speed bump is kind of fun.

If you've researched any topic, you've noticed that its experts don't all agree. This is true of Biblical studies, too. Michael Heiser points out something that might seem obvious but is seldom acknowledged: Such giants of Christian virtue and thought as Augustine, Aquinas, Luther, Calvin, and Wesley arrived at "dramatically different conclusions on many topics in many different passages."[1]

Great. If these brilliant, Jesus-loving giants of the faith can't agree, what is someone like me supposed to do? Well, there is one thing I can do: Join them in the discussion by asking questions.

When it comes to the Bible, we have a tendency to bury our questions, to suffocate curiosity, possibly out of self-protection. Fearful that our questions may be misconstrued as doubt, questioning God, revealing a lack of faith, or being disrespectful, we keep them to ourselves. We would like to do a little research without being judged. Our questions can make us feel vulnerable—they expose our heart's longings as well as how we perceive ourselves, God, and others. Questions open us up to having our worldviews challenged. Also, sometimes we just don't know where to begin to look for reasonable answers, and we'd rather try to muffle the tension of not knowing or not understanding.

Growth happens when we get curious enough to dig for new information. I encourage you to cultivate a mind capable of searching the Scriptures: roll up your sleeves and decide for yourself what to do with the messy parts.

The rest of this book examines some of these Scriptural speed bumps, encouraging you to ask questions. I'll offer cultural context that I hope will help you slow down and take heart: *Helpful answers can be found.* I've chosen passages I found immensely helpful to wrestle through in my own faith journey. Over time, applying the ingredients of cultural context described in the first half of this book brought my dusty theology to life and changed how I live. I hope they will do the same for you.

Violently the Kingdom Advances

I hit one big speed bump during Jesus' description of the role of John the Baptist in the book of Matthew, soon after John's imprisonment by Herod Antipas.[2] Jesus is explaining how John fulfills a prophetic role in announcing the coming of the kingdom of heaven—and then, *bam!* I was jolted by this verse:

"The kingdom of heaven has been forcefully/violently advancing, and forceful/violent men lay hold of it." (Matthew 11:12, emphasis added)

"Forcefully/violently advancing" and "forceful/violent men" sounded cryptic to me, and clunky in English. I immediately wondered: What was the original Greek? Is there a Hebraic cultural underpinning for this particular phrase? Deeply curious, I asked anyone with any theological training: "What does this mean? How was the kingdom of heaven violently advancing? Is this passage justifying violence for believers?" No one, trained or untrained in theology, could offer a satisfying answer. I persisted, hitting this speed bump over and over at full speed.

In my search for answers, I came across materials from the Jerusalem School of Synoptic Research, founded by pastor-scholar Robert Lindsey and David Flusser, the leading Jewish scholar on Jesus at that time. Focused on the Biblical text (lower criticism) and on linguistics, they also applied higher criticism to reading the Gospels as stories about a first-century Jewish rabbi communicating with his immediate audience.

In those days, rabbis functioned like Old Testament prophets; using the *Tanakh* as a mirror and guide, rabbis taught people how to live faithfully in their current circumstances and interpret present-day events through their reading of the text. Rabbis employed well-established hermeneutical principles. Knowing this historical fact led Flusser to suggest that Jesus was using those principles to connect the Hebrew Scriptures (specifically the prophet Micah) to explain John's role in God's larger redemptive narrative.

Digging into this particular messy bit will be very instructive about how rabbis convey information, and will help you learn how to ask different types of questions. The principles of rabbinical interpretation will guide us to uncover an obscure but powerful connection in Jesus' words in Matthew 11:12 to the words of the prophet Micah, which in turn will reveal how God's redemptive plan unfolds. Ultimately, I discovered that this approach answered my urgent questions about violence and the kingdom of God, and at the same time, provided me with tools to help me read the Bible. So, let's slow down and look at the implications of Jesus' words through the lens of a first-century rabbi.

Why So Many Different Translations?

Translating anything from one culture to another is challenging; even more so is translating a text from one language to another. Steven Notley, a distinguished professor of New Testament and Christian Origins at Nyack College, said in a lecture that Matthew 11:12 in Greek is one of the most difficult passages to translate in the whole New Testament.[3] This possibly explains the variety of word choices translators use. Below is a sampling of various English translations of Matthew 11:12. Pay special attention to the underlined phrases.

> From the days of John the Baptist until now, the kingdom of heaven has been subjected to violence, and violent people have been raiding it. (New International Version)

> And from the time John the Baptist began preaching until now, the kingdom of heaven has been forcefully advancing, and violent

people are <u>attacking</u> it. (New Living Translation)

From the days of John the Baptist until now the kingdom of heaven <u>suffers/has suffered violence</u>, and <u>the violent/violent men take it by force</u>. (English Standard Version, New American Standard Bible, New King James Version)

These translations read as if there is a fearsome resistance attempting to slow the kingdom of heaven's advancement—perhaps even one that necessitates a forceful or violent response by God's people. [4] That interpretation could explain John's imprisonment. But how does that work? Does the kingdom advance by means of violent men who then take it by force? Is Jesus justifying, advocating, or even commanding the use of force by his followers? If so, this reading of the passage seems to contradict Jesus' teaching to love one's enemy.

The translations above are the first of three modes of translating we must consider: literal "translation" from Greek into English. The second is "back-translating" the Greek into Hebrew. The third will be "cultural translation": reading this passage from the Hebrew with a first-century rabbinical worldview.

First, let's apply back-translation to this verse. Some scholars hold that Matthew was first written in Hebrew and then translated into Greek. We don't know if that's accurate, but we do know that a *Hebraism* lies behind the Greek. Hebraisms are words or phrases carrying Jewish cultural meaning and nuance, and those are clearly being used here. Below are two English translations of Matthew 11:12 from the Greek into Hebrew and then back into English.

From the days of John (the Baptist) until now the Kingdom of Heaven is <u>breaking through</u> and <u>breakers-through break through</u> with it. (Jerusalem School of Synoptic Research)

From the days of John the Baptist until now, the kingdom of heaven <u>breaks forth</u> and everyone <u>breaks forth</u> with it.[5]

These versions give the impression of the kingdom of heaven breaking forth and initiating a continuing breaking-forth among Jesus' followers.

This translation better aligns with Jesus' teaching in general and infuses readers with optimism rather than bracing them for conflict.

The Gospel of Matthew

As we've learned, knowing an author's background is an important ingredient to help us understand context and audience. Matthew was a most unlikely candidate for a disciple of Jesus. He was a tax collector working in Capernaum, Jesus' base of operations. His fellow Jews would've been hesitant to embrace Matthew as their own, due to his collaboration with the Romans to collect taxes. In addition, handling coins with images of people on them would make any *Torah*-observant Jew unclean. (Exodus 20:4; Numbers 19) Due to Matthew's official position as a tax collector and his potential perpetual uncleanness, he probably lived on the fringes of his Jewish community. Jesus is not deterred by this, and invites Matthew to walk away from his lucrative job to follow him. Ironically, God chooses the one disciple who may have been held at arms' distance from his fellow Jews, and possibly even despised, to be the one to tell them Jesus' story. Despite his probable ostracization from his Jewish community, he demonstrates a thorough understanding of their *Torah*-observant world—awareness and training he may have acquired in his youth, before he became a tax collector.

Matthew employs Hebraic idioms and a style of communicating befitting the rabbinical mindset of his day, which would be understood readily by a Jewish audience. Knowing this, when we come across a confusing passage, our first place to look for clarification should be the Jewish context of the first century.

Expectations Are Everything

In Matthew's account, Jesus answers John the Baptist from within the context of first-century Messianic expectations. Jewish writings from the Apocrypha and the Qumran community give us a sense of how their interpretation of the *Tanakh* provided expectant hope during the two hundred years leading up to Jesus. It was generally believed a forerunner would come before the Messiah, whose arrival they thought was imminent. Then, upon his arrival, the long-awaited Messiah would usher in the kingdom of heaven on earth. John's message of "repent, for the kingdom of heaven is at hand" demonstrates his sense of urgency to prepare for the Messiah's coming.

Reading the Gospels, even for the first time, most of us are already aware that Jesus is the main character, the Messiah. John and Jesus were cousins who grew up seeing each other at family gatherings; when did John come to believe Jesus is the Messiah? We aren't told, but John demonstrates his belief by baptizing his cousin at the beginning of his public ministry. However, John also believes that when the Messiah comes, he will immediately judge the world and usher in God's kingdom. Jesus challenges John's understanding of how and when the kingdom will come. John's unmet expectations are compounded by his imprisonment. Incarcerated and facing imminent execution, John experiences doubt. He wonders if he'd been mistaken about his cousin being the Messiah. So, he sends his disciples to Jesus, seeking a theological answer to his very real, personal, physical and emotional needs.

John's disciples find Jesus and ask him: "Are you the one who is to come?" This question is first-century Jewish code, drawn from the books of Daniel and Enoch, for "Are you the Messiah?"

Jesus replies:

Go back and report to John what you hear and see: The blind receive sight, the lame walk, those who have leprosy are cured, the deaf hear, the dead are raised, and the good news is preached to the poor. Blessed is the man who does not fall away on account of me. (Matthew 11:4-6)

This is fantastic news, because Jesus' statement alludes to six prophetic Old Testament passages describing how people's lives will be changed upon the Messiah's arrival:

1. The blind receiving sight—Isaiah 29:18; 35:5
2. The lame walking—Isaiah 35:6; 61:1
3. Lepers being cured—Isaiah 61:1
4. The deaf hearing—Isaiah 29:18; 35:5
5. The dead being raised up—implied in Isaiah 11:1-2

6. Good news being preached to the poor—Isaiah 61:1-2

Jesus is using a teaching technique of hinting at or alluding to Old Testament passages as a way of communicating in shorthand. His Biblically literate audience would have readily picked up on these references and the context surrounding them, not focusing only on the specific phrases themselves. For example, reading the whole context of Isaiah 35:4 tells us God will be the one who does these things when he comes as the Messiah. These miracles will act as pronouncements of the Messiah's presence as God on earth. Isaiah 61 also affirms the uniqueness of this person by proclaiming that "The Spirit of the Sovereign LORD is upon [him]." Jesus applies all these passages to himself, proclaiming to his audience that he is indeed the Messiah.

However, Jesus leaves out the ending of Isaiah 61:1, "proclaiming liberty to the captives." By intentionally omitting this one phrase while including all the surrounding material, Jesus affirms to John that he is indeed the Messiah but also lets him know he will not get out of jail. John had misunderstood how and when the kingdom would come fully, but Jesus' answer shows him the truth.[6]

Imagine John's emotions: excitement at Jesus identifying himself as the Messiah, combined with confusion and disappointment. John must have pondered how he'd misinterpreted the *Tanakh* regarding how and when the Messiah would inaugurate his kingdom. Jesus does fulfill expectations—just not in the way John had hoped.

The Role of the Forerunner

After this conversation with John's disciples, Jesus addresses the crowd to explain to them how John was the fulfillment of their expectations of Elijah appearing before the Messiah's arrival (a belief still held by many Jews today).[7] This belief originated from the account that Elijah never died, but was instead taken into heaven by a whirlwind accompanied by fiery chariots. (2 Kings 2:11) Elijah is pulled into the discussion when Jesus quotes Malachi in reference to John the Baptist:

I will send my messenger, who will prepare the way before me.
Then suddenly the Lord you are seeking will come to his temple;

the messenger of the covenant, whom you desire, will come, says the LORD Almighty. (Malachi 3:1)

The book of Malachi ends by identifying this person as Elijah, who will come before the dreadful "day of the Lord." (Malachi 4:5) This phrase appears thirty times in the *Tanakh* and is first used by Isaiah, followed by other prophets after him, referring to God coming to judge the earth. Jesus plainly tells his audience that John is "the Elijah to come," which would have been a joyful pronouncement, unleashing an expectation from the audience for Jesus to fulfill the rest of Malachi's prophecy.

At this point, Matthew inserts our perplexing passage: "From the days of John the Baptist until now the kingdom of heaven has suffered violence, and the violent take it by force." (ESV)

The awkward translation confirms, for some, Matthew's Hebrew origins. The Hebrew idioms do not translate well into Greek (let alone English), which led the scholars from the Jerusalem School of Synaptic Research and others to look for an Old Testament passage that Jesus might have been referencing.[8] They concluded that Jesus was teaching from Micah 2:12-13:

> I will surely gather all of you, O Jacob; I will surely bring together the remnant of Israel. I will bring them together like sheep in a pen, like a flock in its pasture; the place will throng with people. The One who breaks open the way will go up before them; they will break through the gate and go out. Their King will pass through before them, the LORD at their head. (ESV)

Leading up to this statement, Micah describes why God's people will be taken into exile. In the first two chapters, Micah makes accusations against the leaders of God's people of greed, theft, and selling God's protection, which will result in a future exile. Chapter two concludes with a message of hope, prophesying a future restoration described as a crowded sheepfold: a metaphor for God's people regathered back in the land of Israel. Then someone will come and break open the door of this sheepfold. Then the Messiah, who was in the sheepfold along with

Scan Here to Watch The Bible Project's Summary of Micah

everyone else, but unrecognized, will lead the way out, thus identifying himself as the king ushering in his kingdom. The passage points to the explosive, but not violent, moment when God breaks into human history.

John the Baptist represented the one who would "break open" the gate of sheepfold. Traditionally, a sheepfold's gate could be a pile of rocks, the shepherd himself, or some other obstacle blocking the entrance. The image of gathering sheep in the pen represents the refugees who began returning from Babylon in a trickle in the fifth century BC. By the middle of the second century BC, after the Hasmoneans defeated the Seleucids and reestablished a Jewish kingdom, Jewish refugees were pouring back in. Jesus' ancestors would have been part of this regathering of God's people to the land of Israel. He is metaphorically in the pen with all the other Jewish people, but unrecognized. When the forerunner breaks open the gate, the shepherd-king comes forth, identifying himself and leading the way to usher in his kingdom. Jesus goes unrecognized as the Messiah until John the Baptist comes and breaks open the way.

Rabbinic Translation

How would Jesus' audience have made this connection between John, the door of the sheepfold, and Jesus as Messiah? To answer that, we need "cultural translation" from Hebrew into a first-century rabbinical worldview. The connection between the New Testament and the *Tanakh* begins with the Hebrew word *peretz*—meaning "to break through, or increase, or spread"—which connects Micah 2 and Matthew 11.[9] Jesus uses the principle of interpretation, created by the great rabbi Hillel the generation before, called *gezerah shavah* (which means "similar law"). According to this principle, two verses thought to be unrelated could be connected by virtue of the same word.[10] In Micah 2:13, the keyword is used twice: "One who breaks open [*peretz*] the way will go up before them; they will break through [*peretz*] the gate and go out." Using *gezerah shavah*, the word *peretz* connects Micah 2 with Jesus' words in Matthew 11, when translated from the Greek to the Hebrew:

"From the days of John [the Baptist] until now, the Kingdom of Heaven is breaking through [*peretz*] and breakers-through [referring to the rest of the sheep] break through [*peretz*] with it."

Jesus speaks as a Jewish rabbi, using *gezerah shavah* to draw upon his audience's knowledge of the Old Testament to explain, with a single word, how Micah's prophecy is being fulfilled in real time.

Bringing Micah 2 forward to Matthew 11, the rabbinical interpretation presents a positive expression of the kingdom of heaven as breaking forth, initiated by John the Baptist and identifying the Messianic king whose followers make the breach wider (breaking forth) as they grow in numbers, advancing the kingdom of heaven.[11] John is right about Jesus being the Messiah; however, Jesus challenges John's understanding of the "age of the Messiah" and when the final judgment will take place.[12] John doesn't fully grasp the enormity of God's grace in delaying his judgment, which allows time for the kingdom to increase.

We can resonate with John's mixed feelings. Praise God for his patience, mercy, and long-suffering: As much as we would like him to return today and usher in his kingdom fully, the longer he delays his return, the more people can come to know him. When he does return, he will come to judge the world, and that day will not be enjoyable for those who don't know him. Nor do I think Jesus will enjoy that day, since he desires all to know him. (2 Peter 3:9)

Jesus, the rabbi, subtly connects John's current circumstances to the Old Testament, engaging and correcting expectations, all beginning with the single word *peretz*. Once I learned this information, that particular speed bump lost some of its bounce. I didn't discover a perfect answer to my question seeking to understand "the kingdom advancing violently," but I did find a place to begin.

My incomplete beginning follows Kenneth Bailey's encouragement to remember that "Our understanding of Scripture must always be open to refinement. All interpretations of Scripture need to be tentatively final."[13] My new understanding of this passage remains open for refinement.

I've become enthusiastically hooked on reading the Bible in this way. I wanted to know: What other connections to the Jewish mindset of the first century could be made to add depth of meaning to familiar New Testament stories? The answer is: Many! For example, I learned that this approach can even help shed light upon larger theological issues like how we define sin, which we will look at next.

Questions

- How does unpacking tough passages, like this one in Matthew, help you in your walk with Jesus?
- What are tools/resources you can now utilize to help you better understand these difficult passages? Is there an ingredient from Part One you find most helpful or interesting?
- As you read this chapter, what "ingredients" did we use to discover the deeper meaning of the story?
- How does understanding a rabbi's use of the Old Testament and the theological worldview of Jesus' original audience help you in your search?
- Do you see yourself as a "breaker-forth" advancing the kingdom today?
- What excites you about seeing God's kingdom move in our modern society?
- Does this impact the way you see your neighbors, coworkers, friends, and family who don't know Jesus?

Additional Resources

Bivin, David, and Roy Blizzard Jr. *Understanding the Difficult Words of Jesus: New Insights From a Hebrew Perspective*

Keener, Craig S., and John H. Walton, eds. *NIV Cultural Backgrounds Study Bible: Bringing to Life the Ancient World of Scripture*

Wilson, Marvin R. *Our Father Abraham: Jewish Roots of the Christian Faith*

Young, Brad H. *Jesus the Jewish Theologian*

The Bible Project: "Old Testament Overviews > Micah"
https://bibleproject.com/videos/micah/

9. What Can Sheep Teach Me About God?

I am the way [path] and the truth and the life.
No one comes to the Father except through me.

—JESUS IN JOHN 14:6-7

Man's chief end is to glorify God, and to enjoy him forever.

—THE WESTMINSTER SHORTER CATECHISM

Sin is losing one's purposefulness.

—MICHAEL HEISER

Living in Israel, there are moments when the Biblical past connects with the present. Some timeless rhythms of life remain unchanged for the people living in Israel today despite millennia of modernization. My wife and I witnessed one such moment while we were enjoying the sunrise from our balcony. As we sipped our tea, we noticed three shepherds, each with their flocks, converge to exchange pleasantries. While they talked, all their sheep melded into one mob of speckled white surrounding their shepherds. We sat mesmerized, wondering how they were going to separate all the sheep. Eventually they shook hands and departed, each heading in different directions, all the while calling their sheep... who all instinctively followed the familiar voice of their shepherd. Amazing! We remembered then that Jesus said, "My sheep hear my voice; I know them, and they follow me." (John 10:27) In that moment, the Bible came to life.

I wonder if there was ever a time when people did not shepherd sheep in this ancient place? So many of the main characters of God's story were shepherds: Abraham, Isaac, Jacob, Rachel, Leah, Moses, King David, the prophet Amos. Jacob describes God as a shepherd when he blesses his sons for the last time.

When Jacob ascribes to God this anthropomorphic image of a shepherd, he is testifying to his sons about God's character: "The God before whom my fathers Abraham and Isaac walked, the God who has been my shepherd all my life to this day." (Genesis 48:15) God provided for Jacob like a shepherd, and he encouraged his sons to trust and walk with this God also.

Imagery of shepherds and sheep fill the pages of the Bible, from Genesis to Revelation. Jesus calls himself the Good Shepherd. (John 10) The relationship between sheep and their shepherd is a favorite metaphor the Biblical authors use to describe our relationship with God.

Before we begin looking at what sheep can teach us about this, please take a moment to write a short definition of the following words: *sin*, *obedience*, and *law*. These words in English conjure up different mental associations and emotions than they do in ancient Hebrew. "The Hebrew language is vivid and poetic because it uses physical imagery instead of abstract words to describe what is intangible."[1] Hebrew word-pictures can help us comprehend abstract, hard-to-visualize aspects of life, such as our relationship with God.

In the next two chapters, let's explore how the Bible communicates our intangible relationship with God through the metaphor of shepherding, as described in ancient Hebrew. Let's begin with the word *sin*.

The Law of First Use—Sin

The law of first use states that the context of a word's first appearance in Scripture colors in its definition: The observable behaviors and attitudes of the characters involved form the definition of the word. We might assume the word *sin* first appears at the Fall in Genesis 3, when eating from the tree of knowledge breaks the relational expectations between Adam, Eve, and God. However, it's not until Genesis 4 that *sin* makes its first appearance, in a warning to protect the relationship between two brothers. The law of first use says the heart of the definition of *sin* is a failure to protect and preserve relationships.

In Genesis 4, both brothers brought an offering to the Lord, who accepted Abel's offering but not Cain's. The Lord said to Cain: "Why are you angry? Why is your face downcast? If you do what is right, will you not be accepted? But if you do not do what is right, *sin* is crouching at your door; it desires to have you, but you must master it." (Genesis 4:6-7, emphasis added) Reading this, we assume Cain knew what kind of offering to bring, but failed to do so. Our modern ears can internalize this exchange like this: *If I do the right thing, then God will accept me. If not, God will withhold relationship from me.*

However, notice that God is still engaging with Cain despite his actions towards him. At no point in the story does God withdraw relationally from Cain, or even directly punish him. His concern is for Cain's relationship with Abel.

The brothers were not in competition with one another for God's approval; both could have brought acceptable offerings. God's response to Cain—"Will you not be accepted?"—expresses the relational intent of the sacrifice. God doesn't need sacrifices; he longs for relationship. The sacrifice represents an external indication of what is in Cain's heart, which God already knows, but Cain doesn't—until he offers the unacceptable sacrifice. God could have justifiably taken offense, but instead he attempts to correct Cain's heart-attitude by pursuing him relationally.

We might hastily identify Cain's sacrifice as the *sin* in this story, because what he sacrificed indicated that he did not highly value his relationship with God. However, the quality of Cain's sacrifice is not the *sin* God warns him about. Cain is overcome with shame, a feeling felt when we fear we've done something that puts a relationship at risk, and we brace ourselves for potential repercussions. Instead of hiding like his parents who felt similar feelings in the Garden of Eden, Cain allows his shame and jealousy to turn into anger (a natural response when we feel vulnerable), recognizing he is at the mercy of the person who he's offended. That is the "*sin* crouching at his door." We too can take out our anger on other people when flooded with emotions. Shame often induces anger, especially when we don't know what to do. In this case, Cain's anger initially manifests as hatred directed back toward himself. These emotions then lead Cain to lash out at Abel—a classic example of projection.

Our focus on Cain's behavior can cause us to miss the heart of the definition of *sin*. The law of first use frames sin as a *relationship* problem, not a *behavior* problem. Sin is the selfishness of failing to consider how our words and actions might affect others. Meanwhile, God's priority is to seek, protect, and preserve relationships, and he desires us to do the same. This is what Paul meant when he said, "consider others better than yourself." (Philippians 2:3)

When we each care for others, we all thrive. In a sense, obeying God is the most self-serving thing we can do, because we are blessed when we obey God in seeking to preserve relationships. God desires us to have life abundantly (John 10:10), which I understand to mean a life lived relationally connected to God and others. Sin creates the opposite of an abundant life. And look what it costs: Cain's failure to master sin resulted in a lose-lose situation. Cain would have been blessed if he brought an acceptable sacrifice, but more importantly, his brother would still be alive and he wouldn't have had to live the rest of his life in fear of vengeance. So much pain could have been avoided.

Who Makes the First Move?

Meeting new people can be awkward. When I first met my wife at a conference, I noticed her reading by herself and I walked up and introduced myself. At the time, I of course had no idea she'd become my wife. Meaningful relationships can begin with a smile and a handshake. But someone has to make the first move.

Throughout the Bible, God is portrayed as continuously initiating with us. With the Hebrews, God initiates by rescuing them out of Egypt and bringing them to Mt. Sinai, and where he publicly declares the unique and special nature of his relationship with them by calling the Hebrew people his "treasured possession." (Exodus 19:5) Ezekiel summarized God's intentions this way: "My dwelling place shall be with them; and I will be their God, and they shall be My people." (Ezekiel 37:27) As with any relationship, intimacy is a two-way street. God's actions and declaration necessitates a response from the Hebrews. Three times they say, "We will *do* [obey] everything the Lord has said." (Exodus 19:8, 24:3, 24:7) The Bible describes our choice to "obey everything" as drawing near to God and walking with him.

But how do we walk with God *specifically*? Unlike all the other gods of ancient Near East cultures, who were often described by their followers as unpredictable, mysterious, and capricious, the God of the Hebrews gave them something like a relational operating manual called *Torah*. God provides relational specifics at Mt. Sinai when he invites the Hebrews into a covenant relationship, sort of like a marriage.[2] As at a wedding, vows are exchanged: God's vows to the Hebrew people are recorded in *Torah*, which also outlines his expectations of the Hebrews—things they must hear, do, guard, keep, and protect in order for their relationship with God to thrive. The specifics of how the Hebrews are to hear, do, guard, keep, and protect their relationship with God begins with the famous Ten Commandments in Exodus 20. This list outlines how to remain relationally connected with God and others; failing to keep them would be breaking relationship and thus be labeled *sin*.

But it doesn't stop with the "Big Ten": Jewish tradition holds that God gave Moses the whole of *Torah* at Mt. Sinai, both the written texts and the oral law, containing even more details of how to relate to God, in addition to the Ten Commandments. Over time, the sages of Israel identified 613 commandments—specific dos and don'ts listed in the *Torah*. However, the list was never intended to be comprehensive, and requires constant interpretation in its application. The Bible is not a divine HR manual, outlining precisely what is permissible and what is not in every circumstance. Being relationally connected with God will always be necessary to know how to walk with him in a particular situation.

After leaving Mt. Sinai, Moses continues to speak with the Lord, face to face in the Tent of Meeting. (Exodus 31:11) He continually seeks the Lord for guidance and wisdom in applying *Torah* to unspecified situations. For example, soon after leaving Mount Sinai, five sisters come to Moses with an issue of inheritance not previously addressed. (Numbers 27) This situation requires Moses to properly discern the relational intent of *Torah*.

Meanwhile, the New Testament records more than a thousand imperatives do-this, don't-do-that statements. Christians selectively choose which ones we think are culturally relevant today. For instance, five times in the New Testament God commands us to "greet each other with a holy kiss."[3] Have you ever been greeted by someone at church with a kiss? Yet, we do expect to be formally greeted by people upon entering church, and if no one did? It would be a sign that something is off. Kiss or no kiss, to not see or acknowledge someone God calls *sin* because we're not valuing relationships.

Still, embracing the primary importance of relationships when defining what constitutes obedience and sin does not stop us from becoming armchair lawyers, creating our personalized lists of acceptable and unacceptable behaviors. From the moment God gave *Torah* to his people, they have debated its application. Our minds focus on the details of how *obedience* and *sin* are defined and miss the connection as to how a particular behavior affects a relationship. Part of our challenge as Westerners is how we translate the word *Torah*; it is often translated into English as *law*, which becomes synonymous with the 613—a list of stuff to do and not do. However, to quote Inigo Montoya from *The Princess Bride*: "I do not think it means what you think it means."[4] Gaining an understanding of the Hebrew word *Torah* will help us appreciate the heart behind what it means to protect a relationship.

What Does *Torah* Mean Relationally?

As discussed in Chapter 7, communication requires a shared language made up of words shaped by common experiences within a social environment. If we lack the visual image the original authors and audience associated with a particular word in the Bible, then our definition of the word's meaning could introduce a subtle misinterpretation, altering our understanding of Biblical concepts. The Hebrew word *Torah*, which is often translated into the English word *law*, is a classic example.

To our English ears, the word *law* describes a code of conduct that is rigid and inflexible (unless you have a very good lawyer!). However, in Hebrew, *Torah* means *direction* or *guide*.[5] *Torah* comes from the root word *yarah*, meaning to cast (Exodus 15:4), to shoot (1 Samuel 20:36), to throw one's gaze (Exodus 15:25), or to teach (Leviticus 10:11).[6] If we don't know these meanings, we can miss the relational intention of the word: *Torah* is a direction to move, with God, as he guides us. Used as a noun, *Torah* results in the Hebrew word for *teacher* (Proverbs 5:13) and *teachings*. (Proverbs 1:8)[7] Moses continually sought clarification from God about how to apply *Torah*, as did every faithful leader after him,

124

constantly reinterpreting the details of how to obey God's commandments specifically to meet the demands of their day. [8] To translate *Torah* as *law* would be like translating *father* as *disciplinarian*.[9] It's true that good fathers discipline, but good fathers also do so much more. Similarly, *Torah* contains much more than impersonal commands. God gave the Hebrews—and us—a relational book, not a law book. What this relationship will look like moving forward from Mt. Sinai begins with God leading the Hebrews to the Promised Land, literally following him like sheep, as the pillar of fire and smoke walked before them like a shepherd through the wilderness. (Exodus 13:21)[10] This description is both literal and emblematic of what it means to follow God.

The rest of *Tanakh* continues to use this imagery of sheep following its shepherd, as well as other word-pictures, to communicate what it means to walk with God... or not. To *walk with God* is another way of saying *obeying* him, which is an elusive Hebrew word to translate into English. Let me explain.

Hebraic Obedience

The meaning of *obedience* is found only in relation to the Good Shepherd and his path. Biblical Hebrew uses active words like "to do, to hear, guard, keep, or protect" to describe how one remains close to the shepherd. These active words in Hebrew are often translated as *obey* in English. To a Westerner, the word *obedience* can carry a negative connotation. We can be motivated to obey to avoid negative consequences, compelling us to do and say the right things in a relationship to earn or maintain acceptance. In contrast, joyful obedience is the desire to care for and protect the other person in the relationship, for their sake as well as our own. We proactively help, encourage, and support one another. We listen and respond. We guard and protect the relationship from harm physically and emotionally. And we keep the relationship a priority. How do we *do, hear, guard, keep,* and *protect* our walk with God?

The Bible says very directly, "Walk in all the way [path] that the Lord your God has commanded you, so that you may live and prosper and prolong your days in the land that you will possess." (Deuteronomy 5:33)

The use of the English word *command* makes it feel like an order: *do this or else*. In this case, the verse speaks to the rewards of walking on God's path. It is helpful to keep this verse and the book of Deuteronomy in context. Deuteronomy is a summation of the first four books of *Torah*. By this point in the story, God had already demonstrated his faithfulness and trustworthiness to the Hebrew people many times over. They have willingly chosen to enter his covenant relationship. With this in mind, the verse reads more like a loving reminder, rather than an order.

The opposite of walking with God is *sin*, choosing to act or respond in ways that do not seek to protect, guard, or preserve the relationship, intentionally or unintentionally. And as with any worthy and honorable relationship, God desires (doesn't demand) a response to his initiation.

Defining Sin in Pictures

Sin is pictured in the Bible as walking away from God and his path, which reflects a heart attitude that no longer desires to preserve the relationship. The Bible describes someone willfully walking away from God's path with the word *wickedness*: a deliberate and definite act of the will. The Hebrew word *rasha* רשע, often translated as *wickedness*, describes this heart attitude: "For I have guarded the path of Yahweh, and I have not walked away [*rasha*] from my God." (2 Samuel 22:22) English translations of this passage vary from *not acted wickedly* to *not turned* or *not departed*. Tangibly, the word-picture of wickedness captures the results of someone who literally turns their back on God, going their own way. Jeff Benner in his book *The Living Words* says:

> There are two ways to leave a trail—by accident, which we may call an error (Psalms 119:176), or on purpose, which we may call defiance. (Isaiah 53:6) Both are *rasha* and have the same results.[11]

Another Hebrew word for *sin* is *khata*, meaning to fail, to leave the path, or to miss the goal. Proverbs 19:2 illustrates this point: "Better the poor whose walk is blameless than a fool whose lips are perverse. Desire without knowledge is not good—how much more will hasty feet miss [*khata*] the way [path]!" *Rasha* describes the heart attitude that causes us to leave the path; *khata* dives into the specifics. This Hebraic concept of sin, to miss the path (of the Good Shepherd), is later translated into Greek for a New Testament audience as "missing the mark," meaning to fail to hit the center of a target in archery. The bullseye is the goal; the amount of sin is the distance measured between the bullseye and where the arrow actually struck.

The Bible uses two other words to further delineate sin: פֶּשַׁע *peša* ("transgression") and עָוֹן *'āôn* ("iniquity"). David uses all three in his prayer in Psalm 51: "Have mercy on me, O God, according to your unfailing love; according to your great compassion blot out my *transgressions*. Wash away all my *iniquity* and cleanse me from my *sin*." The Bible Project's Bad Word series explores the word-pictures behind each of these three words, which all fall into the generic category of *sin* (scan the QR code to watch). Transgression involves betraying trust. Iniquity implies intentional crookedness, taking advantage of someone else. Sin is wronging someone in general, even a stranger, in our shared relational humanity. Each of these words finds their meaning only within the context of relationships with others. David's prayer describes how he broke relationship God and others with his sin, transgression, and iniquity. God longs to forgive and restore relationships. He never expected us to be perfect—God desires us to *want* to repair the relationship. The Good Shepherd demonstrates his trustworthiness and faithfulness, even pursuing when we get off his path. He longs for us to pursue him also, because he doesn't want to see us hurt ourselves.

Scan Here to Watch The Bible Project's "Bad Words" Series

The Character of a Shepherd

Shepherding sheep is hard work. I know (*yada*) this—well, I *yada* about three hours' worth. I wanted to experience what it was like to shepherd sheep because this metaphor seemed so vital to understanding the heart of God and our relationship. I asked my friend if I could spend the afternoon with him while he tended his flock. Three hours in the scorching sun watching sheep eat was incredibly boring most of the time, but I learned that shepherding requires a person to be watchful and vigilant, because something might happen at any moment that endangers the sheep (or the sheep might endanger themselves).

To grasp this deep abiding relational nature of God's character, it is helpful to understand the responsibilities of a shepherd and why so many Biblical authors lean into this metaphor to try and communicate God's intangible love for us. The job description for a shepherd can be found in the famous Psalm 23. Let's read it closely to know the job requirements but also to discover the heart motivation of a shepherd.

Notice the verbs the psalmist uses: *makes, leads, restores, guides, prepares, anoints.* Because the shepherd does these things, the sheep lack nothing. They feel safe enough to lie down in green pastures (a very vulnerable position), knowing the shepherd is protecting them. They have no worries about finding water, trusting the shepherd knows where to find it. Enjoying a right relationship with the shepherd, they fear no evil, experience comfort, enjoy restored relationships with their former enemies, and are blessed with refreshing oil and abundance. None of these things happen without great effort and intentionality on the part of the good shepherd. He cares for his sheep out of his immense love for them. This is his instinctual nature; he is who he is (the Lord *is* my shepherd). His decision to act in love is effortless, because we are his "treasured possession." The actions of the shepherd display his character.

The verb is *is* the present form of the irregular verb "to be"; it indicates a state of being. The Lord *is being* my shepherd. When God spoke to Moses from the burning bush, he told Moses his name: "I AM who I AM." (Exodus 3) Scholars vigorously debate how to translate this form of the verb "to be" from Hebrew into English, because God is describing his very essence. The word-pictures of a good shepherd help us grasp the concept of God's character.

When Jesus says, "I am the good shepherd" in John 10:11, his audience hears him saying, "I am God coming to be the Good Shepherd." Jesus is claiming to be the embodiment of the divine shepherd described in Psalm 23. Jesus' motivation for doing this is found in the center of Psalm 23, which is a Hebraic *chiasm*: a balanced Hebrew poem, with the important take-away found in the middle. That central phrase is: "For you are with me." (Psalms 23:4) God wants to be with us, and so he came from heaven to earth to be with us and show us how to walk with him.

Feeling the Metaphor

Healthy relationships are mutually beneficial. In this case, the shepherd does a lot of work to maintain his relationship with his sheep. They rely upon the shepherd for everything. In return, sheep provide a source of milk, wool, and (occasionally) meat—you don't want to eat your principal investment. They are also incredibly vulnerable animals who possess no means of combative self-protection. They have no claws or sharp teeth. They are slow, non-aggressive animals who lack the ability to evade predators. If they happen to tip over, they need assistance to right themselves or they will eventually drown, as fluid will fill their lungs. Sheep are also unable to discern good water from brackish water, and they have been known to knock themselves out while attempting to get a bug out of their ear by hitting their head on a rock.[12] In the Biblical analogy, we are the sheep (Psalm 78:52, Matthew 9:36, and John 10)! God is the Good Shepherd (doing most of the relational work). He initiates with us, communicates our value to him, sacrifices for us, protects and provides for us, and all he wants in return is that we stay connected to him on a daily basis.

Each morning, sheep follow behind their shepherd, led by his voice, to hillside pastures carved with dozens and dozens of paths. At times, the specific path matters, requiring the sheep to follow the shepherd precisely on his path which then leads back to home, peace, and security. In those moments, all other paths lead the sheep away from the good shepherd and away from the provision and protection he provides. The *path* becomes a metaphor often used by the prophets to describe us choosing to obey God by walking with him.

The prophet Jeremiah grew up in Anathoth, a town on the edge of the Judean Wilderness, where sheep go to graze during the rainy season. He uses the imagery of shepherding throughout his book.

For example, "I thought you would call me 'Father' and not turn away from following me." (Jeremiah 3:19) This is relational shepherding language. He later emphasizes the necessity of walking God's path: "Stand at the crossroads and look; ask for the ancient paths, ask where the good way is, and walk in it, and you will find rest for your souls. But you said, 'We will not walk in it.'" (Jeremiah 6:16) Jeremiah's words imply his audience knows of the path's existence and could ask for directions. Either they refused to ask, or they definitely chose not to walk in that path, like a sheep without its shepherd, to their own demise.

Sheep rely solely on their shepherd for everything, which raises the question, "Why would anyone, sheep or human, walk away from God?" Describing sin as walking away from God implies that trust has somehow been broken between the sheep and the shepherd—so much so, that the sheep are willing to venture out on their own.

Bad leaders erode trust. Prophets chide kings, rulers, priests, and even other prophets, for acting like self-centered, irresponsible shepherds. Jeremiah calls Judah's leadership inept shepherds:

> My people have been lost sheep; their shepherds have led them astray and caused them to roam... They wandered over mountains and hills and forgot their own resting place. (Jeremiah 50:6)

Bad leadership causes suffering, producing skepticism and hesitancy to trust or follow any leader ever again—even God. That's why Jeremiah gives them a warning: "'Woe to the shepherds who are destroying and scattering the sheep of My pasture!' declares the LORD." (Jeremiah 23:1)

Jesus, too, echoes the Old Testament prophets when he confronts the neglectful leaders of his day. As the Gospel of Matthew tells us, he sees the results of poor shepherding and grieves: "When he saw the crowds, he had compassion on them, because they were harassed and helpless, like sheep without a shepherd." (Matthew 9:36-37) The phrase *sheep without a shepherd* first appears in Numbers 27:17, when Moses prays for his own replacement:

> May the Lord, the God of the spirits of all mankind, appoint a man [Joshua, but now Jesus] over this community to go out and come in before them, one who will lead them out and bring them in, so the Lord's people will not be like sheep without a shepherd.

Jesus replaces Moses, Joshua, and all previous leaders to regather God's scattered sheep, providing them security, provision, and protection. Jeremiah speaks of this restoration and return through this metaphor: "Flocks will again pass under the hand of the one who counts them." (Jeremiah 33:13) Jesus comes as the Good Shepherd to fulfill Moses' and Jeremiah's words once and for all.

Sheep who are trying to faithfully follow the shepherd can get lost. And even a good shepherd can have sheep who are willfully stubborn, despite their best efforts to lead well. The sheep's attempts to procure the essentials of life apart from the shepherd will ultimately leave them even more dissatisfied, vulnerable, and unprotected. Life only works when we are with the Good Shepherd, because his path is the only path that leads to life. Regardless of how one finds themselves off the path, it will result in death: "This is the fate of those who trust in themselves... Like sheep they are destined for the grave, and death will feed on them." (Psalms 49:13-14) God has compassion for both the lost and willfully stubborn; he seeks to find them all.

God's superpower is his ability to respond in love when offended by pursuing us to restore our relationship, as he did with Cain. He never needed Cain's sacrifice. He longed for Cain to value their relationship as much as he did. Nor does he need anything from us. Samuel describes this when he says: "Does the Lord delight in burnt offerings and sacrifices as much as in obeying the voice of the Lord? To obey is better than sacrifice, and to heed is better than the fat of rams." (1 Samuel 15:22) Hosea goes even further: "For I desire mercy, not sacrifice, and acknowledgment of God rather than burnt offerings." (Hosea 6:6)

God pursues us to preserve and repair our relationship, "to be with us." The sacrificial system God instituted at Mt. Sinai was for us, not for God. He doesn't need our sacrifices. The sacrificial system was a way to tangibly demonstrate our desire to repair our relationship with God when we disrupt it. The sacrifice removed guilt and shame by symbolically retracing steps taken away from the path, and instead taking different steps to actively draw near to God.[13] Today, we sacrifice our pride instead of sheep, taking responsibility for our actions and words that have hurt others, because we choose to value relationships more than we value being "right in our own eyes." (Proverbs 14:12)

Redefining Our Relationships

Look back at the definitions you wrote down at the beginning of the chapter. How has gaining a Biblical definition shifted your understanding of sin, obedience, and law? Both *sin* and *obedience* are words which find their meaning and definition within a relationship. If a relationship holds little value, then defining sin is meaningless, since there's no relationship worth sustaining, keeping, or preserving. *Torah* provides God's wisdom in how to be in relationship with him and others. However, most of us can't simply decide to stop being people who feel most comfortable with tight definitions and concrete lists of specifics. The people in Jesus' day wrestled with the same inclination—remember those 613 laws? They debated how to precisely fulfill each one of them down to the smallest detail (more on this in the next chapter). But think about the friends and family in your life: Could you make a list of rules, and a perfect explanation for how to follow and apply each one, for every circumstance? And even if you could, would following that rulebook be enough to keep you in a healthy relationship with every person you know and love? We could never come up with an exhaustive list of right behaviors that would keep us always in the right relationship. Relationships are delicate and complex; they require constant thoughtfulness and attentiveness to the other person—in God's case, a sensitivity to listening for the Shepherd's voice as we follow him.

Let me give you two examples. I was turning thirty and my beloved Cubs were coming to Cincinnati, where I lived at the time. My friends were gathering to celebrate my birthday by going to the game together. I commented to my best friend, "I can't wait to get a dog and a beer." He reminded me that one of my guests was a recovering alcoholic. In that moment I had a choice: Do I care more about my desire to celebrate my birthday the way I'd been looking forward to and anticipating, or about protecting someone else from an addiction? I chose to forego the birthday beer. It didn't even feel like a sacrifice.

Another time, I was with a group of people who knew I worked with a missionary organization. Some assumed I would be very stiff and legalistic and would certainly not drink alcohol. However, on that night I did enjoy a beer, and I had a great conversation about Jesus with someone who would have probably not approached me otherwise. I felt safe and relatable to them.

It is tempting to set up guardrails like the 613 laws, outlining specific behaviors to protect our relationships with God and others. If we sat down together and compiled a list, I'm sure we'd eventually agree our list was reasonable. We might debate some of our choices, challenging each other's understanding of sin and obedience, which is healthy. However, if our guardrails become our focus, then we may unintentionally divert our attention away from enjoying the relationship in the first place. We get preoccupied over not offending someone—often, a hypothetical someone. We then forget to get good at sensitivity and reconciliation, because guess what? No matter how carefully we plan, sooner or later we're going to offend someone. Then what do we do?

The cautionary guardrail approach describes a fear-bonded relationship. Living in a constant state of fear of rejection drives us to be hypervigilant, producing joyless compliance and obligatory obedience. This attitude misses the heart of why we choose to stay close to God and not to walk away from him (*sin*), because we enjoy being with the shepherd.

In the next chapter, we will explore how to joyfully walk with God and what to do if we get lost.

Questions

- How does understanding the shepherd-sheep metaphor impact your understanding of what it means to follow God?
- Who is someone in your life who you've willingly followed? What made you want to follow them?
- Is asking for forgiveness challenging for you? If so, why?
- Have you ever expressed being disappointed with someone? What were your intentions in sharing your feelings with that person?
- Can you remember a time when you received forgiveness you knew you didn't deserve? How did that impact you?
- Have you experienced healthy shame?
- Read Psalm 23. Using the ingredients we discussed in Part One and the deeper knowledge of the sheep-shepherd metaphor we learned in this chapter, what do you see differently? Does it enrich your understanding of this famous passage of Scripture?

Additional Resources

Comer, John Mark. *The Ruthless Elimination of Hurry*

Hurnard, Hannah. *Hinds' Feet on High Places*

Jennings, Timothy R. *The God-Shaped Brain: How Changing Your View of God Transforms Your Life*

Wilder, Jim, and Michel Hendricks. *The Other Half of Church: Christian Community, Brain Science, and Overcoming Spiritual Stagnation*

Wilder, Jim, and Ray Woolridge. *Escaping Enemy Mode: How Our Brains Unite or Divide Us*

The Bible Project: "Bad Words of the Bible"
https://bibleproject.com/videos/collections/bad-words/

10. Walking the Ancient Path

Whether you turn to the right or to the left,
your ears will hear a voice behind you, saying,
"This is the way; walk in it."

—*ISAIAH 30:21-22*

Walking with someone indicates desire or willingness to be physically close, which implies a level of intimacy, acceptance, and trust. Our decision to walk with God must be a choice, a desire on our part to draw near to him, in response to God drawing near to us.

The first people to *walk with* God were Adam and Eve. (Genesis 3:8) Others whom the Bible specifically describes as *walking with* God include Enoch (Genesis 5:24), Noah (Genesis 6:9), Abram (Genesis 17:1), Isaac (Genesis 48:15) and Jotham. (2 Chronicles 27:3) Hezekiah reminds God how he "walked before you [God] in faithfulness and with a whole heart and have done what is good in your sight." (2 Kings 20:3) Reflecting God's character is evidence of a person who is walking with God. (Micah 6:8) "Walking with God" became Biblical shorthand for a connected and faithful relationship with God.

We know we can struggle to walk towards God (that is, to trust him). Why? Well, Adam and Eve walked and talked with God yet still questioned the one rule he gave them. Now, to be fair, the serpent planted the seed of doubt in Eve's mind, asking: "But did God really say..." (Genesis 3:3) Very early in the story, the Bible tells us there is an entity that desires to get in between us and God, with the ultimate goal of persuading us not to trust him. Adam and Eve's failure to obey God resulted in them being escorted out of the Garden away from his full presence, in order to save them from living forever with a knowledge of good and evil. (Genesis 3:22) Even what we may perceive as punishment by God, making them leave the garden, was for their benefit. They lost their innocence, but God still maintained a relationship with them, even though it wasn't at the level of intimacy they previously enjoyed.

The first three chapters of the Bible explain the state of our spiritual and physical condition. We see it every day as we observe people struggle to obey the most basic and common-sense rules, which would protect them. The Bible's remaining 1,186 chapters relate God's pursuit of us, his work to get us home to the full relational intimacy previously enjoyed in the Garden. This restoration begins when God invites a shepherd named Abram to walk with him. The Hebrew word *halak* הָלַךְ means *to walk*; it's one of the most common idioms used in the *Tanakh* to communicate *obedience*. Abram's obedience to walk with God is the start of God's restoring the entire world to himself. Through God's relationship with Abram, he defines obedience as walking in a right (connected) relationship with him. Let's explore what this means.

God Partners with Us

God often partners with people to accomplish his plans, putting their dynamic relationship on display so that the world can witness God's work to restore relationships. For this purpose, God chooses to partner with Abram. While he is living in the land of Ur, God interrupts Abram's life and promises him an amazing future:

> I will make you into a great nation and I will bless you; I will make your name great, and you will be a blessing. I will bless those who bless you, and whoever curses you I will curse; and all peoples on earth will be blessed through you. (Genesis 12:2-3)

This promise is formally ratified in a gruesome covenant ceremony in Genesis 15, with the terms specified later in God's command: "Walk before me and be blameless." (Genesis 17:1)

The word *covenant* literally means to cut. In Genesis 15, God tells Abram to bring to him five specific animals; after cutting the animals in half, he places the halves opposite each other. Their blood pools in a small gully between the halves, forming a stream of blood. Abram knows exactly what is happening. God is inviting him into a formal covenant, a binding agreement in which the greater party sets the terms with no negotiations, and the lesser party either accepts the agreement or walks away.[1] The greater party walks through the blood-path first, followed by the one accepting the terms. In doing so, both parties pledge to follow the terms of the agreement—or become like one of the animals whose blood now covers their feet. The intent of the gruesome ceremony is to *cut* this moment of commitment into their memory.

After preparing the animals, Abram is overcome by great darkness. He fears for his life, knowing he will soon be a dead man because he can't keep the terms of the covenant (although we the reader don't find out exactly what those terms are until Genesis 17). Two figures do walk through the blood path to ratify the covenant. God, as the greater party, passes through first, depicted as a smoking fire pot or furnace. Then the image of a flaming torch passes through, taking the place of the unconscious Abram. This torch represents the Messiah (Jesus), who will eventually take the place of Abram (and his descendants), receiving the punishment required for our failure to keep the covenant.[2] God will keep his part of the covenant perfectly, forever. This covenant explains God's fidelity to us throughout the rest of the story.

In ancient Near-Eastern covenants like this one, the greater party often also names or renames the other person. Names reflect a person's character and purpose, and their new name serves as a reminder of this new covenant to be lived out. God changes Abram's name, "exalted father," to Abraham, "father of many." Abraham is the beginning of God's restoration plan for all humanity—he will be the father of many, who will bless the entire world by revealing who God is through their relationship with him.

How to Be Blameless

Many interpret the word *blameless* in God's covenant as God requiring perfection from Abraham and his descendants if they want to be in relationship with him. However, God knew from the beginning that neither Abraham nor his descendants would or could keep the covenant blamelessly. Sometimes, our theological preconceptions insist that perfection is required to be in relationship with God; theology can be construed as clear-cut, but relationships are messy.

Theological assertions like this one describe the facts of our spiritual reality. Our sin does break fellowship with God. But theology can fixate on our responsibility for sin and miss God's heart-motivation to persistently and patiently pursue us to restore our relationship with him back to the full intimacy experienced in the Garden. But first, God wants us to realize that we desire the same thing. We have a choice: We are not robots programmed to respond as per God's prewritten code, forced to love him in return. Instead, God longs for us to freely choose to want to be with him. We demonstrate our desire to be with God by acknowledging our sin, asking for forgiveness, and choosing to walk with him through our obedience. That's why Jesus says: "If you love me, you will keep [obey] my commandments." (John 14)

God's command to Abram, "Walk before me, and be blameless," is a four-word sentence in Hebrew, לְפָנַי וֶהְיֵה תָמִים הִתְהַלֵּךְ, spotlighting the word *tamiym*. [3] Attempting to capture the essence of God's command in English, different translators lean on phrases such as *be perfect, be trustworthy, be pure-hearted, be devout, do what is right*, and (in Eugene Peterson's wording) *live to the hilt*. The popular NIV, a version which translates concept-to-concept rather than word-for-word, adds *faithfully*, attempting to infuse the relational nature into what God is saying to Abraham: "Walk before me *faithfully* and be blameless."

As I mentioned in chapter 9, no single Hebrew word exists equivalent to the English word *obey*. The Hebrew words *hear, do, keep, guard, preserve*, and *walk* are all often translated as *obey* in our English Bibles. Further criteria for what it means to obey blamelessly will be given to Abraham's descendants at their covenant ceremony at Mt. Sinai, where God reiterates his command to be blameless (Deuteronomy 18:13), which simply means we are to be "complete, whole, entire" in our relationship with God. God desires us to willfully choose to pursue him and him alone.

God offers the Hebrews an exclusive relationship, like a marriage, in which they commit to trust him alone to provide for, care for, and protect them. The forty-days' journey from Egypt to Mt. Sinai is God's courtship of the Hebrew people, leading up to their official marriage. During this time, God demonstrates his deep commitment to the Hebrews, who play hard-to-get. Even before arriving at Mt. Sinai, the Hebrews struggle to trust God. After miraculously walking through the Red Sea, they question whether God can provide them food and water, complaining against him different four times. At Mt. Sinai, while Moses is receiving the terms of the covenant from God, they have an "affair" with the Egyptian goddess Hathor (represented by the Golden Calf), crediting her with leading them out of Egypt. They then spend forty years in the desert because they don't trust God to defeat the giants in the land of Canaan.

However, God's commitment to the Hebrews (and us) is not based on their (or our) response. He remains faithful to the covenant regardless of our behavior. This kind of deep, committed love changes people. God wants to court the whole world to be in a relationship with him, so he invites them to witness his gracious love lavished upon the Hebrew people—and upon us.

Bless the World

God's promise to Abraham is that the whole world will be blessed through him and his descendants. This begins when he calls the Hebrews to be a kingdom of priests and a holy nation—set apart and distinct. (Exodus 19:6)[4] The desolate region of Mt. Sinai provides an ideal, solitary place to live set apart. However, being set apart and distinct requires a contrasting reality to be set apart and distinct from: God never intended the Hebrews to stay at Mt. Sinai. They need to learn how to follow him in the midst of engaging a larger world in order to fulfill the promise given to Abraham: "All peoples on earth will be blessed through you." (Genesis 12:3) They depart from Mt. Sinai with the tabernacle, *Torah*, and God's presence (as a pillar of fire and smoke) to guide them, like a shepherd does, through the wilderness in which they'll end up wandering for the next forty years.

After they finally settle in the Promised Land, no longer isolated, members of each subsequent generation will need to learn to trust God for themselves, this time surrounded by the Canaanites, Philistines, Ammonites, Amorites, and Moabites. Additionally, God places them geographically on the international crossroad between two great empires: Egypt and Mesopotamia. God intentionally sets his people in a location from which they can influence the whole world. However, this location also exposes them to external influences from a constant influx of international travelers touting the power of *their* gods, as proven by their military and economic success.

The Hebrews often abandon their fidelity to Yahweh and instead pursue the gods of the nations around them, leading them to sacrifice their own children, neglect the needy, and inconsistently pursue a faithful relationship with the Lord. They put their trust in other gods and kings to meet their needs. The story of the Old Testament makes the case that no one is able to live a blameless life. But when we're reading the story, the challenge is that our attention can be drawn to the Israelites' behavioral choices, overlooking the core issue: Their hearts were far from the Lord. (Isaiah 29:13; Ezkiel 33:31)

The Hebrews fail to be blameless far more often than they succeed. Eventually, God sends them to Babylon for seventy years, forcing them to let the land rest as he commanded them.[5] The generation that returns from exile in Babylon rebuilds the temple with a renewed sense of fidelity to God. But it doesn't last long. Just read the Books of Ezra and Nehemiah: You'll see there that their faithfulness to living distinct, holy, and blameless lives is mediocre at best. They continue to struggle to live in such a way that the world may know God. Now, what do you think: Maybe more rules could solve this problem?

Relationship, not Rules

As I discussed in chapter 2, obeying the *Torah* became a focus of many in Jewish society by the time of Jesus. Leading up to the first-century-AD, sages identified 248 positive and 365 prohibitive statements in *Torah* as specific guidance for living a holy or blameless life. Different Jewish groups debated the specifics of how to live blamelessly. Sadducees, Herodians, Pharisees, Essenes, Zealots, Hasidim, and Boethusians are just a few of the twenty-six to twenty-nine uniquely identifiable groups of Jews in the first century.[6] Each had its own beliefs and practices about obeying these 613 commandments.[7] While these different groups debated the specifics, the heart-motivation behind the obedience for many for them was to walk with God. This can be lost on us as 21st-century outsiders, since our legal minds gravitate towards the nitty-gritty details of their debates on how to obey God specifically. We are also not immune to debates over how to precisely obey God and can unintentionally create our own version of the 613 commandments. Desire to attract and keep

God's favor, instead of focusing on being in a relationship, can cause us to seek formulas to follow in order to guarantee relational outcomes. Using the Bible as case law, we judge others for not agreeing with our understanding of obedience. This attitude has more to do with making ourselves feel better (often at the expense of others) than with loving God.

We talk about grace and love, but, given enough time, written and unwritten rules form organically within every group, setting parameters or expectations for joining and maintaining one's membership in that group. This is human nature. Even the most hardened gangs live by rules, which must be followed to maintain acceptance by the group. All relationships need boundaries to thrive. We all long to find "our people" and feel like we belong.

However, if fear of rejection is our motivation for complying with expectations, then the relationship suffers from codependency—which is neither life-giving nor joyful. Obedience becomes transactional when our focus shifts to keeping rules and judging others for not keeping them, rather than on loving God and others. When some people look at Christianity, they can get the idea that we think people have to live a certain way in order to be accepted by God, when actually it's meant to be the opposite. We experience a sense of belonging with God, which then changes how we live.

Tanita Maddox's research offers a glimpse into perceptions of Christianity among many members of Gen Z who describe Christianity as "unsafe, intolerant, judgmental, inauthentic and irrelevant."[8] To some people, Christianity, the Bible, and God can seem like obstacles to living a life of freedom. According to Maddox's study, the fundamental question Gen Z asks is: "Will your truth take away my freedom?" This question seems very reasonable, given their perception and experiences of Christianity. The misperception is that we need to change in order to be accepted by God. In God's reality, he already accepted us when Jesus took our place on the cross, receiving what we deserve. The question is whether or not we *want* to be in a relationship with God. He continually extends his grace, waiting for us to *yada* him, inviting us to ask for his forgiveness and receive it. Experiencing genuine forgiveness and acceptance draws us to *want* to walk with God. And then we begin to live differently, out of joy rather than fear or obligation.

Following Commandments

After we choose to follow Jesus, what does relational obedience look like? Two Hebrew words are helpful here: *derek* דֶּרֶךְ and mitzvah מִצְוָה. The Hebrew word *derek* means *path* or *way*. The meaning of this word developed over thousands of years in the context of shepherding. It occurs in Jeremiah 6:16, which says: "This is the way [*derek*]; walk in it," meaning God has one path for us to follow.

Derek feels similar to the word *Torah*. In fact, *Torah* provides the guiding principles and direction to walk God's *derek*, which is actually embodying what God says. We've all experienced the disconnect between the two. It is hard to do what Jesus said consistently, even while walking in his direction. The issue is our hearts, not our desire. In Hebrew, our heart is the place where we make decisions. No amount of making intentional decisions will consistently override our sympathetic nervous system's automatic response. We need a heart-transformation of our being—a rewiring of our inner self to change how we respond, which we will discuss in greater detail in the next chapter (here's a sneak preview— God gives us a new heart). Experiencing the genuine, healthy, and loving belonging that God provides causes us to want to walk more closely with him. Drawing near, we subconsciously begin to act like him, slowly transforming our character to be like his. We start responding like God without having to think about it. We only truly change when we experience being accepted and appreciated by someone whom we genuinely want to be like.[9] Rules may influence our behaviors, but unlike relationships, they never change our hearts.

We could never come up with enough rules and guidelines to help us navigate every possible scenario. When Moses left Mt. Sinai, I suggest the most important thing he took with him was not *Torah*, but God's presence. And when we joyfully walk with God, like Moses, we slowly begin to see the world as God does and walk out his principles of love, valuing relationships, rather than needing specific rules of which there never would be enough anyway.

Torah and *mitzvah* also seem similar in English. *Mitzvah* is often translated in English as *commandment*, which sounds like an order given by someone in authority whom we are obligated to obey.[10] The word command in English has a similar connotation, as does the word *law*: Both must be followed, or we'll face the consequences. As we learned with *Torah* and its Hebraic understanding not being as rigid as our English word *law*, *mitzvah* (*tsvah*) means *to direct* (Deuteronomy 1:19), *to show*, or *to point out*. It's a relational word, meaning something like a shepherd showing us a path we can choose to walk or not.

Understanding the heart of the word *mitzvah* makes many Scripture passages easier to understand. For example, Psalm 119 uses the word *mitzvah* in almost every other line. Most translations use the word *commands*; this makes it sound as if we don't have a choice. However, if you substitute *directions* for *commands*, it reads like the Lord's loving encouragement to his sheep, rather than orders for his soldiers to obey or suffer disciplinary consequences.

Following God's path—obeying him—is the gift we give ourselves, leading to deeper intimacy with the Lord to experience his freedom.

Misreading Isaiah 30 as a Westerner

Misinterpreting the heart language of the Bible affects our understanding, potentially causing us to misapply what we read, resulting in immense hurt and confusion. A classic example is how we read and understand Isaiah 30. Through the prophet Isaiah, God tells us: "Whether you turn to the right or to the left, your ears will hear a voice behind you, saying, 'This is the way; walk in it.'" (Isaiah 30:21) Our Western ears perk up, hearing God's willingness to guide us, filling us with confidence that he will provide us personal directions as we chart our self-determined course—like in the Disney move *Ratatouille*, with Remy the rat literally pulling the strings that guide Alfredo's cooking decisions. But that's not the right word-picture at all. God is guiding us to *his* path: not one driven by our ambitions to achieve, and not one of our own creation where we ask God to bless the plans we've made.

As we saw in Chapter 9, we can only begin to grasp the meaning of Isaiah's statement "this is the path, walk in it" when we understand the relationship between a shepherd and his sheep. Reread Isaiah 30; where is the voice coming from? The voice in verse 21 comes from behind, telling us the sheep are no longer following the Good Shepherd; instead, they are leading themselves and pursuing their own path. If God were leading, then he would be walking in front with his sheep following his voice. The direction of the shepherd's voice tells us he is pursuing a lost sheep.

This matches the larger context of the whole chapter, in which Isaiah calls God's people to repent, to turn back from going down to Egypt to seek Pharaoh's protection. (30:2) Historically, this refers to the coming invasion from Sennacherib and the Assyrian army. Almost a thousand years after God's people left Egypt, they're still tempted to go back, trusting in Pharaoh to save them rather than God alone. On paper, this makes sense: The Egyptian empire is one of the most powerful in the region. However, ever since Mt. Sinai, God has asked the Hebrews to trust in him to provide and protect them, even from the Assyrians. Isaiah describes God as the Good Shepherd, pursuing the Hebrews who are willfully getting themselves lost by seeking Pharaoh's protection rather than God's. But Pharaoh can't save them; only God can. Ironically, Sennacherib subdues Egypt while God miraculously saves King Hezekiah and Jerusalem.

Anyone can become lost, especially when feeling afraid or threatened. Panic causes us to seek immediate solutions, often getting ourselves even more lost. But despite straying far from the Good Shepherd, we can have confidence that he will find and rescue us. We just have to stop moving and cry out.

God's Covenantal Pursuit

Later in Isaiah 30, Isaiah encourages his readers: "People of Zion, who live in Jerusalem, you will weep no more. How gracious he will be when you cry for help! As soon as he hears, he will answer you." (Isaiah 30:19) When a sheep is lost, its only hope is to cry out. Its bleating will act as a beacon for both the wolf and the shepherd. But how did the sheep get lost in the first place? Please take a moment to watch this video from SourceFlix. In it, you will see a willfully lost sheep choose its own path, placing itself in danger. You will also see a shepherd searching for his sheep. Notice how the shepherd responds to his sheep when they finally

Scan Here to
Watch a Lost
Sheep Get
Rescued

reunite. He doesn't hit it, scold it, or put a rope around its neck. He calls it, pets it, reassures it, and invites it to follow him back to life.

This is the story of the Bible: God fulfills his covenant relationship faithfully by endlessly pursuing a people who perpetually and willfully go their own way, forgetting their source of life.

We will stumble and find ourselves off God's path, because we will not be perfect. Walking the path was never about being perfect; it's about trusting that the Good Shepherd will pursue us when we call out. Unfortunately, our frequent missteps can lead us to believe God is disappointed in our lack of maturity to trust him, and we imagine him becoming impatient with us. These feelings are how we feel about ourselves, not how God feels toward us. It is impossible for God to feel disappointment. Existing outside time, he knows the past, present, and future. He never expects one thing and gets another; he never says: "I didn't see that coming." Just as God told Abraham his descendants would be enslaved in Egypt years before it happened (Genesis 15:13-16), nothing we do surprises him either. Does knowing this change your desire to cry out to him? It did for me. It makes me willing to cry out as soon as I realize I'm lost.

Jesus, the Good Shepherd, pursues us. We call out, acknowledging that we know we are lost and need help. The Good Shepherd's grace and love are such that he takes the initiative to pursue both the willfully stubborn and untrusting as well as those who don't even know they are lost, because he longs to be in relationship with us.

We often can't see clearly, which is why Jesus says, "my sheep hear my voice, I know them, and they follow me" (John 10:27): God desires us to hear his voice and follow him. It takes time to learn to hear the shepherd's voice, discerning it among all the others. In our next chapter, a man is going to come to Jesus and ask him specifically how to walk with God. Little does he know he is listening to the Good Shepherd's voice. Will he follow? Will you?

Questions

- Has your trust in God changed as you explore cultural context?
- How does realizing God is not disappointed with you change your desire to approach him?
- Do you feel that obeying God comes at the cost of your personal dreams and desires?
- Do you feel God's love is contingent upon your obedience?
- How do you know when you're lost relationally or spiritually?
- What emotions do you feel when you are lost? How do you respond? How does God respond?
- What helps you hear the Good Shepherd's voice more clearly? Or, is the thought of hearing God's voice a new concept to you?
- What stops you from wanting to cry out to God?
- Do you believe God pursues you? What would you do differently if you believed that he does?
- How do the Hebrew definitions & heart language of the words *derek* and *mitzvah* reshape how you read Scripture as a whole?
- Would you say you are walking the ancient path, or have you simply found it and are waiting to begin?

Additional Resources

Brown, Tommy. *The Ache for Meaning: How the Temptations of Christ Reveal Who We Are and What We're Seeking*

Living Hope Ministries. "SourceFlix | Visual Media Demonstrating the Bible Is True" https://www.youtube.com/watch?v=2lIUBYFIfTU

Manning, Brennan. *Abba's Child: The Cry of the Heart for Intimate Belonging*

Wakefield, Norm. *Equipped to Love: Building Idolatry-Free Relationships*

11. Going to Heaven

*Is the Bible an encyclopedia book of doctrines
or a book of faith intended for the faithful?*

—JORDAN BAJIS, COMMON GROUND

The Bible itself can be one giant speed bump. It's a collection of sixty-six books, written over roughly a thousand years, in three languages, by forty or so different authors. The faithful have poured over the Scriptures for centuries, attempting to highlight unifying themes so that it could be read cohesively. Competing theologies abound, offering differing ways of putting the puzzle pieces together, each with its own nuanced theological conclusions. What sometimes gets left behind in the process?

People. Not *what*, but *who*.

Theology can be a helpful tool in understanding how the Bible fits together as a whole document only if we don't forget the end goal: our relationship with the Lord. Indulging the desire to perfect our theology, we can argue vehemently for our theological position and unintentionally end up worshiping our doctrines, or even the Bible itself, instead of the God of the Bible. There is no better example than the fiercely debated speed bump: "How can I get into heaven?"

In the story we'll examine in this chapter, Jesus encounters a man who seems to be asking this very question. The man willingly humbles himself to approach Jesus, exposing his personal perception of his spiritual state. Their exchange touches upon theological issues of obedience to *Torah*, eternal life, and our relationship with God here on earth before we die.

During this deeply theological exchange, the Gospel of Mark gives us a glimpse into the heart of God: "Jesus looked at him and loved him." (Mark 10:21) Jesus' motivation to correct this man's theological misperceptions is driven by his love for the man and his desire that he would experience a vibrant relationship with God—now, and for eternity.

After witnessing this intense line of questioning, the disciples have questions of their own. Jesus addresses these too, and offers an equally compassionate warning to them (and us) in a parable, which we will explore in the next chapter.

Sharing an Efficient Gospel

Americans tend to be pragmatic people, valuing efficiency and productivity; we like to chart the most direct course to our desired destination. Applying this mindset to sharing the Gospel, we often desire to get straight to the point. This process begins by condensing a thousand-page book into bite-sized pieces of valuable theological information: none more important than how to be in a right relationship with God.

In the early 20th century, evangelists began to implement what is known as "the sinner's prayer" as a streamlined answer to this question.[1] One version of the prayer goes like this:

> Lord Jesus, I need You. Thank You for dying on the cross for my sins. I open the door of my life and receive You as my Savior and Lord. Thank You for forgiving my sins and giving me eternal life. Take control of the throne of my life. Make me the kind of person You want me to be.[2]

This efficiently sums up what many consider to be the way to begin an eternal relationship with God. However, efficiency isn't always Jesus' highest value when trying to share his Gospel with someone. He demonstrates this when the man in our story asks him: "What must I do to inherit the kingdom of heaven?" Our ears hear him asking: "How do I get to heaven?" Well, he is, and he isn't.

Before answering, Jesus engages the man by asking questions to understand his perspective. He could have answered quickly. Instead, Jesus' questioning communicates a desire to know him, and for him to know himself, inviting him to put his theological cards on the table. His questions challenge both the young man and the disciples in their understanding of how to live in the kingdom of heaven now.

The Gospel is about being in relationship with God, which in my own life is often messy, and at times extremely inefficient as God corrects my understanding of who he is. Relationships marked by authentic care are seldom efficient.

Setting the Scene of the Story

Roughly 80% of the Bible is narrative: That means it tells stories. The word *story* can cause us to think what is presented is fictional. This is not necessarily the case: We tell true stories all the time, and so does the Lord. God presents deep truths about himself, creation, sin, salvation, and redemption, mostly through story. Rabbis in general read the Bible as a story and assume God communicated with great intentionality, so every jot and tittle was written for a reason.[3] God's intentionality also includes the sequence of events recorded within an individual book of the Bible. Therefore, it is our job as the reader to figure out the connections between adjacent stories.

The story I want us to look at next is found in Matthew 19, Mark 10, and Luke 18. The preceding narrative in all three Gospels describes parents bringing their children to be blessed by the most prominent rabbi of their generation. The idea of blessing others, especially children, may be a universal custom in Judaism.[4] The disciples appear to be bothered by the interruption and attempt to act as crowd control. Jesus, valuing people, demonstrates to his disciples that people are the whole point of all this theological knowledge. These two adjacent stories seem to be unrelated, but they both use the phrase: "enter the kingdom of heaven."[5] That clause is the ingredient that connects them.

The Rich Young Ruler

Above this story, your Bible may have the header "The Rich Young Ruler." This title is a composite from Matthew 19:22, which identifies him as "young," and Luke 18:18, which calls him a "ruler." The use of the title *ruler* leads some to speculate he is head of a local synagogue. [6] He addresses Jesus as "teacher" in Matthew and "good teacher" in Mark and Luke. The Hebrew equivalent for teacher is *rabbi*, a polite way to address a sage in a Jewish setting.[7] The man identifies Jesus as a Jewish sage, a learned man of *Torah*, and he seeks to know Jesus' view on how to walk with God.

He is a man of means and prominence within his community, but by running to meet Jesus, this man humiliates himself publicly: holding up his expensive robes, exposing his legs, getting sweaty, falling onto the ground, and dirtying his fine garments—these actions are no small thing in a status-conscious culture. (Mark 10:17) He is one of only twelve men in the entire Bible who willingly shame themselves by running.[8] Who is the most prominent person you can think of? Imagine that person running and falling at someone's feet with a whole crowd of his subordinates and neighbors watching! We get a small glimpse into this man's sincere desire to pursue Jesus by his willingness to do something so undignified.

What Is Eternal Life?

After running to Jesus, this young man strikes up a conversation with Jesus by asking: "What good thing must I do to get/inherit eternal life?" Translating this passage into Hebrew from the Greek, Robert Lindsey connects it to Micah 6:8, which asks: "What good does the Lord require of you?" Some suggest this follows a first-century interpretation of Micah which held that one could perform good deeds to obtain eternal life.[9] Jesus' response in the Gospel of Matthew, "Why do you ask me about what is good?" reflects this possible understanding that only doing the good deeds of *Torah* is good.[10] This interpretation flows well into Jesus' next statement: "If you want to enter life, obey the commandments." Jesus gives the man his answer of how to walk with God: *do* (obey) *Torah*. However, contrary to appearances, Jesus isn't preaching a works gospel but rather a relational gospel, as we'll see shortly.

If we've spent much time in an Evangelical church, the young man's next question, "What must I do to have/inherit eternal life?" probably rings theological alarm bells in our ears. We don't *do* anything to earn or acquire our salvation... right? And yet Jesus responds with words that people outside of Judaism may perceive as a claim that one obtains eternal life by observing the commandments. [11] Is he saying "doing" something can earn eternal life? Yes—but also no. Stay with me here.

The story of the Hebrews is a story of God's grace, from Genesis through Revelation, leading us to eternal life with God. When they cry out to God in Exodus 2:23, they don't even know God's name. He rescues them out of Egypt, fulfilling his covenant promise to Abraham, displaying his grace by parting the Red Sea, providing food and water for them in the wilderness, and giving them the *Torah* at Mt. Sinai. The eternal God initiates a covenant relationship with them, starting at Mt. Sinai and stretching into eternity.[12] So eternal life began with God's gracious acts of deliverance out of Egypt, and now the Hebrews live eternal life in the present, walking with God by obeying *Torah*, and this walk continues after death into eternity. That is why the man's question doesn't make sense. God's people don't *do* anything to inherit eternal life; they already have it by walking with God as a member of God's family.

Walking with God here on earth is challenging. He commands the Israelites to be blameless, giving them *Torah* so they know what to do, and the rest of the story is God's never-ending pursuit of this relationship despite their lack of fidelity. The prophets Jeremiah and Ezekiel acknowledge our inability to obey *Torah* and foretell God's promise to end the cycle of unfaithfulness when the Messianic king comes. He will put his law in our minds and write it on our hearts. (Jeremiah 31:33; Ezekiel 36:26) To "do" *Torah*—to walk perfectly in a right relationship with God—requires a heart transformation. Here in this New Testament story, this man is unaware that this Messianic prophecy is being fulfilled right in front of him. He responds to Jesus by asking which specific commandments he should keep to acquire a right relationship with God for eternity. His question reveals his theological misunderstanding of eternal life. He thinks it's something to obtain rather than a relationship to be lived.

Something to Do

Part of his confusion here is the emphasis on keeping *Torah* to prove to himself and others he is walking with God, which will then later lead to eternal life. So, Jesus begins his discussion with the rich young ruler by listing five of the ten commandments, then he adds "love your neighbor as yourself," all as things to do. (Leviticus 19:18) The first four of the ten commandments detail the relationship between us and God, and the remaining commandments outline how we should treat each other. Jesus cites commandments five through nine without mentioning the tenth: "Do not covet." Why leave this off his list? Maybe the man is coveting something? Yet he tells Jesus he's kept all the commandments since he was a boy. If this is true, then why does he lack assurance that he is walking with God? Jesus is taking time to help the man see his own heart.

If his first question about doing something to earn eternal life did not trigger us, then his claim of having "kept all the commandments" probably will. We might quote Paul in Romans 3:9-18: "There is none righteous, no, not one..." [13] But Jesus doesn't go there. This man's emotional state already indicates something is spiritually off, so Jesus offers him something to do to put an end to his emotional distress. In doing this, Jesus helps the man discover for himself what is blocking him from walking with God, revealing what he's coveting.

The man asks Jesus for something to do to assure himself of God's acceptance. The Greek verb tense used here implies a once-and-done action. [14] Some rabbis' interpretation of Micah 6 suggested that one could procure eternal life by performing a single good deed (one grand gesture). In contrast, Jesus and other sages speak about the necessity of observing all of Torah. [15] James, a disciple of Jesus, taught what he learned from his rabbi: "For whoever keeps the whole law but fails in one point has become guilty of all of it." (James 2:10) Jesus taught his disciples to keep all the law, yet this man is asking for one grand gesture to do. Obliging his request for one impressive action that will save him, Jesus now exposes what he really wants: relationship.

Become a Disciple

Here's Jesus' one huge command. Jesus tells the man: "Sell your possessions and give to the poor, and you will have treasure in heaven." [16] This stops the man in his tracks, and he turns around and walks away, unwilling to do this one grand gesture. Many readers mistakenly assume Jesus is asking the man to become poor and destitute, which doesn't seem like a wise thing to do. Jewish sages understood that giving away all one's wealth could have unintended consequences if those generous people became a burden on the community themselves. They taught that one could not give away more than 20% of one's wealth. [17] It seems likely that this is what Jesus meant, but this man is unwilling to give away even twenty percent of what he owns.

Jesus kindly leads the man to a deeper understanding of God, himself, and *Torah* because his request reveals that the man covets his stuff, particularly the comfort, control, and protection his position and money provides him. Jesus challenges the man to walk with God by letting go of social status and material security to follow him. What we can overlook here is the tagline invitation Jesus offers after he sells his possessions: "Come, follow me." This phrase is a formal invitation to become one of Jesus' disciples. Jesus invites him to give up his comfort, security, and control over his life to follow in the dust of his rabbi's sandals wherever he goes, to learn to walk with God like one's rabbi.[18] Not an easy life—and he walks away.

Did you catch that? The man walks away from the very assurance he so desperately seeks by literally walking away from God. Jesus offers him an ongoing relationship walking with God, rather than a checklist of things to do to acquire a ticket to heaven. One doesn't earn a future eternal life, which is then awarded later like a payout from a retirement account; one walks with God relationally now and forever. That's what eternal life is, and it begins now. Observing *Torah* is an outward expression of an inward desire to be in a right relationship with God. Some keep *Torah* to avoid God's punishment with the desire to earn eternal life when they die, as a reward to living a righteous life, but the sages address this issue by clarifying that one obeys *Torah* out of love (for God), not obligation or duty to earn a reward.[19]

We do not know this man's heart, but I believe he sincerely desired to walk with God. What he did not fully grasp is that walking with God requires following him, which means letting go of control and remembering that eternal life is inherited by being a member of God's family.

God's family began at Mt. Sinai, by his grace, where he chose the Hebrews. Their promised inheritance of eternal life is a relationship with God, passed down from generation to generation beginning with Abraham. This relational inheritance cannot be earned; it is simply received by being part of the family. The rich young ruler, as a Jew, is already part of God's family, possessing the very inheritance he is coveting. [20] He has either forgotten or misunderstands that his inheritance is a relationship to be lived, not something to possess.

Nevertheless, God invites him to participate in expanding God's family by joining Jesus on his mission.

Through Jesus, God's family will grow to include the whole world to fulfill the promise made to Abraham in Genesis 12. How do you become part of God's family? You need to be born into it, both Jews and Gentiles. This is why Jesus uses the language of being "born again" in John 3 with Nicodemus, a Jewish leader. He comes to offer everyone the opportunity to be a member of God's family by being born into it through Jesus, receiving the inheritance of eternal life now and walking with God into eternity. Everyone, Jew and Gentile, needs to be born again to be a member of God's family.

The rich young ruler doesn't fully understand how to be part of God's family. The Gospel of Matthew describes him as being young, possibly referring to his spiritual maturity. Jesus' questions help him to know what is in his heart and tells him that eternal life begins now by walking with God on his terms. Rejecting Jesus' offer, he walks away sad, anxious in his lack of assurance of eternal life.[21] To our western ears, it sounds like he walks away from salvation by rejecting Jesus' invitation. Others say this is a story about the cost of discipleship. I think it is a little of both. Despite the man's position, wealth, and self-perceived faithfulness to God, he lacks assurance he's in a right relationship with God. He wants what God offers, eternal life, but on his own terms. Without recognizing what he's doing, he chooses to literally walk away from the path the Good Shepherd is calling him on.

The Story After

The disciples witness this exchange, which stirs up lots of questions. They must have felt stunned, wondering: What just happened? Had this man turned down an invitation few receive from Jesus, one they all had accepted? After they witness this startling exchange, Jesus then tells them of the relative ease with which a camel can pass through the "eye of a needle" in comparison to a rich person trying to get into heaven.[22] In rabbinic literature, this same phrase is used to convey the idea that repentance begins with a small opening, the size of the eye of a needle, and then grows.[23] The camel sticks his nose through a gap in a tent flap, then his head, and next thing you know, his whole body is inside the tent!

This man is the epitome of someone appearing blessed by God, given his wealth and status within the society, which raises the question in the minds of the disciples: "Who then can be saved?" Jesus tells them: "With man this is impossible, but with God all things are possible."[24] Then, the disciples begin to compare themselves to the rich man. They'd all given up everything to follow Jesus and wonder "Will our sacrifice be rewarded?" Jesus assures them of the great reward and honor awaiting them, in addition to the eternal life they already have by walking with him now.

What if the rich man later repents, receiving eternal life in heaven, while enjoying a comfortable life here before then, unlike the disciples? How would you feel about someone who lives however they want, only to accept Jesus on their deathbed and receive the same reward? The disciples (and we) potentially misunderstand the blessing of experiencing the kingdom of heaven on earth just as much as the rich man, even while the disciples are living in it.

Matthew 19 ends with Jesus saying: "The first will be last and the last will be first." This phrase bookends the parable that follows, which we'll discuss in the next chapter. Why? Jesus desires to warn his disciples of potential dangers ahead—and, like the rabbi he is, he presents the potential hazards with a story.

Questions

- Have you been operating under the belief that you have to earn salvation or earn your place in God's family? How do you become a part of God's family?
- Have you ever valued man-made doctrine over relationship? What does that look like?
- How have you interpreted the story of the rich young ruler story in the past? Has anything changed now?
- What does it look like for someone to walk with God in our modern world?
- What would you need to see in your life to know that you have eternal life now?
- How would you feel if you got to heaven and found out everyone got in? Why? What do your feelings tell you about how you see God and salvation?
- Why are stories such a powerful tool to communicate our thoughts, feelings, and experiences? How do you see this play out in Scripture?
- How might you be like the rich young ruler in this story?

Additional Resources

Comfort, Ray. *Hell's Best Kept Secret*

12. Who Can Be Saved?

Parables enlighten and instruct,
but often with a message that people do not want to hear.

—KLYNE SNODGRASS

A rabbi who gives a teaching without two parables
is like giving someone a jar to carry without any handles.

—RABBINICAL SAYING

Do I understand that how I see me
is the greatest evidence of my theology?

—BILL THRALL, TRUEFACE MINISTRY

A Conversation with my Grandma

I grew up living next door to my grandparents. Towards the end of my grandmother's life, she lived with us, and I'd shuttle her back and forth to the local senior center. While driving, I'd ask her questions about her life, and she'd share stories I'd never heard before about growing up in a Jewish family. I had never seen her practice any faith except hard work and commitment to my grandfather. During one of those drives, our conversation turned to my father, who had recently become a follower of Jesus. She didn't think God could forgive him for all the things she thought he'd done, but I said that Jesus can forgive anything. She questioned whether God would be that forgiving, so I shared with her a parable of Jesus from Matthew 20:

For the kingdom of heaven is like a landowner who went out early in the morning to hire men to work in his vineyard. He agreed to pay them a denarius for the day and sent them into his vineyard. About the third hour he went out and saw others standing in the marketplace doing nothing. He told them, "You also go and work in my vineyard, and I will pay you whatever is right." So they went. He went out again about the sixth hour and the ninth hour and did the same thing. About the eleventh hour he went out and found still others standing around. He asked them, "Why have you been standing here all day long doing nothing?" "Because no one has hired us," they answered. He said to them, "You also go and work in my vineyard."

I asked my grandmother, "What do you think these workers get paid?" She responded: "I don't know." So I continued:

When evening came, the owner of the vineyard said to his foreman, "Call the workers and pay them their wages, beginning with the last ones hired and going on to the first." The workers who were hired about the eleventh hour came and each received a denarius. So when those came who were hired first, they expected to receive more. But each one of them also received a denarius. When they received it, they began to grumble against the landowner. "These men who were hired last worked only one hour," they said, "and you have made them equal to us who have borne the burden of the work and the heat of the day." But he answered one of them, "Friend, I am not being unfair to you. Didn't you agree to work for a denarius? Take your pay and go. I want to give the man who was hired last the same as I gave you. Don't I have the right to do what I want with my own money? Or are you envious because I am generous?" So the last will be first, and the first will be last.

My grandma's response: "That's not fair."

And she's right. On the surface, taking offense at this equal pay for unequal work seems completely reasonable. American culture values fairness, equity, and earning one's keep.

If we interpret the wages in this parable as a metaphor for salvation, we might think: "Ah, I get it—we don't earn our way into heaven, and it doesn't matter when someone makes that decision—whether early in life or late." That interpretation might not help us feel less resentful, but it might make us feel guilty about our resentment!

In the previous chapter, a rich young man came to Jesus with a theological question about eternal life, to which Jesus offered a relational answer. After witnessing the exchange between the two, the disciples asked questions like my grandmother's: What if this man, who rejects Jesus' offer, enjoys a full life of (perceived) comfort and ease, in comparison to the disciple's life, only to ask for forgiveness towards the end of his life and walk with God into eternity? Is it fair he should receive the same reward of eternal life as the disciples?

The disciples' questions expose their theological beliefs, and Jesus' response goes well beyond the theological mechanics of how one gets to heaven to take aim at how we can joyfully live in God's grace now. Eternal life is being with God now *and* forever. To challenge their thinking, Jesus tells the parable of the vineyard workers to his disciples.

Ask Questions

The rich young ruler and the disciples both asked questions; so did my grandmother. I'm encouraging you to do the same. God welcomes our questions; like all of us, he longs to be understood. What questions came to your mind when you read this parable? Applying some of the principles we discussed in the first half of the book, we need to ask some foundational questions to put this story into context:

1) What is Jesus' location geographically?
2) What stories come before and after?
3) To whom is he speaking?
4) How does this piece fit into the larger narrative?
5) Why do the disciples (and we) need to know this?

An often neglected but helpful piece of information is geography. Knowing the story's location clues us into the audience as well as the environment. The authors of the New Testament often utilize what Dr. Thomas Dixon of Campbell University calls *theogeography*: the layering of New Testament stories onto the same general location as an Old Testament setting to connect the themes of the two stories. In this instance, Jesus travels from the Galilee through a place called "Judea beyond the Jordan" on his way to Jerusalem to celebrate the Passover feast. (Matthew 19:1) This feast commemorates God's deliverance of his people out of Egypt. Deuteronomy 16:16-17 commands all righteous male Jews to convene in Jerusalem annually to celebrate the three pilgrim feasts: Passover, Shavuot, and Sukkot. Jesus is obeying the *Torah* by making his tri-annual pilgrimage and is passing through this place.[1]

Jews traveling from the north through this region, like Jesus and his disciples, would often traverse the eastern side of the Jordan river to avoid contact with Samaritans, with whom they'd been feuding since returning from exile in the 5th century BC.[2] They would then cross the Jordan river at a location opposite Jericho to begin their ascent to Jerusalem. This well-traveled location is traditionally believed to be the location of Jesus' baptism (although other options have been identified), Elijah's crossing of the Jordan before he was taken up to heaven in a whirlwind (2 Kings 2:11), and Israel's crossing into the promised land under Joshua's leadership.[3] *Jesus* is the Latin form of the Hebrew name *Yeshua* (*Joshua* in English), and, like Joshua, Jesus will cross the Jordan to lead his people into a new kind of promised land, inaugurating a new kingdom—and also like Joshua, not without a fight. This location has some serious theogeography! Here, Jesus enjoys one last moment of calm before ascending to Jerusalem and the chaos of the cross that awaits him.

The Power of a Story

Stories get our attention. People put down their phones, stop doodling, and give their eyes and ears when someone tells a story. Amid constant stimulation vying for our attention, stories cut through our mental white noise. I'm sure competition existed for people's attention two thousand years ago, but obviously not nearly as much as today. For rabbis, parables function as closing arguments—practical, applied wisdom packaged in a story—to get people's attention and challenge them to act. As fictional stories, parables draw upon source material from aspects of people's everyday lives and their shared history—as in

Scan Here to Watch Brad Gray Explain Parables

"There once was a king...." If the character steps outside the bounds of expected behavior, that deviation serves as a clue. Rabbis employ these powerful stories with the intent to stir emotions and elicit a response, often delivering a message difficult for the audience to receive.⁴ Typically, a parable aims at a specific audience as the targeted listeners identify with one of its characters, with the dilemma of the main protagonist becomes the audience's call to action. One of the first parables in the Bible occurs when Nathan calls out King David after his affair with Bathsheba, which we discussed earlier in Chapter 5. A parable's real-life scenario packages a rabbi's practical application of his interpretation of Torah, and the listener typically must choose between only two courses of action: The hearer must either act upon the wisdom offered in the story, or else remain unchanged. After hearing Nathan's story, David repents, choosing to reconcile with God.

To our ears, parables hit like cryptic riddles requiring further explanation due to our unfamiliarity with the cultural framing of the parable, which the original audience would have grasped more easily. Sometimes, however, a parable ending could be equally as challenging for the original audience as for us. Even the disciples ask Jesus to explain several of his parables. This parable requires no explanation of who its target audience is: Jesus tells this parable to his disciples in response to their questions regarding the rich young ruler.

The Story Before

Leading up to this parable, all three Gospel accounts include the back-and-forth between Jesus and the rich young man, sparking questions from the disciples. The disciples would like to know if their decision to follow Jesus, leaving family and comfort, will be rewarded. Jesus assures them that their decision shows more wisdom and maturity than the most accomplished person in town. He promises them they'll sit as judges over the twelve tribes of Israel and receive a hundredfold reward—and, as a bonus, they'll inherit eternal life.

After reassuring them, Jesus challenges his disciples by adding: "But many that are first will be last and the last first." In the Gospel of Matthew, this statement ends chapter nineteen, but chapter twenty is a continuation of the same story. The parable Jesus is about to tell his disciples will challenge them (and us) over having compassion for the lost. In this case, the lost person is the rich young ruler who just walked away from the very relationship he needed most, remaining lost because he didn't understand that eternal life (living in the kingdom of heaven) starts now. The disciples' emotions are swirling after they witness this exchange, and Jesus seizes the moment to tell a tale of vineyard-workers.

The Characters of the Story

In the parable I recounted to my grandmother, the "master of the house" metaphorically represents God, and his vineyard symbolizes the kingdom of heaven here on earth. Acting as a foreman, God hires people to work in his vineyard: an offer extended both to the disciples and to the rich young ruler. The master continues to hire more workers throughout the day, and only at the end of the workday does the challenge embedded in the parable reveal itself, exposing the heart-attitude of the workers who were first hired—the disciples.

The cultural context of this parable is the harsh reality of life as a subsistence farmer in the first century, difficult on its best day and impossible on its worst. Scholars estimate that the Romans imposed tax rates of between fifty and eighty percent, effectively sentencing the population to unending survival mode. [5] Due to inability to pay these taxes, many workers became tenant farmers on land they'd previously owned, or were forced to seek work as day laborers. As they woke up each morning, their emotional reality included wondering how to survive the day, provide for their families, and avoid unpleasant engagements with the Romans.

Imagine the joy of those hired in the early part of the morning, rejoicing as they walk to the master's vineyard. What a sense of relief, knowing their family would eat that day! With their emotional and physical needs met, those hired first probably celebrate as others join them throughout the day. But then something shifts. The joyful camaraderie turns into resentment, directed not at their fellow workers but towards the generous master, culminating in the claim that he's treated them unfairly. After they've spent the day gratefully enjoying a sense of relief from their daily struggles to provide for those they loved, those feelings evaporate due to this perceived injustice, despite receiving the pay promised to them. Their accusations reveal that they harbor an expectation of fairness instead of celebrating and honoring the master's generosity (grace) to others who are in need like themselves. The order in which the master chooses to pay the workers unmasks the hidden expectations of fairness in those hired first. Since they worked through the heat of the day, they expect the pay to be prorated for those who did not.[6] How quickly their emotions shift from joyful gratitude for God's provision to demanding fairness, overlooking God's graciousness in hiring them in the first place!

Now, if the workers intentionally showed up later in the day without a good reason, their delay in seeking work could be seen as a reflection on their character. But we are not told those details. We don't know whether everyone was seeking work at the same time, but the master only chose a few each time he visited the marketplace. Maybe those hired later lived farther away from the marketplace and had a longer walk to get there before they could offer their services. Regardless of the circumstances, the demands for fairness coming from those hired first are not for more pay for themselves, but for their suffering fellow Jews to receive less. Their heart-attitude exposes their lack of compassion; they are on a slippery slope that could lead to pride, arrogance, ingratitude, and even jealousy.

Comparison Steals Joy

The tension of the parable reaches its peak when the workers hired first discover that everyone receives the same pay. Keep in mind, this parable is told because the rich young ruler walks away from choosing to follow Jesus: He potentially represents those hired later in the day if he repents and comes back to the "marketplace" looking for "work." In the meantime, to the disciples (the first workers), it looks as if those who delay this choice live an easier life. My grandmother and the disciples both ask: "Is this fair?"

The disciples have some faulty assumptions about those hired later, which could lead to comparison. It's been said that "Comparison is the thief of joy."[7] When our appreciation shifts from focusing on what we have, to noticing only what we don't, our gratitude begins to erode. Gratitude is the very fuel necessary of joy and how quickly we (and the workers hired first) can become ungrateful, forgetting the grace we've been given to work in God's field in the first place! What the disciples have yet to fully appreciate is the blessing of living connected to Jesus while working in the master's field, which is eternal life now. Those hired later receive the same pay, but experiencing emotional relief from the daily struggle to survive is the true prorated reward. Those who delay working in the master's field experience the natural consequences of living in a constant state of stress, worry, and anxiety until they are hired.[8] Delaying your decision to walk with Jesus takes a toll on your emotional and physical health. As for the rich young ruler, he may come back to Jesus, but in the meantime he will continue to live with the anxiety that drove him to seek Jesus in the first place.

Sacrificing for the Lord

Comparison not only robs us of joy; it can also lead us to become prideful. Those who choose to work in the fields first can begin to admire themselves for being wise enough to accept the master's offer, while judging those who delay or refuse as being foolish. To call someone "foolish" is to comment on their intelligence and character. This attitude can lead to feelings of prideful self-righteousness, resulting in a lack of humility and compassion for others.

In our pride, we could proclaim we're denying ourselves things of this world. Concealed in this statement is a subtle and backhanded way of feeling better about ourselves while judging those outside of the master's field for being lost. Those who delay accepting the master's invitation spend their lives chasing mirages, attempting to fulfill their needs with things that never fully satisfy, which often leaves them more disappointed and discouraged. Life Model Works, a Christian counseling organization focusing on relational transformation, uses the acronym BEEPS to describe temporary fixes we attach ourselves to instead of attaching to people and God in joy. BEEPS stands for Behaviors, Events, Experiences, People, or Substances.[9] These large categories can be filled in lots of different ways, but they all can quickly become habits that turn into unhealthy addictions. While working in the master's field, we can pridefully judge others for indulging in their BEEPS, when we really want to as well but choose not to. We call this "sacrificing for the Lord" to make ourselves feel better despite being secretly jealous, wishing we could have the same experiences. Working in the master's field doesn't guarantee every one of our heart's desires will be met, because not all those heart's desires are good for us. But we are always with the Master and can grow to trust his knowledge of what *good* is.

Not all BEEPS are inherently unhealthy, but they become detrimental to us when they function as a substitute for God or self-medicate our pain and loneliness with temporary relief, taking our time, energy, and focus away from building genuine healthy relationships. Life Model Works believes that our fundamental need is to be relationally connected to the Father. Feeling known and accepted by God fills us with overflowing joy, one of the fruits of the Spirit in Galatians 5, which spills outward for others. Nothing else compares to experiencing the life-sustaining joy of working alongside the master in his field. If we know that life is found only with the master in his field, then why would we see working there as a sacrifice? We are spared much pain and heartache by not pursuing BEEPS for their unintended purposes. However, the enemy from Genesis 3 never stops trying to erode our trust in the Master.

Satan's Spin on the Story

While we're working in the master's field, our enemy hopes to stoke feelings of discontentment, causing us to question God's trustworthiness. Forming strong bonds of trust takes time, so the enemy seeks to sow seeds of doubt, tempting us to revert to trusting in ourselves to meet our needs. [10] The seeds he sows come in the form of sophisticated advertisements, goading us to compare ourselves to others who seem to be enjoying what we long for ourselves. All it takes is a perfectly framed social media post to prick our hearts and stir up our unmet longings. "They look so happy," we lament, "and here I am, sacrificing for the Lord by working in his fields!"

These moments serve to remind us of our unmet longings, which the enemy hopes will cause our feelings of joy to fade and be replaced by second-guessing God's goodness and faithfulness. He wants our work in the master's field to feel like a sacrifice, drudgery, or even boredom. Consider this thought for a moment: Think of the master's field as sacred space, like the Garden of Eden. There, God commissions Adam and Eve to tend and protect his Garden. But then they fail in their task. I wonder if Eve's curiosity about the forbidden fruit comes from boredom and discontentment. The enemy, seizing the opportunity, asks her a question that merely encourages her to act upon her feelings—but the result is disastrous. We face the same temptation daily to reach for things we know will not satisfy our deepest desires. Seeking some temporary relief, we pursue BEEPS, and they work—but only for a moment. Our curiosity is abated briefly, but then we are reminded once again that BEEPS fail to give us sustaining joy.

Failing to trust the Lord and buying into the enemy's false advertisement unleashes a fresh cycle of shame, now doubly intense because we believe we should've known better. In these moments, we can be driven to work harder to regain God's favor, convinced God's patience and grace are in limited supply. This striving is the opposite of the Gospel and is kryptonite to our joy. When will we feel like we've done enough to repair our relationship with God? Never! As Jesus communicated to the rich young ruler, no amount of effort is enough to earn what we already possess. Perhaps now we might have some compassion for the young man who desired to do something to know God accepted him.

Reverse-Engineering the Gospel

We can strive to prove ourselves worthy in almost every aspect of our lives. The evidence for our lack of faithfulness seems far greater than moments of obedience to Jesus that make us feel worthy, so we worry: Am I worthy of the pay I receive at work? Am I worthy of being loved by others? Am I worthy to be called a follower of Jesus? The most dangerous anxiety might be: Am I proving myself worthy for God to have chosen me? This can lead us to attempt to reverse-engineer the Gospel, looking for evidence we've done enough while working in the Master's field to be worthy of receiving his grace in the first place.

We can doubt our worthiness when we hear statements like: "Jesus died for you, so you should..." The word *should* here is shame-based language. When used in this manner it is meant to manipulate us to strive to justify our worthiness by acting in a certain way. Coercing someone to produce a desired response might alter their behavior, but it never fills anyone with joy—including God. What lies behind this type of 'you should' language is the implication that a person is ungrateful and if they were grateful, they'd live accordingly. Jesus does not demand we prove ourselves worthy; he came to pronounce that we are worthy. Living in this reality produces genuine gratitude and joy, which is hard to fathom when so many have so seldom experienced this radical kind of unconditional love and acceptance.

We cannot fake feeling accepted by God or living securely in his grace. Spend enough time with someone and you can begin to discern where they're struggling. While speaking at an Athletes in Action event I attended, Bill Thrall insightfully asked: "Do I understand that how I see me is the greatest evidence of my theology?"

How I treat myself reflects how I really believe God sees me, beyond what I say or hold to be theologically true. Personally, I can be critical, judgmental, and disappointed in myself, perceiving I'm failing to live a life worthy of God's grace. Is this how God views me? No! But my feelings of shame are very real, driving me to try harder as I feel responsible for letting God and others down. Stuck in a cycle I can't get out of, my striving to prove myself worthy seems to only validate my feelings of unworthiness.

Answering this question may help to break the cycle: Why did Jesus die on the cross? We might quickly answer: "To pay for our sins." That's the right answer—to a different question. It explains *what* he did, not *why*. The reason that the God of the Universe came in human flesh, died on the cross, and resurrected three days later, was to be in a relationship with us now and forever. That's why the author of the letter to the Hebrews wrote that Jesus endured the cross and discounted its shame "for the joy set before him" (Hebrews 12:2)—the joy of reuniting with us. Understanding his love, accepting responsibility for our sins, and repenting ushers us into this relationship we call salvation. But before we choose to walk with Jesus, he demonstrates our innate value to him by his death and resurrection. (John 15:13) God sees us as worthy before we ever respond in kind, not because we did respond, and not because he knows with perfect foresight that we will respond in some particular way.

This is the definition of grace: Unmerited favor. Grace is an extremely hard concept to grasp. Scholars debate whether grace even needs a response from us: Martin Luther said no, Calvin said yes.[11] A core tenant of Biblical *theology* tells us we are all unworthy to receive God's grace, because we've turned our backs on God. True! But the *story* of the Bible is about God's extraordinary actions to restore our relationship, because he believes we are worthy. God's amazing grace remains constant and is the only antidote to our shame and striving.

A Parable for the Disciples (and Us)

The parable of the vineyard workers is told to the disciples as a cautionary tale. Jesus invites those who were hired first and anyone who follows him later to be filled with compassion for those hired last. Those latecomers, like my grandmother, missed out on experiencing genuine joy all the years they weren't working in the master's field, at a great cost to themselves and others. Our compassion for the lost can short-circuit any attempts by the enemy to persuade us to become prideful or judgmental, feeling we deserve something more. Eternal life is walking with Jesus and begins the moment we accept the invitation to work in his field. This is the reward: living connected with the master now.

In the next chapter, we will look at a story of Jesus healing a blind man. The process of his healing illustrates how we experience the kingdom of God here on earth through trusting and obeying his words.

Questions

- Do you struggle to feel worthy and accepted by God?
- If you're a follower of Jesus, what were the circumstances that led you to make the decision? If not, is there something holding you back?
- How has God shown you that he cares about you and the desires of your heart?
- Where have you wrestled with believing that God is trustworthy?
- Have you struggled with comparison with others?
- Are there any BEEPS (Behaviors, Events, Experiences, People, Substances) sidetracking you from your walk with God?
- What assumptions do you have about people who don't follow Jesus?
- Can you identify with the potential hazard of becoming prideful and judging those who do not know and follow Jesus the same way you do?
- When was the last time you talked to someone about what Jesus has done in your life? How do we make Jesus the hero of our stories?

Additional Resources

Chan, Francis, and Preston Sprinkle. *Erasing Hell: What God Said About Eternity, and the Things We've Made Up*

Lynch, John, Bruce McNicol, and Bill Thrall. *The Cure: What If God Isn't Who You Think He Is and Neither Are You?*

Manning, Brennan. *The Ragamuffin Gospel*

Snodgrass, Klyne R. *Stories with Intent: A Comprehensive Guide to the Parables of Jesus*

Young, Brad H. "Jesus and His Explosive Parables | The Teaching Series." https://walkingthetext.com/the-teaching-series/mini-series/jesus-and-his-explosive-parables/

13. I Want to See

If you hold to my teaching, you are really my disciples.
Then you will know the truth, and the truth will set you free.

—JESUS IN JOHN 8:31-32

What is truth?

—PILATE'S QUESTION TO JESUS IN JOHN 18:38

If you want to experience the life of Jesus,
you have to adopt the lifestyle of Jesus.

—JOHN MARK COMER

Defining the word *truth* is challenging. Have you ever engaged in an argument with someone who responded: "That's not true"? Truth, for most westerners, means agreed-upon facts reflecting our perception of reality. Conflict occurs when different versions of truth collide, leading to heated conversations seeking congruence between witnesses to answer the question: What is real?

We can ask the same question about the Bible. How we define "truth" in relation to the Bible impacts our ability to accept that relational concepts like sin, justice, salvation, and righteousness are real.

Conversations about truth can quickly turn philosophical or theological because we don't all see and experience the world in the same way. I affirm the existence of absolute or objective truth: a non-subjective reality that exists outside of ourselves, like gravity. No matter how fervently I believe I can fly, if I act on my belief by jumping off a cliff with no safety gear, I'm going to hurt myself. Yet people can choose to deny the existence of God's absolute truth, creating their own personal alternative realities that can be equally harmful. Many misperceive the absolute truths of God's love, sin, redemption, salvation, and eternal life. Choosing to ignore God's truth can make living life very challenging, because his truths explain reality just as much as gravity does.

A Jewish person in the first century AD would not define "truth" as objective facts, but rather by how one lived a life of obedience with God.[1] This, too, was subjective within Judaism then (and now), as no consensus existed on how to live a blameless life of obedience in every situation. However, there was one common consensus. Despite the differing rabbinical schools of interpretation about how to obey the 613 commandments blamelessly, the *truthfulness* of one's interpretation was demonstrated by the *integrity* with which they practiced their beliefs.

One aspect of Jesus' life that was so attractive and compelling was the integrity with which he lived what he believed and taught about how to walk blamelessly with God. So, when he says, "you shall know the truth and the truth shall set you free," he is identifying himself as the source of truth and freedom if we follow his example. Jesus' profound statement acts as a pivot point between three seemingly unrelated stories in the Gospel of John. Connecting the narrative of these stories that span three chapters in our English Bibles serves as an object lesson for the freedom and healing available when we choose to live out God's truth. The lead-up to Jesus' famous statement about the truth involves him disrupting the high priest (while he is conducting a ceremony in the temple!) by making a shocking identity claim.

Traveling for the Feasts

Our story begins in John 7, with Jesus in the temple celebrating the Feast of *Sukkot*. *Sukkot* was one of the three pilgrim feasts that required all males to travel to Jerusalem. However, scholars debate whether every man in Israel possessed the financial means to do so and are unsure whether that law was always strictly observed by everyone.[2] As my professor Paul Wright often said, "There is what the Bible prescribes, and then what it describes. The two don't always match." Some historians suggest it might have been considered enough to make this journey once in a lifetime.

We may wonder, then, how often Jesus traveled to these feasts during his life on earth. The Bible doesn't exactly answer that question, since each Gospel provides us only snapshots of Jesus' life. If you combine all four Gospel accounts and account for the overlapping stories, you'll see that they add up to only about seventeen to nineteen days of Jesus' life, total! Obviously, then, we don't possess full accounts of his travel itineraries. Yet we can get some hints. According to Luke's Gospel, twelve-year-old Jesus traveled with his family to Jerusalem to celebrate the Passover. (Luke 2) John's Gospel records Jesus observing three Passovers and one *Sukkot*.[3] These passages give the impression that Jesus, a rabbi desiring to live out *Torah*, regularly traveled to Jerusalem three times a year for each of the three pilgrim feasts. Obeying this commandment may have been extremely inconvenient, but it seems likely that Jesus made this trek three times each year.

The Feast of *Sukkot*

Most commandments in *Torah* require some interpretation for their application. For instance, Leviticus 23 gives us ten verses outlining how to celebrate the Feast of *Sukkot*. The generations of sages leading up to the first century fleshed out specifics, adding layers of symbolism and details as to how to commemorate God's provision for the Israelites as he brought them through the desert into the promised land.[4] *Torah* commands the people to "rejoice before the LORD" by waving "leafy branches," which rabbis identify as palms, willows, and myrtle. (Leviticus 23:40)[5] Each branch recalls a stage of God's provision on their journey to the Promised Land: Palms remind them of when God provided shelter in the wilderness, willows remind them of when they crossed the Jordan, and myrtles commemorate settling into the land itself. Moments in their history to remember and celebrate indeed.

Sukkot also celebrates the fall harvest of grapes, olives, and pomegranates after a long rainless summer. The dry season ends between September and October. The early winter rain begins in October/November and continues through early spring (March/April), which sustains the crops the rest of the year. Without these rains, nothing will grow. So, the sages added an extra-Biblical aspect to celebrating *Sukkot*, called the water drawing ceremony, in which they asked God to send rain.[6] For seven consecutive days, the high priest leads a procession to the Pool of Siloam (Jerusalem's only water source) to collect a golden pitcher of water; he then returns up the steep incline to the temple and pours the water upon the altar as an offering. This offering of water follows the concept of first-fruit offerings: giving God the first of what you have and trusting him to provide what is needed moving forward. The water-pouring ceremony acknowledges that God is the provider of rain; pouring out the water rather than using or storing it demonstrates their trust in him to send rain again.

Elijah gives an example of this practice when he confronts the prophets of Baal on Mount Carmel. The events leading up to this moment begins when King Ahab marries Jezebel, the daughter of the king of Tyre, whose main god is Baal. (1 Kings 16:31) King Ahab starts worshiping Baal, leading his fellow Israelites to do the same. Deuteronomy 11:16-17 specifically warns against worshiping other gods, saying that if they do, God "will shut up the heavens, so that there will be no rain." When Elijah douses the sacrifice with water, it hasn't rained for the previous three and a half years; he's not trying to make the wood harder to light so much as he is asking God to send rain. He offers the little water he has to God, displaying his active trust in him to provide rain.

This brings us back to water-imagery at *Sukkot*. The seven-day feast concludes with the high priest collecting the water in the same way he has on the previous seven days, except this time he circles the altar seven times, reminding everyone of Israel's conquest of Jericho and their entrance into the promised land. The worshipers shout praises to God, asking him to send rain. The waving branches produce what sounds like rain reverberating throughout the temple. As the high priest ascends the altar one last time, a hush of reverence ripples through the hundreds of thousands of worshipers crowding the large temple complex.

Suddenly, at this solemn, reverential moment, Jesus jumps up and shouts: "If anyone is thirsty, let him come to me and drink. Whoever believes in me, as the Scripture has said, streams of living water will flow from within him!" (John 7:37-38) This is astonishing behavior: Jesus disrupts the climax of this holy ceremony by loudly announcing that he is the source of living water.

Apart from the interruption, what makes his statement so bold is Jesus' claim to be God; yet we won't pick up on that fact without a deep knowledge of Scripture. His stunning announcement is hidden within the

Jewish way of communicating truth indirectly, but his fellow worshipers get it immediately even though he does not include the specific Old Testament references. In several passages (such as Jeremiah 2:13 and Isaiah 12:3; 35:6; 44:3; 55:1; 58:11), God portrays himself as both the provider of living water and as the water itself: the source of life. The water is both metaphorical and a manifestation of God the life-giver. If we are unaware that the *Tanakh* personifies God as living water, we'll miss Jesus' self-proclamation. Those in attendance receive Jesus' message loud and clear: The temple authorities immediately try to arrest him because they understand his claim to be God. A debate ensues over Jesus' declaration: Is this man a troublemaking nobody, they ask, or a prophet— or is he the Messiah?

The Woman Caught in Adultery

The day after identifying himself as God, Jesus returns to the temple for the eighth day holy assembly. (Leviticus 23:36) A crowd gathers to hear him teach, which undermines the rabbinical authorities and makes them feel threatened. Anticipating a moment like this, the Pharisees and the teachers of the law have prepared to confront Jesus by bringing before him a woman caught in adultery. Their intention is to "test" Jesus, "that they might have some charge to bring against him." (John 8:6) Humiliating her by making her stand in front of the crowd, they ask Jesus: "In the Law Moses commanded us to stone such women. Now what do you say?" (John 8:5)

According to *Torah*, no forgiveness is possible for having an affair; the Bible prescribes death to anyone caught in adultery. (Leviticus 20; Deuteronomy 22) But *Torah* is not a legal system as we think of ours today; it is meant to provide guidance and wisdom to make life livable while honoring God.[7] Only the Sanhedrin, the religious ruling council, could condemn a person to death, and they avoided doing so as much as possible. In the *Mishnah*, collection of rabbinical commentary on the *Tanakh*, Makkoth 1:10 states:

> A Sanhedrin that puts a man to death once in seven years is called a murderous one.

Rabbi Eliezer ben Azariah said, "Or even once in seventy years." Rabbi Tarfon and Rabbi Akiba said, "If we had been in the Sanhedrin, no death sentence would ever have been passed."

The Sanhedrin went to great lengths to avoid putting people to death even though they had the right to do so. But how will Jesus apply *Torah*?

These teachers of the law believe that they have Jesus cornered. In Jesus' day, the Sanhedrin can deliver a death sentence, but only the Romans possess the legal authority to carry out capital punishment. If he follows the letter of the law and initiates stoning this woman, then he puts himself in conflict with the Romans. But if he responds by letting this woman go unpunished, then he contradicts *Torah*. Everyone witnessing this moment must realize this is a trap, because only the accused woman is present; where is the man with whom she is accused of having an affair? The Pharisees probably set up this woman as a pawn in their scheme to discredit Jesus, who just yesterday claimed to be God.

In response, Jesus doesn't speak; he kneels, and begins to write in the dust. We want to know *what* Jesus writes. A more Hebraic question is: *Why* does he write? The answer, of course, is found in the text:

> O LORD, the hope of Israel, all who forsake you will be put to shame. Those who turn away from you will be written in the dust because they have forsaken the LORD, the spring of living water. (Jeremiah 17:13 NIV, emphasis added)

He's writing condemnation in the dust for those who turn away from him! The Pharisees recognize the reference to Jeremiah and realize what Jesus is communicating, which sets up his next statement. He pauses, then says: "If any one of you is without sin, let him be the first to throw a stone at her." Then he returns to writing, reinforcing his statement. And the message is received: The crowd of Pharisees slowly melts away, oldest to youngest.

Now alone with this woman, Jesus corrects her behavior without condemning her, while also not condoning her sinful actions. He says: "Woman, where are they? Has no one condemned you?" She responds, "No one, Lord." And he concludes: "Then neither do I condemn you; go now and leave your life of sin." (John 8:11) He interprets *Torah* through the lens of Micah 6: "He has showed you, O man, what is good. And what does the Lord require of you? To act justly and to love mercy and to walk humbly with your God." Jesus says this mercy extends even to adulterers, and he shames those who know the text but don't live it and are willing take advantage of this woman for their own purposes.

The crowd sits in dazed silence. They've just witnessed Jesus go toe to toe with the theological experts of his day! In that powerful moment, Jesus doubles down on his divine claim to be God. He says: "I am the light of the world. Whoever follows me will never walk in darkness but will have the light of life." (John 8:12) According to the *Talmud*, four menorahs lit up the temple courts during the Feast of *Sukkot*.[8] I can picture him pointing to the extinguished menorahs as he makes his assertion to be the source of light. Through his interpretation of *Torah*, Jesus claims to be the source of life (living water) as well as the light to walk on God's path.

Object Lesson of Truth

The Pharisees hear Jesus' claim to be the Messiah, which sparks a lengthy debate in John 8 about witnesses. According to Deuteronomy 19:15, two witnesses are required to validate someone's testimony. Jesus tells them that he is his own witness and his father is the other, but they don't know him. Ouch! He states plainly that these religious leaders don't have a relationship with God. The debate continues over Jesus' identity, with Jesus telling them where he is going (to be with the father), referencing his future crucifixion and the necessity to believe in his claim to be God, who forgives sins. During this exchange, the Pharisees hope to discredit Jesus, but their plan backfires as many put their faith in him. (John 8:30)

Jesus now directs his attention to those who believe in him. "To the Jews who had believed him, Jesus said, 'If you hold to my teaching, you are really my disciples. Then you will know the truth, and the truth will set you free.'" (John 8:31-32) I identify this statement as the fulcrum of these stories. Leading up to this moment, Jesus dramatically claims to be God, disrupting one of God's seven appointed festivals and then causing a stir again in the temple courts the next day. He displays his knowledge and application of *Torah* by decisively convincing the religious leaders of his position. Then he tells those same religious leaders his Father is God, which means he is the Messiah.

Many first-century Jewish people believed the Messiah's arrival was imminent. They debated the nuances of who the Messiah will be, what roles he'll fulfill, and what his arrival would look like.[9] Now, Jesus stands in front of the crowd, identifying himself to be the long-awaited Messiah, God on earth, who knows the *Torah* so well he can stupefy the greatest rabbinical teachers of their day. He tells those who believe in him as Messiah how to live out his interpretation of *Torah* to experience the reality of his claim to be God. This culminates in a practical object lesson in John 9. Jesus' statement "You will know the truth, and the truth will set you free" is an invitation to walk God's path.

We need to unpack Jesus' statement phrase by phrase to fully grasp what he is saying. This quote begins with the word "Then," which means we need to consider what precedes it. What comes before the often-quoted phrase is: "If you hold to my teaching, you are really my disciples." (John 8:31) When we hold to Jesus' teachings (meaning when we do what he commands), then, we come to know (*yada*) the truth, which sets us free. This is how people will know we are Jesus' disciples.

The Hebrew word *talmid*, meaning disciple, describes someone who mimics or repeats what their rabbi does, even if they do not understand his actions immediately. By following their rabbi's example, living out *Torah* like him, the disciples experience the wisdom and experiential knowledge of their rabbi. Then they go and live likewise, teaching others to do the same. Knowing intellectually what Jesus said is not enough to reap the benefits. Only through doing (holding) his interpretation of *Torah* will we fully enjoy the lived experience of the freedom he offers.

In many parts of the Middle East, people will not usually ask you what you believe; instead, they will probably say: "Let me watch your life for twenty-four hours, and then I'll tell you exactly what you believe." Our actions demonstrate what we believe. While this approach makes total sense, Western culture makes allowances for people to say they believe in something even if their actions do not match those beliefs. This is a Greek mindset, separating heart, mind, and soul, explaining the incongruencies between our beliefs and actions.

Inheriting this mindset through our culture, we can get stuck on Jesus' command in John 8:31 to "hold to my teachings." The word *hold* can cause us to slip back into that Greek framework, suggesting that we must work hard to grasp and cling to his teaching intellectually.

However, to hold to your rabbi's teachings means to embody them, not merely know them intellectually. Thus our actions, how we live out *Torah*, demonstrate that we're disciples of a particular rabbi.

Jesus' disciples included more than just the twelve. At one point, he sends out seventy-two disciples. (Luke 10:1) Where did these other disciples come from? Jesus focuses on training up the twelve, but others chose to follow him as well. The phrase 'followed him' is vague in English. But in Hebrew, this phrase describes the actions of someone who is a disciple or follower of a particular rabbi. In John's Gospel, Jesus delivers a particularly challenging teaching in the synagogue in Capernaum; the result is that "many of his disciples turned back and no longer followed him." (John 6:66, emphasis added) So, when John mentions "those who believed in him," he's referring to those in the crowd in addition to the twelve disciples who accept Jesus to be the Messiah: the only forgiver of sins who lives out truth by rightly applying *Torah* in his walk with God. When the disciples live out Jesus' teachings, then they "are really [his] disciples." In Jesus' rabbinical worldview, our beliefs and actions are inseparable. Only in doing (holding to) his interpretation of *Torah* will we fully enjoy the lived experience of the truth and freedom he offers.

How to Know the Truth

As we have discussed before, to know something Hebraically means knowing through experience: the Hebrew word *yada*. "To know the truth" implies an experiential rather than merely intellectual understanding of the truth. Jesus is speaking to a Hebrew audience who share this understanding of the word. Linguistically, the Greek word used for 'know' in John 8:31 is the same word later used in the 3rd-century BC Greek translation of the Old Testament (called the *Septuagint*). For example, in Genesis 4:1, Adam "knew" Eve, and she conceived. To really know something or someone must happen through experience—all the more so when truth is embodied in a living person.

Here's my paraphrase of what I believe Jesus is saying: "If you do my teachings, then you are really my disciples. Then you will experience the reality of who I am and *yada* that what I'm saying is real and true. Experiencing me like that will set you free." What are we being set free *from*? Sin—which hinders our ability to know God fully and live in healthy relationships with others. We are also set free *for*—freed up for experiencing a true walk with God now and free to share this truth with others. Jesus as a rabbi is teaching his disciples to live in loving obedience to what the Father taught him. (John 8:28-29) When we obey, doing what Jesus said, we *yada* the freedom he offers. *Knowing* the truth is not enough; we've got to *do* the truth to experience it.

We Fight Freedom

Living in God's freedom requires us to see the world from his perspective. For this to happen, we need to let go of our strongly-held but potentially inaccurate beliefs. The Pharisees reject Jesus' claim to be the Messiah and his interpretation and application of *Torah*.

Jesus tells them "...everyone who sins, is a slave to sin." (John 8:34)

But the Pharisees declare: "We are Abraham's descendants and have never been slaves of anyone. How can you say that we shall be set free?" (John 8:33) Maybe they've literally never been slaves, but neither their heredity nor spiritual piety can make someone immune to sin. The consequences of sin Jesus refers to is the warping of how we see God's reality, which distorts how we see our identity. The Pharisees claim to see God and themselves clearly, but Jesus offers them corrective lenses to help them see they are living with a misconstrued sense of reality. They are faithful and passionate, but blind. To live in God's reality will require them to let go of their perceived identity and notions about what it means to be part of God's family. Living in God's reality, free from sin, makes someone a child of God. They believe just being born a Jew makes them part of Abraham's family. Being Jewish may give them a head start, but God says that everyone is able to be part of God's family.

Family of origin is everything within the cultural context of the Middle East. Even today, when you travel there, people will often ask you: "What is your name and where are you from?" Your name reflects your character and family's reputation; where you come from tells them your wider identity as part of a people group: "Oh, you're from the United States."

In this passage, Jesus uses imagery of the *bet av* (the father's house), which is woven all throughout *Tanakh*. This makes sense, since it was written to a culture in which the family unit provides one's sense of belonging, identity, security, and future. Jesus contrasts a child of the father with a slave. In Jesus' time, wealthy households typically owned slaves who were required to obey their masters. [10] However, God's children obey him not out of obligation or coercion, as a slave does, but by choice. To be a slave to sin means that sin rules us—it tells us what to do. Here, then, the Son of the Father stands in front of the Pharisees, offering them freedom from the slavery of sin, but they reject Jesus' claim of being the Messiah and the truth he offers them.

Continuing, the Pharisees challenge Jesus' family identity by questioning his knowledge of his father. Frustrated, they finally accuse him of being a Samaritan and demon-possessed. (John 8:48) This heated debate over truth ends with Jesus' drop-the-mic statement: "I tell you the truth, before Abraham was born, I AM!" Here again, he claims to be God. The "I am" statement is sometimes capitalized in our Bibles, because many scholars connect these words with God's sacred name Yahweh from Exodus 3—when Moses asks, "Who are you?" and God responds, "I AM." Horrified by his claim, the Jews pick up stones to stone Jesus for blasphemy. But he fades into the crowd. (John 8:59)

We are about to reach the climax of this three-chapter story. Jesus indirectly claims to be God in John 7, but now at the conclusion in John 8 he emphatically states he is by invoking God's sacred name. They hear him clearly: so clearly that they want to kill him for blaspheming God by claiming to be him. They realize that the freedom Jesus offers everyone can only be experienced by knowing and obeying him. The Pharisees embody the concept of living in obedience to God—what was considered truth—yet Jesus says they are in sin and blind. This would have shocked not only the Pharisees, but also everyone who views their practice of righteousness as exemplary. Engaging the Pharisees on their terms, Jesus tells them he is God come down from heaven to rightly interpret and apply *Torah*: that he is the truth they say they are seeking. If they want to live in freedom, then they must follow him.

As Jesus leaves the temple courts to avoid being stoned, his next encounter with a blind man drives home his teaching on how to experience the freedom he's offering.

Live It to Know It

The narrative in John 9 opens with "As he went along," which leads me to infer that Jesus and his disciples are leaving the temple grounds after the previous story. The importance of this specific location will become more relevant as the story continues. Just then, they encounter a blind man. The disciples ask Jesus who sinned—this man or his parents— to cause the man's blindness. Their question reflects the prevailing belief that God gives people what they deserve and, specifically, that congenital disabilities were punishments from God for sin. Jesus dismisses this idea, saying: "This happened so that the work of God might be displayed in his life." (John 9:3)

Jesus reiterates that he is the light of the world, here to do the will of God until he leaves. This work of God will require the blind man to do what Jesus says in order to experience the truth so he can be free, in this case, from his blindness (think about the Pharisees from the previous story—and us). Spitting on the ground, Jesus places mud on the blind man's eyes, then tells him to go to the Pool of Siloam and wash. This is the same pool where the high priest collects water for the Feast of *Sukkot*, which just ended.[11] Mentioning this location connects us back to the story in John 7. The blind man most likely would have heard Jesus' claim to be God in the temple, and (unlike the Pharisees) he will act upon what Jesus says.

The location of this encounter is significant because, if we are correct and this exchange takes place outside of the temple, the blind man is about a half mile away from the Pool of Siloam. The paved road to reach the pool bends steeply downhill. Why make a blind man walk this difficult half-mile journey? Why make this man's healing contingent upon completion of Jesus' instructions, when Jesus typically heals people immediately with little to no effort on their part?

The answer may be found in Jesus' promise: "If you do what I say… then you shall experience the truth [that I am God on earth], and you'll be free [from sin]." However, if the blind man fails to follow Jesus' instructions, he remains blind. In this way, the blind man becomes a living parable of Jesus' recent teaching. Essentially, Jesus is asking him: "Do you believe in me and my words enough to act on them?"

He does, and receives his sight. He is set free because he *meets* Jesus, *hears* him, *and follows* his instructions. The freedom Jesus offers can only be experienced when we accept that he is God and faithfully obey his instructions. Jesus is God's truth and reality.

Do You Want to See?

The Pharisees are blind and "slaves to sin," having forgotten that the purpose of their obedience to *Torah* is to walk with God. Having lost this relational insight, they're unable to see God even when he's standing right in front of them. To the Jews around them, the Pharisees are the embodiment of truth because of their faithful integrity in acting out their interpretation of *Torah*. The Pharisees themselves confidently believe that they are sons of Abraham due to their piety and heredity. But Jesus tells them their interpretation of *Torah* has become a slave master. They miss the whole point of enjoying being a son who obeys the Father out of love, not duty and obligation. A true son of Abraham would recognize Jesus as the Messiah, God on earth, and obey his interpretation of *Torah*. Jesus came to set everyone free, including the Pharisees, but instead they argue with God because they can't see him for who he is. They remain slaves, locked in a prison of their own creation, unable to live in God's freedom.

Everyone is spiritually blind until they meet Jesus and acknowledge him as Lord. But we can't stop there. Knowing theological facts about Jesus is a necessary start—but to *yada* (experience) his freedom, we've got to actually live out what Jesus says to do. Then we are really his disciples and members of God's family. This becomes possible when we are set free from the prison of our sin. But sometimes our personal prisons of sin become so comfortably familiar they are difficult to leave.

The movie *Shawshank Redemption* illustrates the importance of knowing our true identity and how that allows us to live in freedom, despite our circumstances. The story begins with Andy Dufresne being falsely accused and convicted of murdering his wife. Incarcerated, he finds himself immersed in a world that believes he is guilty. Except Andy knows that he's innocent, and lives accordingly, with dignity. The prison guards notice his sense of self-worth and despise him, seeking to break his will; they desire to convince him he deserves his fate. However, prison doesn't change what he knows to be true about himself. His fellow inmates marvel at Andy's courage to hold onto his dignity, because even though some of them claim to be innocent, they know they are guilty. Their long confinement serves only to entrench their shame-filled identity. Prison becomes weirdly comfortable as they've come to agree with how the world sees them—convicted men, forever stained, with no hope of redemption. As much as they might say they long for freedom, being released from prison secretly frightens them.

Freedom can feel scary, because it requires us to know who we are and what we truly desire and then take the responsibility to pursue what we believe will bring us life. Andy Dufresne knows exactly what would bring him life and shares his dreams with his closest friend Red, who responds: "Hope is a dangerous thing. Hope can drive a man insane." Red understands how prison institutionalizes a man, suffocating hope of seeing themselves any other way.

Similarly, before meeting Jesus, all we've ever known is slavery and following the orders of our sinful compulsions. Then Jesus comes along, opens the prison door, and says, "You're free to go." Staring at the open cell door, all we have to do is get up off our cot and walk out the door to enjoy the freedom Jesus offers. But we might hesitate. Our new-found freedom can feel awkward and even intimidating. One character, after decades of confinement, commits suicide once he is released, unable to handle his unfamiliar freedom. I'm convinced that many followers of Jesus are not experiencing the abundant life Jesus promises because they have yet to leave their prison cells, even though they know they are free. Courage is required to leave behind all we've known.

Our sin can blind us, causing us not to see who and whose we are. Having lived so long in our sin, we accept our identity as sinners, even after coming to know Jesus. Nowhere in the New Testament are believers called "sinners." Instead, we're called "saints"[12] and sons and daughters (children) of God. [13] We have a new family and identity. During the argument with the Pharisees, Jesus states, "So if the Son sets you free, you will be free indeed." (John 8:36) Our freedom is experienced in living like Jesus, which begins when we acknowledge that he is God, the creator of our reality.

Intellectually, we may accept that Jesus died and resurrected to set us free from our prison of sin. But we can become paralyzed by the responsibility of freedom. We stare at the open cell door, knowing we are free to leave at any time, but fear causes us to cling to our old identity and blinds us to what is possible. We know the truth, but we don't know (*yada*) the truth, because we've yet to follow Jesus' instruction and go and wash the mud from our eyes, allowing us to see ourselves as God sees us— his beloved children. Living in our new identity will take some time to get used to—and it will probably feel very awkward and even uncomfortable at first. But Jesus is with us as we slowly take our first steps out of the dark cell and into the sunlight of our new identity.

Jesus freeing us from sin and giving us a new identity is the Good News. As we follow Jesus, we have the opportunity to share his truth with others, demonstrated by how we live our lives in freedom and love. Filled with the Holy Spirit, we become a temple of God (1 Corinthians 3:16), which means, in a sense, we usher people into the presence of God who dwells in us.

God's priests in the temple had this same responsibility. But by the time of Jesus, the priesthood had become political and corrupt. In the next two chapters, we will see how Jesus pursues them even while they plot his demise.

Questions

- Which ingredients from Part One stick out to you as you explore this story in John? Did you discover anything new as a result?
- How do you define truth? Do you believe there is absolute truth? Why or why not?
- How does the 1st-century Jewish definition of 'truth' impact your understanding of this Scripture?
- Do you celebrate and express gratitude for God's provision and presence in your life? How?
- What is the difference between having beliefs and living beliefs? How do you hold to Jesus' teaching?
- How have you experienced the freedom Jesus has given you?
- Are you living in your identity as a child of God? How has that changed your life?
- Is there any area of your life where you struggle to have hope? Why? What is one step you can take to embrace the hope we have because of Jesus (Hebrews 10:23)?

Additional Resources

Boman, Thorleif. *Hebrew Thought Compared with Greek*

Brickner, David. *Christ in the Feast of Tabernacles*

Comer, John Mark. *Practicing the Way: Be with Jesus. Become like Him. Do as He Did.*

Edersheim, Alfred. *The Temple: Its Ministry and Services as They Were at the Time of Jesus Christ*

14. Two Men Meet Jesus

The Son of Man came to seek and save the lost.

—JESUS IN LUKE 19

Anyone can get lost, even those whom God chose to serve him in his temple: his priests. Priests in the ancient Near East served as caretakers of their god's sacred space, conducted worship, and functioned as intermediaries between a god and its people. They were also supposed to emulate the god they worshiped by displaying its character and nature in their lives. To engage with a priest, in a sense, was to engage with the god whom that priest served and worshiped. This is the mission God of the Hebrews gave to all his people at Mt. Sinai, not just a chosen few among them, so that the whole world would come to know him. (Exodus 19)

However, when the day arrives for all the Hebrews to receive God's instructions and to be commissioned as his priests, they become fearful. Gathering at the foot of the mountain, they see lightning-laden smoke covering its peak as thunder crashes and trumpet blasts emanate out of the darkness. The people's hearts fill with fear (awe), and they decline his invitation and ask Moses to be their representative. (Exodus 20:19) While Moses meets with God on behalf of the people, the golden calf incident takes place. God responds by singling out a single tribe, Moses' brothers the Levites, to be his priests for the people. This one tribe will teach and train the others to know who their God is and how to engage with him.

God's priests are still human, after all, and lose their way many times over the centuries. By the time of Jesus, they have lost their way yet again. Jeremiah's chastisement of the leaders of his day (which we read in Chapter 9) could be repeated and applied word-for-word in Jesus' day. They, too, could be accused of scattering the sheep as well as refusing to go and search for them. The priests God chose to serve him are not reflecting his character; how will God respond?

In this chapter, we'll read how God himself comes down to gather his sheep whom his priests have scattered; in the next chapter, we'll discover how Jesus pursues even those who are responsible for scattering them.

A History of the Priesthood

In ancient texts, gods are described as living in sacred, otherworldly spaces. When a god chooses to live on earth, he requires sacred space here as well, typically in a temple. At Mt. Sinai, God instructs the Hebrews to build him a tabernacle: a place for him to dwell among his people. (Exodus 25:8-9) Unlike a permanent temple in which gods dwell, the portable tabernacle demonstrates that the God of the Hebrews moves with his people as they travel to the Promised Land and ultimately to a permanent dwelling place in Jerusalem. The priests are responsible for transporting the tabernacle and its contents through the wilderness as the people are led by Moses, Aaron (the first high priest), and their sister Miriam. After the death of Moses and Aaron, the baton of spiritual leadership is passed down through the line of Aaron to a newly appointed high priest in each generation. In the absence of a king, the high priest becomes the default leader, called an *ethnarch*, which is a non-royal representative of a particular people group. This situation occurs when the exiles return from Babylon because no one from the line of David assumes leadership as king.

During this time, the high-priestly line of Aaron develops its own distinctive theology as it begins to engage in politics, carving out space for itself in the larger world beyond the temple walls. By the time of Jesus, the role of high priest has become a political appointment, serving at the pleasure of King Herod and the Roman overlords. The high priest presides over the temple and its revenue stream; a powerful position, to be protected at all costs, but de-emphasizing the spiritual purpose of the original calling. Unfortunately, this is not the first time God's chosen priestly leaders fail in their mission to represent him well. But now, for first time in history, God himself comes down to earth in the flesh to address them personally and regather the sheep they've scattered. What will God say? Jesus' disciples witness him pursue the lost, and call those who lost them, back to himself.

The Importance of Jericho

Our story begins outside of Jericho, a geographically strategic city, as Jesus is passing through on his way to Jerusalem to celebrate the Passover. Luke 18 tells us Jesus is "near to Jericho" when he encounters "a blind man [...] sitting by the roadside begging." (Luke 18:35-36) Where is Jericho? Why Jericho? Why was the blind man there?

The city of Jericho predates Abraham by seven thousand years, making it one of the oldest known cities in the world. Jericho is an oasis town on the edge of the Judean Wilderness, colored lush green by Elisha's Spring, which still provides water for the city today. If you stand on top of Old Testament Jericho (Tel el-Sultan) and face east, you'll see a thin line of green several miles away, in the middle of the valley: That's the Jordan River. At your back, the Judean Mountains begin their quick ascent into the interior of the Promised Land.

Ancient Jericho sits at the strategic junction point for east/west traffic. To the east, Jericho connects with the eastern kingdoms of Moab, Ammon, and the Amorites, all prominent in Israel's early history. Jericho's pivotal economic location makes it one of the most frequently mentioned cities in the Bible (58 times). Shortly before Jesus' day, Herod built one of his seven palaces here to control trade and serve as a tangible reminder of his prowess and wealth to all who passed through, before they ascended to his capital. To the west, three roads diverge out of Jericho, following natural topographic contours, to reach the ridge of the Judean mountains. These three roads then connect to the central north-south route cutting through the middle of Israel, linking the cities of Hebron, Bethlehem, and Jerusalem, all the way northward to Shechem. The southernmost of the three branches leads directly to Jerusalem. Jewish pilgrims traveling from the north and the south funneled through Jericho on their way to Jerusalem. This makes Jericho a strategic location for beggars to engage with large numbers of faithful Jews as they make their way to the temple.

A Man in Need of Being Seen

Sitting next to the roadside on the outskirts of Jericho, a blind beggar hears people beginning to stir; someone tells him: "Jesus of Nazareth is passing by." (Luke 18:37) He senses the crowd swelling with excitement as people anticipate encountering one of the most prominent rabbis of their generation. At this time, admiration for rabbis cuts across all socioeconomic levels. Many rabbis are known for treating the common person with the same dignity as anyone else, displaying concern for the poor and downtrodden. None exemplifies this more than Jesus, so it's no wonder this man wants to meet him.

Mark 10 records this man's name as Bartimaeus. Names reflect a person's character in many cultures, and Bartimaeus can carry two different meanings. *Bar* means *son* in Aramaic. *Timaeus* as a noun means honor; as a verb, it means to be *unclean* or to be *filthy*.[1] Both meanings carry significance. To God, Bartimaeus is a son of honor, but to many of those who are supposed to represent God on earth, he is seen as unclean, a son of filth.

Desiring to get Jesus' attention, the beggar shouts: "Jesus, Son of David, have mercy on me!" This title references the Messiah's kingly lineage as given in 2 Samuel 7:16, when God tells David, "Your house and your kingdom will endure forever before me; your throne will be established forever."[2] The crowd rebukes the blind man for interrupting the moment, but he persists in trying to get Jesus' attention and shouts even louder, asking for mercy. Although he's blind, he can see that Jesus is the Messiah. The story continues:

> Jesus stopped and commanded him to be brought to him. And when he came near, he asked him, "What do you want me to do for you?" He said, "Lord, let me recover my sight." And Jesus said to him, "Recover your sight; your faith has made you well." And immediately he recovered his sight and followed him, glorifying God. And all the people, when they saw it, gave praise to God. (Luke 18:40-42)

Why is this man begging specifically here? Well, in the first century, giving alms to the poor was considered a righteous, God-honoring act that demonstrated you were in right relationship with God because you acted like him.[3] Walk through the streets of Jerusalem today, and you'll hear people begging and saying *"Tzedek,"* the modern Hebrew slang word for "Be righteous." Similarly, this man places himself on a strategic thoroughfare, knowing that pilgrims, who desire to be righteous especially on their way to the temple in Jerusalem, will pass through Jericho. It's prime real estate for the business of begging.

In most English Bibles, those pesky sixteenth-century chapter breaks interrupt the flow of the story, which can lead us to think this is the end—but it's just the beginning of the second part of a three-part story.

Entering Jericho

After Jesus' encounter with Bartimaeus, he is still outside the city of Jericho. The story continues in Luke 19 with a curious detail: "Jesus entered Jericho and was passing through." (Luke 19:1) Today, we might not think much about this because we travel with purpose, valuing efficiency of time and punctuality—but in the Middle East, everything revolves around relationships, which gives us a clue to Jesus' motivation. Jesus anticipates being delayed by people desiring to host him as he passes through Jericho. Given the limited travel routes to Jerusalem, it was a safe assumption that Jesus would eventually pass through their town on his way to celebrate the Passover. All the prominent people of Jericho would have welcomed the opportunity to host one of the most renowned rabbis of their generation and had probably prepared to do so. This would include city officials and religious leaders. But Luke 19:1 gives the impression that Jesus' intention is to "pass through"—hinting he doesn't wish to accept anyone's invitation and thus delay his journey.

Religious leaders such as the Sadducean Priests lived in Jericho, preferring the location's mild winter climate.[4] This detail adds validity to Jesus' parable in Luke 10 about a priest and a Levite traveling to Jericho from Jerusalem. Other prominent people living in Jericho included the chief tax collector, Rome's official regional tax representative. This is where a man named Zacchaeus enters our story: "He was a chief tax collector and was wealthy." (Luke 19:2) Taxation in Jesus' day functioned as a means of power and control imposed upon them by their enemy,

Rome. Zacchaeus fulfills his responsibilities to collect local taxes, passing the funds along to the next person up the governmental chain—eventually to Herod, then through all the additional bureaucratic stops along the way to Caesar in Rome. Each layer of bureaucracy expects a cut of the proceeds. This grift creates an excessive tax rate, and Zacchaeus is the face of the exploitative organization. This makes him one of the most well-known and most despised people in town.

In this story, Zacchaeus does something shocking and unexpected. He wants to see Jesus, but he's short of stature and can't see over the crowd. So, he runs ahead and climbs a sycamore-fig tree for a higher vantage point. Like the rich young ruler, Zacchaeus demonstrates his sincerity by his willingness to humble and shame himself, first by running, and then adds to his undignified behavior by climbing a tree. Known for its low-hanging branches, the sycamore-fig tree makes for easy climbing, while producing low-quality fruit often eaten by the poor. Ancient Jewish sources tell us that these trees were not permitted to grow within the city limits.[5] That means the interaction about to take place must happen before Jesus enters the city proper and has opportunities to receive invitations from the social elite.

Jesus Pursuing the Lost

Parallels exist between Zacchaeus and Bartimaeus: Both men are excluded from the community, and both desire an encounter with Jesus. Bartimaeus doesn't know he will meet Jesus, let alone have his request for healing be granted. Nor can Zacchaeus anticipate what is about to transpire: "When Jesus reached the spot, he looked up and said to him, 'Zacchaeus, come down immediately. I must stay at your house today.' He came down at once and welcomed him gladly." (Luke 19:5) How does Jesus know this man's name? I don't think any God-powers or Jedi mind-tricks are needed. Noticing Zacchaeus in the tree, the crowd probably mocked the most well-known and disliked person in town by name. And like Bartimaeus, who unexpectedly meets Jesus and has his sight restored, Zacchaeus also meets Jesus and has his human dignity restored. His name also has two meanings: "God remembers" or "God is pure/clean."[6] God remembers him, seeks and finds him in Jericho, and restores his purity, despite how his fellow Jews view him.

We've already seen that, due to the nature of his work as a tax collector, Zacchaeus' fellow citizens view him as conspiring with the enemy, which makes him socially unpopular; even worse, his constant contact with Roman money makes him ritually unclean. Roman coins often bore images of the emperor, gods, or goddesses, thus violating the second commandment, which forbids making graven images. Touching such money, according to some rabbis, makes a Jew unclean. As a tax collector, then, Zacchaeus potentially lives in a perpetual state of ritual impurity, socially isolating him from the Jewish community due to his religious defilement as well as his distasteful political position. Members of the crowd call Zacchaeus a sinner, implying his state of impurity. (Luke 19:7) It's no wonder, then, that Jesus' request to stay at Zacchaeus' house stuns them. If Zacchaeus is unclean, then whoever he touches or touches him will become unclean as well. All righteous Jews guard their ritual purity, especially priests and rabbis.

Although becoming unclean is not a sin (since it's impossible to avoid amid everyday life), the process of purification is time-consuming, and necessitates isolating oneself from others to protect them from becoming unclean as well. If Jesus enters Zacchaeus' home, he risks becoming unclean on his way to celebrate the Passover; the extra time needed for purification might cause him to miss the celebration. But the potential for becoming ritually impure never seems to stop Jesus from engaging with unclean people.

Zacchaeus responds to Jesus' astonishing generosity by saying: "Look, Lord! Here and now, I give half of my possessions to the poor, and if I have cheated anybody out of anything, I will pay back four times the amount." (emphasis added) That word *if* could also be translated as *since*. Many readers and scholars assume Zacchaeus has acted like a typical tax collector, taking more than was owed and skimming extra off the top. This incident reminds us of when some tax collectors at the Jordan River respond to John the Baptist's call for repentance and get baptized. After they immerse themselves in the river, they ask John, "What should we do?" John responds by telling them: "Don't collect more than you are required to," which illustrates the near universality of such exploitative practices. (Luke 3) However, it is also possible that Zacchaeus' use of *if* might allow him to save face publicly in an honor/shame society: It leaves room for the impression that maybe he has not acted dishonorably. In either case, he first responds to Jesus' offer with generosity, giving half of what he has to the poor, and then possibly out of conviction to make things right, stating he'll reimburse any victims four times what he stole.

Where does he get the idea of paying back four times? From Scripture! Several possible sources exist. Leviticus 6:5 says to pay back one-fifth after financial fraud. Exodus 22:1 addresses the issue of replacing a stolen animal by making restitution four or five times the animal's value. Zacchaeus must know these texts.

After engaging with the most notorious person in town, Jesus senses the tension rising from the crowd and addresses them by saying: "Today salvation has come to this house, because this man, too, is a son of Abraham." Zacchaeus is a Jew, not a Roman. Who knows the last time anyone embraced him as a son of Abraham? And now the most famous rabbi of their day is going to have lunch at this sinner's house, preemptively shutting down potential invitations from respected and notable figures of the town. In this way, Jesus restores Zacchaeus' dignity as a son of Abraham and a child of God.

The Good Shepherd Has Come

In his statement that salvation has come to Zacchaeus' house, Jesus makes use of a double entendre. His salvation-declaration simultaneously acknowledges Zacchaeus' repentance, while making a reference to himself: *Jesus* in Hebrew, *Yeshua*, means "God saves." Literally, Jesus is God's salvation coming to Zacchaeus' house. The exclamation point of this story is Jesus announcing to the crowd that he is the Messiah who has come, but he does it in the indirect Jewish way of communicating through the people's shared knowledge of the text. Jesus adds: "For the Son of Man came to seek and to save what was lost." Many Bible editions don't cite an Old Testament reference here in their footnotes, yet this is one of those 1,600 connections to the Old Testament found in the New Testament. Jesus quotes Ezekiel 34 and adds the 'Son of Man' reference from Daniel 7:13-14:

For thus says the Lord GOD: Behold, I, I myself will search for my sheep and will seek them out. As a shepherd seeks out his flock when he is among his sheep that have been scattered [lost], so will I seek out my sheep, and I will rescue [save] them from all places where they have been scattered on a day of clouds and thick darkness [...]. I myself will be the shepherd of my sheep, and I myself will make them lie down, declares the Lord GOD. I will seek the lost, and I will bring back the strayed, and I will bind up the injured, and I will strengthen the weak, and the fat and the strong I will destroy. I will feed them in justice. (selected portions of Ezekiel 34:11-16)

When rabbis quote Scripture, they customarily say, "It is written..." first. By not adding this introductory statement, Jesus implies that he himself is the embodiment of Ezekiel 34 and Daniel 7. These passages would have exploded in the ears of the crowd, who would have heard Jesus declaring himself to be God himself coming down from heaven to seek out the lost as the Good Shepherd. His biblically literate and astute audience would immediately pick up on the implication of these references. Now you can, too!

Two Stories; One Point

When we read both stories together as one, we see how Jesus announces he is the Good Shepherd who has come down from heaven and (in this story) searches for one guy whose name means "son of honor/filth" and another whose name means "God remembers—God is pure/righteous." Both men experience exclusion from their communities. One is poor, blind, and alone, but can see who Jesus is; the other is wealthy and probably living in one of the nicest homes in town, but socially isolated, unclean, and shunned by the community. Jesus meets both men's greatest needs, but more importantly, he demonstrates their innate value by seeing them and engaging them.

God incarnate does what those who were supposed to be his representatives on earth fail to do. Those neglectful shepherds are as lost as those they fail to lead. After Jesus' encounter with Zacchaeus, he addresses those lost shepherds by telling a parable. Jesus clues in the audience of the parable's target by quoting Ezekiel 34 as a *remez*, which opens with a condemnation of the leadership of Israel:

> Prophesy against the shepherds of Israel... Woe to the shepherds of Israel who only take care of themselves! You do not take care of the flock. You have not strengthened the weak or healed the sick or bound up the injured. You have not brought back the strays or searched for the lost. You have ruled them harshly and brutally. So they were scattered because there was no shepherd, and when they were scattered they became food for all the wild animals. My sheep wandered over all the mountains and on every high hill. They were scattered over the whole earth, and no one searched or looked for them... Because my shepherds did not search for my flock, but cared for themselves rather than for my flock... the Sovereign LORD says: I am against the shepherds and will hold them accountable for my flock. I will remove them from tending the flock. (selected from Ezekiel 34:1-10)

The Sadducees living in Jericho might understand that Jesus is using Ezekiel to refer to them. They had not sought out Bartimaeus nor Zacchaeus. And yet, as we'll see in the next chapter, Jesus pursues the very shepherds whom God condemned in Ezekiel 34—even though they don't know that they're lost.

Questions

- When you walk into a room, do you assess where you are in the social pecking order?
- Have you ever felt like Bartimaeus or Zacchaeus—ignored, overlooked, or excluded?
- Think of a time when you felt seen and heard by someone whose opinion you highly valued. How did it make you feel?
- Have you ignored, overlooked, or excluded others, thinking of them as socially unclean? What stopped you from acknowledging them?
- Have religious leaders let you down? How did this impact your faith? What have you done to recover?
- What does it mean to you that Jesus intentionally engaged with the unclean and messy people in this story?
- Knowing the importance of the Old Testament and its impact on how we interpret the stories of Jesus, how will you read the Bible differently?

Additional Resources

Biblica's *The Books of the Bible: New Testament* (printed in 1861 without chapter and verse divisions).

All nine books in the *Cultural Studies* series by Kenneth E. Bailey, along with any of his articles you might find.

15. Open for Business

Woe to the shepherds of Israel who only take care of
themselves!
Should not shepherds take care of the flock?

—EZEKIEL 34:2-3

Truth is always strange...stranger than fiction.

—LORD BYRON, DON JUAN

He is no fool who gives what he cannot keep
to gain that which he cannot lose.

—JIM ELLIOT

Good stories elicit feelings, inspiring people to live differently. The *aha!* moment often hits when hearers see themselves in the main character. They witness the fallout of certain behaviors, and the impact attitudes have on others, as a spectator. Then, feeling convicted, they have a choice to make. People often avoid changing until they've experienced the negative impact their actions have on the lives of others and develop empathy,[1] but stories let us preview this effect through our imaginations. If we're receptive to their lessons, stories can accelerate our growth and even, sometimes, let us skip right past the part where we make a painful mistake, live selfishly, and cause others pain. Jesus' audience in Luke 19 is about to experience this for themselves.

With the word-pictures from Ezekiel 34 ringing in people's ears, Jesus tells them a parable—because "he was near Jerusalem, and the people thought that the kingdom of God was going to appear at once." (Luke 19:11-12) The target audience of Jesus' parable are those shepherds who've muddied the water and scattered the sheep. They're lost themselves and don't realize it—they need their relationship with God restored before they can fulfill their purpose and pursue the sheep they've neglected. This is the goal of a parable: restoring relationships—not only relationships between the shepherds and their sheep, but also between the shepherds and God.

How Will the Messiah Come?

Jesus' actions, words, and miracles fulfill many of the Messianic expectations of people in the first century. When Jesus casts out a demon from a deaf-and-mute man (a miracle many believed only the Messiah should be able to do), the crowd wonders: "This man cannot be the Son of David, can he?" (Matthew 12:23-24)[2] After his three years of public ministry, Jesus' reputation has spread widely across Judea, creating a growing anticipation that he could be the Messiah. For instance, he enters Jericho on his way to Jerusalem to celebrate the Feast of Passover: Many Jews believed that the Messiah would arrive in Jerusalem during this feast (which commemorates the time God freed his people from their bondage in Egypt), proclaim his kingdom, then defeat the Romans.[3] The book of Zechariah identifies the location of the Messiah's pronouncement—the Mount of Olives—followed by an ensuing battle in which he vanquishes his enemies in the Valley of Jehoshaphat[4] and then judges the world. This location also corresponds to the belief that the Messiah would come from the east; in the book of Ezekiel, the Spirit of God left the temple heading east and would return from the east to the Temple. As Jesus is about to ascend up to Jerusalem to celebrate the Passover, traveling from the east, the anticipation in the crowd grows. They wonder: Is he the one?

History Repeating Itself

Aware of all these expectations, Jesus tells this parable to the crowd:

A man of noble birth went to a distant country to have himself appointed king and then return. So, he called ten of his servants and gave them ten minas. 'Put this money to work,' he said, 'until I come back.' (Luke 19:12-13)

A historical scenario like this one had happened some thirty years earlier after the death of Herod the Great, who ruled Israel for almost four decades. During his reign, he displayed political shrewdness, architectural genius, and paranoia—leading him to kill one of his wives, his brother-in-law, an uncle, and three of his sons.[5] Josephus records that Herod died in Jericho after rewriting his will, in which he divided his kingdom among his three surviving sons, naming his son Archelaus ruler of Judea. However, Herod lacked the authority to give this financially lucrative position away without Caesar's approval. Therefore, Archelaus and his brother Antipas sailed off to Rome to contest the will, each seeking to be named the sole ruler.[6] But the Jewish people did not wish either of these men to become king, and also sent a delegation to Rome to contest Herod's will (the will that named Archelaus ruler of Judea; Archelaus had already killed three thousand Jews since his father's death).[7] Their efforts failed and Caesar confirmed Herod's will, dividing his kingdom among his three surviving sons: Archelaus, Antipas, and Philip.

The opening of Jesus' parable would have resonated with his audience, reminding them of their recent past. This parable echoes Jews thirty years earlier, who said of Archelaus: "His subjects hated him and sent a delegation after him to say, 'We don't want this man to be our king."

Jesus continues: "He was made king, however, and returned home. Then he sent for the servants to whom he had given the money, to find out what they had gained with it." (Luke 19:14-15) What is left unspoken is the length of time between the master's departure and his return home. How long do you think it would take to sail from Israel to Rome, get an audience with Caesar, present your case, wait for an answer, and then finally return home? Depending on the time of year and the prevailing winds, travel alone could take at least three months if all went smoothly and easily up to six months or more if it did not.

During this uncertain time of travel, the servant's loyalties back home were tested. What if he dies on the way, or returns without the title? Some would be tempted to switch their loyalty, making a politically shrewd decision for self-preservation. Backing a losing candidate could cost someone their life. But remaining faithful to the eventual successor in such a time of political ambiguity, demonstrating their devotion and loyalty, would surely be rewarded. Remembering all that political intrigue and ambiguity involving Herod's sons thirty years earlier creates emotional tension for the audience in this parable.

What Is the Master's Business?

In the story, Jesus tells about a man of noble birth who summons his servants—the people who work for him and know him well. They all receive the same resources: a *mina*, which equals about a year and a half's wages. How successfully will each servant allocate their resources to follow their master's instructions while he is away?

Keep in mind, the subjects hated this man. Those resources provided to each servant is supposed to be used to conduct their master's business in his absence. The servants wouldn't see themselves as the master's business partners, but as his representatives. The way the servants conduct their master's business will signal to his future subjects what the master's priorities are and what kind of a ruler he intends to be. In this way, the servants will help the people who currently hate the master come to know him the way they do. When the master returns, their success will be measured by the response he receives from the people upon coming home. Will they receive him gladly? Or remain hostile?

A minimum of three months is a long time to conduct the affairs of an unpopular person in a small community, let alone a year. But then one day, their master returns as king—with full authority now vested in him. He then calls his servants to give an account:

> The first one came and said, 'Sir, your *mina* has earned ten more.'
> 'Well done, my good servant!' his master replied. 'Because you have been trustworthy in a very small matter, take charge of ten cities.' The second came and said, 'Sir, your *mina* has earned five more.' His master answered, 'You take charge of five cities.' (Luke 19:16-18)

The first servant produced a tenfold return on the king's investment and the second servant a fivefold return. The master commends both servants for being "trustworthy" and rewards them accordingly. Another translation often used here is "faithful"; both carry the same concept, but with a slightly different flavor. As Americans, we probably equate the trustworthy/faithful actions of the first two servants with productivity and profitability, because our culture often celebrates people who achieve business success, like Bill Gates, Elon Musk, Jeff Bezos, etc. Our cultural values can cause us to misinterpret the reason for the servants' success. Let me provide some examples of how different cultural values can influence how we understand this parable.

Every culture possesses core values that individuals' decisions subconsciously filter through. Individuals calculate the potential outcomes of their decisions to produce the best results based on the highest values of their society. When communicating the Gospel cross-culturally, we must present it in a way that demonstrates how Jesus meets a particular culture's most cherished emotional needs.[8] The needs of each culture are often different. For example, in many parts of the former Soviet Union, a prevailing unspoken need is for power and control. Why? For centuries, Russians were ruled by a very few, first by czars and then by elites within the communist power structure. A small circle of people decided the fates of millions, while the vast majority felt helpless to impact their lives. Therefore, they sought to exert their power over any aspect within their sphere of influence to feel like they had some control in their day-to-day lives.

My wife experienced this cultural attitude while shopping at a grocery store in the former Soviet satellite country of Belarus. As she approached the checkout counter, the woman operating the cash register (the only cashier in the store) noticed her and slapped down a sign in Russian which said, roughly: "Be back in five minutes." She proceeded to step outside to smoke a cigarette, forcing everyone to wait for her. In doing so, she exerted her power over what was probably the only aspect of her life that she controlled.

Americans have unique cultural priorities too. We tend to highly value and honor efficiency, pragmatism, and profit. These priorities can cause us to miss the point of the parable, to our own spiritual detriment. The master commends the first two servants for being trustworthy/faithful, not for being profitable. While our cultural values draw our attention to the increase they produce, Jesus' audience would have focused on the process, not the end results. Their faithfulness amid potential dangers displays their relational connection with the master, which compels them to risk their lives to honor his instructions. Living and working in the master's home, these servants know (*yada*) the master and his character. They've experienced how the master lives with integrity in his relationships. The *mina* given to his servants represents their valuable experiential knowledge of the master, which he wants others to know—especially those who hate him. Their mission is to share their knowledge of the master with everyone, and their success will be measured by their faithfulness to make him known under tremendous social pressure. Their fidelity to the master is what they are commended for, not their return on investment.

If we read this parable with American values of productivity and profitability, we risk taking responsibility for things outside of our control. The parable doesn't tell us exactly how the master is received upon his return home. The increase of *minas* by the first two servants implies some of the people's attitude towards the master changed, but not everyone's. Only God can draw people to himself. (John 6:44) What the servants can control is their faithfulness in making the master known (*yada*) to as many people as possible before he returns. But Americans, driven to produce numbers, can beat ourselves up trying to convince people who don't want Jesus to be king over anything that they should accept him as their personal king. We can see ourselves as failures if people remain unconvinced. We can be dissatisfied with the number of those who believe, assuming that there should be many more. However, we're not responsible for how people respond. Our job is to make Jesus known by conducting his business, faithfully representing who he is to everyone we meet.

I believe our passion for faithfully making Jesus known is directly correlated to how well we *yada* him ourselves. That's the challenge with the third servant.

The Third Servant Is the Key

Not all his servants know the master well enough to live a life of faithfulness. When the third servant addresses his master, we discover the problem is not his work ethic, but rather his assumptions about the master's character:

'Sir, here is your *mina*... I was afraid of you, because you are a hard man. You take out what you did not put in and reap what you did not sow.' (Luke 19:20-21)

One could argue the third servant made the wisest decision. Desiring to remain neutral (and safe, so he thought), he chose not to publicly identify with his master and simply wait out the results. He returns the money in full, so he cannot be accused of theft. This seems to display incredible shrewdness navigating this potentially dangerous political situation.

However, the *mina*'s value as currency is only as good as the servant's relational knowledge of his master, and the third servant buried what little knowledge he possessed. His lack of knowledge of his master becomes apparent when he describes him as "a harsh man." Some could interpret his description of the master as a Middle Eastern compliment. In the world of roaming nomads, to be able to "take what you did not put in and reap what you did not sow" exemplifies cunning and strength. But not so in a settled agrarian society. The servant possesses a distorted view of his master's intentions and motivations. His language suggests the master acquired his position through dishonest means. Worse, this servant has adopted the citizens' negative perception of the master, despite having the opportunity to know him by working in his employ.[9] The master confronts his perceptions of him when he replies:

I will judge you by your own words, you wicked servant! You knew, did you, that I am a hard man, taking out what I did not put in, and reaping what I did not sow? Why then didn't you put my money on deposit, so that when I came back, I could have collected it with interest? (Luke 19:22-23)

The master expects results, especially when he provides the means to produce them. However, the servant could not have put his money on deposit, because it's against *Torah* to charge interest. And if the servant took his *mina* to the bank, he would risk publicly identifying himself as being a steward of the master's affairs, making his loyalties known publicly. The servant desires to stay quietly neutral. His *mina* was worthless anyway because he doesn't see the master for who he is, despite having worked in his house. Truly, this servant has nothing to put on deposit, nothing to share with those who hated his master.

Don't Miss God's Grace

In the end, the master reallocates his resources to those who are faithful, while maintaining a relationship with the third servant. The master continues:

> Then he said to those standing by, "Take his mina away from him and give it to the one who has ten minas." "Sir," they said, "he already has ten!" He replied, "I tell you that to everyone who has, more will be given, but as for the one who has nothing, even what he has will be taken away. But those enemies of mine who did not want me to be king over them—bring them here and kill them in front of me." (Luke 19:24-27)

Notice that the wicked servant is not fired, nor kicked out of the house, nor is he included in those whom the master orders to be killed. The servant lacks the means to make the master known, but hasn't lost his place within the home. Though completely undeserving, he remains employed by the master and can enjoy living under the master's care and protection. At the heart of his disobedience (sin) is his disbelief in who the master is; only time together will correct his misperception. God's extravagant grace extends even to those who live in the master's house but don't fully know him.

This parable begins with servants receiving gifts they neither earned nor deserve and ends with enemies being told what they deserve—but the parable doesn't make clear whether they receive it.[10] For the master's enemies, fear of political retribution is real. However, God's grace extends even to them. We Westerners might assume that because the master says to kill his enemies, that's what happens. But, crucially, the parable ends without saying whether the executions took place. That's important! Nothing in the Middle East is straightforward; everything is negotiable, driven by desire to maintain relationships. The parable's conclusion is open-ended, leaving the master's enemies an opportunity to repent.

Parables Aim to Restore Relationships

Remember, this is a fictional story meant to spark repentance—turning back to a relationship. We can assume the punishment was immediately carried out in the story, which would mean there was no opportunity for the enemies to change. However, in real life, conflicts resolve when forgiveness is extended and received, especially when both parties are allowed to save face.

I witnessed such relational restoration play out first-hand about twenty years ago. We started a basketball tournament in Bethlehem and quickly learned fights were commonplace during the games. Attempting to discourage this behavior, we implemented a rule: if a player started a fight, he would be banned from participating in the remainder of the tournament. However, fights continued. In one game, the best player in the country pushed an official while arguing a call. Chaos erupted as players and fans flooded the court, and a mêlée ensued. The consequences should have been straightforward. But in a culture that values relationships and honor over end results, the broken relationships required restoration. All the officials refused to referee if this disgrace wasn't dealt with; the team said they would withdraw from the tournament if their player wasn't allowed to play. What a mess! The best player in the country believed the referee had dishonored him, so he felt justified, while the referee was publicly humiliated. How to restore honor while saving face, even for those who caused the mess?

After three days of negotiations, a gathering was held in the home of the official who was publicly shamed. The player responsible, along with his entire team, attended. Tea was served, and, after a short while, the player's father stood up and acknowledged how his son's actions had brought shame upon the official's family. He asked forgiveness, and then the player apologized directly to the official, in front of his family. They shook hands, and it was over. Honor was restored and the player saved face by being allowed to continue participating in the tournament.

The parable ends when the nobleman says: "Those enemies of mine who did not want me to be king over them—bring them here and kill them in front of me." In the Middle East, a statement like this might be just the beginning of negotiations.

Call to Repentance

The purpose of the parable is to cause the target audience to consider which servant they are in the story. Whom is Jesus calling to repentance? By citing Ezekiel 34, Jesus claims to be God incarnate who has come to "seek and save the lost," while at the same time confronting those who scattered his sheep in the first place. The master, Jesus, has returned as king to see how faithful his representatives, the priests (some of whom happen to live in Jericho), have been while he has been away. By using the *remez* of Ezekiel 34, he indirectly accuses the priests—as God's representatives on earth—of scattering his sheep, never bothering to seek them.

Working in concert with Rome, the 1st-century priestly class—Sadducees—focused on politics and personal wealth rather than faithfully ushering people into God's presence by displaying his character. They were given authority and resources, but they did not use those resources to pursue people like Bartimaeus and Zacchaeus. Like the third servant, they didn't see God clearly; despite knowing him and serving in his house, instead they pursued a life of greed and comfort. They buried their relational treasure because they didn't believe in God's redemptive grace in the here and now, nor in an afterlife. They also never expected to see God face to face, in either this world or the world to come. Now God appears standing in front of them, calling them to repent. God's grace even extends to those shepherds—the Sadducees—who were far off the path and didn't know it.

Make Him Known

In Matthew 25:14-30, we hear Jesus telling the same parable to the disciples on the Mount of Olives, although the "talents" there are not distributed evenly, but according to one's abilities. Essentially, Jesus tells his disciples that he is going away, and they will be his representatives until he returns. He tasks them with conducting his "business" in a world that doesn't want Jesus to be king.

Jesus is asking the same of us. It's like being asked to sell Red Sox gear outside their archrivals' Yankee Stadium. The world isn't going to want to buy what we have to sell; in fact, they may even be hostile to any suggestion of their need for Jesus. Moreover, the American productivity mindset causes us to focus on what we perceive to be the end results, on making stuff happen for God. But our job is only to faithfully conduct his "business"; God is the one who changes hearts. Along the way, the Holy Spirit empowers us, and we're equipped and strengthened by our personal relational experiences with the Master.

How do we make Jesus the hero of our stories? Being "open for business" is the daily invitation to faithfully abide in the Master's love and share it with others, even with those who hate him. I believe this is accomplished through noticing others and engaging them genuinely. People need to know that God sees them in their pain, isolation, shame, and unworthiness.

Some servants will seem to be more successful than others in making Jesus known. That is not the point. Our instructions are to know (*yada*) the Father's love and live in it. This experiential knowledge is our resource, our *mina*, to faithfully share with others what our master is like and how some may have a misperception of him. We have all been given a *mina*, a measure of faith, and as it grows, so will our joy and fruitfulness in making Jesus known. (Romans 23:3) To be about our Father's business means we are relationally available and treat the next person we meet as Jesus would. When we do, God's kingdom is proclaimed and begins to grow.

Ultimately, we desire people to place their trust in Jesus and believe in him. The word *believe* can mean different things to different people. In the next chapter, we will explore what it means to believe in God.

Questions

- Which of the three servants do you identify with? Why?
- Have you ever felt guilt and shame for not doing enough as a follower of Jesus? What do you do with those feelings?
- Have you felt prideful about what you believe you have done for Jesus? What do you do with those feelings?
- How do you experience Jesus in a personal way?
- As a follower of Jesus, what is your role in sharing the Good News of Jesus with the people around you?
- Are you confident about sharing the Gospel with others? Why or why not?
- How does knowing and feeling God is active in your life impact your desire to share him with others?

Additional Resources

Bailey, Kenneth E. *Jesus Through Middle Eastern Eyes: Cultural Studies in the Gospels*

Levine, Amy-Jill. Short *Stories by Jesus: The Enigmatic Parables of a Controversial Rabbi (Annotated Edition)*

Wilder, Jim. *Renovated: God, Dallas Willard, and the Church That Transforms*

Willard, Dallas. *Life Without Lack: Living in the Fullness of Psalm 23*

16. Believe

Believe!

—TED LASSO

I believe; help my unbelief!

—MARK 9:24

The New England Patriots were down 28-3 to the Atlanta Falcons midway through the third quarter of Super Bowl LI. Tom Brady's thoughts in that discouraging moment were: "You can look at that situation and basically quit and say, you know, [expletive] it. We have no shot of winning,' or you can say, 'This is going to be an amazing comeback.'"[1] With the score 28-9 heading into the fourth quarter, no one anticipated what was about to transpire. Five minutes into the fourth quarter, after a New England field goal, Patriots wide receiver Danny Amendola shouted: "Gotta believe, bro." Fellow wide receiver Julian Edelman responded: "Gotta believe. Gotta believe, boys." Two touchdowns and two two-point conversions later, the last one coming with fifty-seven seconds remaining, the Patriots had scored nineteen improbable unanswered points to send the game into overtime, eventually clinching the greatest comeback in Super Bowl history. The players' ability to believe made the comeback possible.

The word *believe* in English is used in many ways. It can communicate what we *think*, *know*, and *like*: "I *believe* this to be true." "I *believe* that is accurate." "I *believe* this is best." People also say they "believe in themselves," ascribing their success to their self-belief. One's ability to believe thus takes on a life of its own, becoming an elusive quality that some seem to have while others don't.

Self-doubt is very real. Those who achieve somehow overcome their self-doubt, causing others to wonder how they did it. The struggle against self-doubt is a shared human experience, which is why we gravitate to stories of heroes who conquer their fears. Their ability to believe in themselves often begins with an infusion of confidence from an outside source: a ring, a sword, an invitation, a revelation of their true identity. Their new-found belief leads them to attempt tasks previously believed to be impossible. Then the plot twists: They lose the very thing they believed gave them their abilities, only to realize they had what they needed within themselves all along. These stories broadcast the message that if we only believe in ourselves, we can do anything.

Biblical Belief

The word *belief* in various forms is used over two hundred times in the Bible, depending on which translation you're using; the majority are found in the New Testament. The word is not used as a motivational tool to inspire belief in oneself, but rather to encourage belief in someone else. Believing in Jesus being the Messiah, the Son of God, becomes the focus of the New Testament—a belief that causes us to live differently.

From the beginning, God's desire to restore the world to himself would be accomplished through his son, the Messiah. The lineage of the faithful leading to him starts with Adam, then proceeds through Seth, Noah, and Shem, eventually leading to a man named Abram, whom God invites into a covenant relationship. Before their covenant ceremony, the narrator of the stories says: "Abram *believed* the Lord, and [the Lord] credited [that belief] to [Abram] as righteousness." (Genesis15:6, emphasis added) This is the first appearance of *believe,* אמן, in the Bible. What is "credited to him as righteousness" are his actions leading up to this moment that demonstrate his belief in God.

What did Abram's belief look like? Let's examine his life to see how he embodied what it means to believe in God—and what will be asked of him as he continues to believe in God in his life ahead.

Just Minding His Own Business, Until...

Abram is living in a place called Ur when an unknown God says to him: "Leave your country, your people, and your father's household, and go to the land I will show you." (Genesis 12:1)

Consider what God is asking of him: He invites Abram to leave his extended family, identity, religion, culture, protection, financial security, and stable future to follow a God he's just met, letting go of everything he knows and understands about the world—all his inherited generational knowledge—to travel to a place with no tangible means of support, security, or knowledge of the people he will encounter or the land in which he will live. Most importantly, Abram does not know (*yada*) this God whom he just met and now must decide to trust him with absolutely everything, including his life and his legacy.

To encourage Abram, God casts a vision explaining how he is participating in something much bigger than himself. God promises Abram that if he follows him, God will make Abram into a great nation, impacting the entire world:

> I will make you into a great nation and I will *bless* you; I will make your name great, and you will be a *blessing*. I will *bless* those who *bless* you, and whoever curses you I will curse; and all peoples on earth will be *blessed* through you. (Genesis 12:2-3, emphases added)

What does it mean to bless someone? The Hebrew word to *bless* or to *praise* is *barukh* בָּרֵךְ, which also means "to kneel." The root word for *knee* is *berek* בֶּרֶךְ. The use of both of these words is seen in 2 Chronicles 6:13, where Solomon "knelt down בָּרַךְ on his knees בֶּרֶךְ before all the assembly of Israel, and spread out his hands toward heaven." The word-picture here is that to bless someone means to bend the knee as if to present a gift to another person. In doing so, the giver makes themselves smaller, and the person standing to receive the gift appears bigger, more visible. To bless someone is to direct others' attention to them.

God blessed us when he became small in his incarnation so that we could become big.[2] In turn, we can bless the Lord by kneeling, which makes him stand out and be noticed; we acknowledge that he is worthy of worship when we point others to him. Indeed, God blesses Abram so that he in turn will bless the whole world by pointing them to his God.

Abram's Journeys

Abram and his family pack up everything they can carry to follow the Lord, leaving Ur, along with his father Terah, and his nephew Lot. Traveling the Fertile Crescent trade route, they settle in Haran.[3] After his father's passing, Abram becomes the patriarch of his family at the age of seventy-five. Journeying south into the land of Canaan, they stop near the town of Shechem by the oak of Moreh. (Genesis 12:6) God appears to Abram and repeats his promise that he will possess this land: A nomadic shepherd will become a landowner. Owning land signifies strength and permanence, demonstrated by one's ability to acquire, keep, protect, and cultivate a piece of land. So Abram builds an altar. Why? What purpose does an altar serve?

A pile of arranged stones, an altar marks a particular spot. Shepherds often set up *ebenezers*—piles of stones—to mark their paths and provide directions back to where they came from. An altar functions similarly, but instead of marking a path to lead us somewhere, it can mark the location where God once spoke to someone. The idea is: if God spoke here once, maybe he will speak with me again at this same place. Both Abraham and Jacob build altars marking places where God speaks to them. They want to be able to find those exact spots again in the future.

In many ancient Near-Eastern cultures, gods were localized to a region or connected relationally to a specific people. That's the reason temples were built in specific locations: to identify the dwelling place of a particular god. The idol inside the temple marked the presence of the god itself; the image made of wood and stone was thought to act as a conduit for the god to speak with his people.

At this place near Shechem God says to Abram: "To your offspring I will give this land," (Genesis 12:7) so Abram builds an altar on the spot as a reminder of God's promise about this theogeographically important location. Two other patriarchs—Abraham's son Isaac and his grandson Jacob—will pass through Shechem during their travels, following in Abraham's footsteps. When the Israelites enter the Promised Land, God commands Joshua to lead the people to Mount Gerizim and Mount Ebal, near Shechem, to reaffirm the covenant. Many centuries later, Jesus also passes through Shechem, connecting his story with the Patriarchs'.

It all began when Abram believed God enough to follow him to this place. But his faith will be tested.

Egypt and Back

While Abraham lives in Canaan, famine strikes. To survive, he travels to Egypt, the only place where food can be found. Concerned about his wife Sarai's protection, he asks her to tell everyone that they are brother and sister. (Genesis 12) Many readers quickly besmirch Abram's character, accusing him of lying or of using Sarai as a human shield. This may be, but it's also possible that something quite different is going on.

The Egyptians think Sarai is very beautiful. (Genesis 12:14) Her attraction isn't necessarily based on physical attributes, since women in that culture wore veils and covered their bodies from head to toe. Sarai's allure most likely has more to do with possessions, resources, and the perceived strength associated with her family of origin. Abram, as the patriarch of the clan, has amassed great wealth in livestock by this point. To the Egyptians, he likely represents a larger nomadic tribe with the skills to thrive in a harsh environment—no small feat—since they view everything east of their territory as a mysterious land full of demons and other unknown dangers. In their minds, Abram must possess great strength and courage to survive in those elements. In addition, we later find out that Abram has 318 fighting men at his disposal. (Genesis 14:14) That number seems insignificant to us today, but at the time it represented a substantial military force. The Egyptians see Abram as someone to be taken seriously, especially if he represents an even larger tribe.

Pharaoh, however, was the leader of a great kingdom; he could have killed Abram and taken Sarai, along with all their possessions. However, if Abram represents a smaller clan from a larger tribe, then killing him could invite problems. The easiest way to resolve the issue is to create an alliance. As discussed in Chapter 5, marriage in the ancient Near East had more to do with cementing alliances than with romance. Think of Solomon and his seven hundred wives and three hundred concubines: Each of those women functioned as her father's representative or ambassador to the most powerful ruler in the region. To solidify a geopolitical alliance, the cultural expectations required formal negotiations to finalize the terms of an arranged marriage. The Genesis text alludes to Pharaoh discreetly snatching Sarai, taking her to become his bride without following this expected protocol. (Genesis 12:15) Had Pharaoh followed cultural expectations instead, he would have afforded Abram an opportunity to clarify his relationship with Sarai.

Now, it is likely that Sarai was Abram's half-sister, sharing the same father but different mothers. Abram says as much in Genesis 20:12. In the ancient Near East, sibling marriage wasn't an uncommon practice; its purpose was to keep resources circulating within the family. Sarai could be both Abram's wife and sister. God gets Pharaoh's attention when Pharaoh realizes that Sarai is Abram's wife. Possibly as an acknowledgement for his rash decision to snatch Sarai, Pharaoh makes restitution, and the couple leave Egypt wealthier than when they arrived. Surviving both the famine and potential death at the hands of Pharaoh, they return to Canaan, back to the place where Abram built a second altar between Bethel and Ai. (Genesis 13:3-4) Throughout all these trials, Abram is learning to trust the Lord's provision and protection.

The next piece of the story is Abram and Lot separating, with Lot moving east and Abram southwest toward Hebron. (Genesis 13) While both settle into their new locations, Lot is caught in the crossfire between rival kings and is taken captive—along with his family and possessions—by four kings from the north. Abram and his 318 fighting men pursue Lot's captors all the way to Dan in northern Israel and rescue him and his family. (Genesis 14) Returning to Hebron, he travels down the watershed ridge route, passing near the city of Salem (later called Jerusalem). Here Abram is met by a priestly king named Melchizedek (Genesis 14:18) and begins to fulfill his mission of blessing God by making God's name known. He also discovers he is not alone in worshiping his God; we're told that Melchizedek is a priest for God Most High, and he blesses Abram before he departs: "Blessed be Abram by God Most High, Creator of heaven and earth. And blessed be God Most High, who delivered your enemies into your hand." (Genesis 14:19-20) In a culture where all events, good or bad, are attributed to a god, Abram points people to his God, who is the God and like no other, as the source of all his success and blessings.

An Acknowledgment, Not a Pronouncement

We read in the opening verses of Genesis 15 that after this encounter with Melchizedek, "the word of the Lord came to Abram in a vision":

> 'Do not be afraid, Abram. I am your shield, your very great reward.' But Abram said, 'O Sovereign LORD, what can you give me since I remain childless and the one who will inherit my estate is Eliezer of Damascus?' And Abram said, 'You have given me no children; so a servant in my household will be my heir.' (Genesis 15:1-2)[4]

Abram challenges God by asking, essentially, "What's the point of having you as my shield and great reward if I don't have a son to pass it on to?" Being married half a century to Sarai has not produced a child for Abram, in particular a son whom he can raise to take over leading and protecting the family.

God directs Abram to step outside his tent and look up at the stars as an indication of the vast numbers of his future children and the scope of their influence:

> Then the word of the LORD came to him: "This man [Eliezer] will not be your heir, but a son coming from your own body will be your heir." He took him outside and said, "Look up at the heavens and count the stars—if indeed you can count them." Then he said to him, "So shall your offspring be." <u>Abram believed the LORD, and he credited it to him as righteousness.</u> (Genesis 15:1-6, emphasis added)

Abram's belief forms the cornerstone of our faith: God's grace is received by believing, not earned through one's actions. This is absolutely true. However, in this instance, I think God is acknowledging Abram's long-existing belief rather than pronouncing it as beginning at that moment. Why? Because it is difficult to separate beliefs from actions. Abram demonstrated his belief/trust in God to bring him to this specific place and time, where they are now establishing the formal covenant described in Genesis 15. But there is one essential piece missing from Abram's life: a son who will carry on the family's lineage. Abram challenges God to prove that he can do what he says. He can't become a great nation if he has no heir to continue the family line. God tells him to look at the stars and promises: "So shall your offspring be." Abram believes God will provide him a son—his belief in God's covenantal promise is what is credited to him as righteousness. But Abram's belief in that particular pronouncement isn't based on nothing. God has proved himself trustworthy to Abram many times over leading up to this point. Abram will need to remember God's past faithfulness while he waits another twenty-five years until Isaac is born.

Because of their belief, both Abram and Isaac become faithful generational links in the lineage of the eventual Messiah, to bless the entire world. The blessing the Messiah brings with him to the world is the understanding that we are saved by grace. God's pronouncement of Abram being credited with righteousness becomes a theological lynchpin in the New Testament for this belief. While addressing the high priest in Acts 7, the disciple Stephen explains how his hope in Jesus as the Messiah is rooted in Abraham and in God's fulfilling his promises to Abraham now through Jesus. Paul later dedicates an entire chapter to Abraham in Romans 4, explaining that it was not Abraham's outward acts of *Torah*-keeping that saved him, but his faith in God and his promises. Like Stephen, Paul quotes Genesis 15:6, both here and in the letter to the Galatians. This concept of being saved by faith and not by works is foundational in our understanding of God's love being a free, unmerited gift of grace. However, our beliefs drive our actions. It is impossible to separate the two.

Belief as a Feeling

As a Chicago Cubs fan, I begin every new season with the "belief" that this is going to be their year. Then it finally happened in 2016. The time between championships for the Cubs franchise was almost as long as Abraham's wait for Isaac. We can read events in the Bible as happening in quick succession when the narrator skips over the intervening time, but years pass, sometimes decades, between recorded events separated by only a few sentences. Holding on to our belief over long years is an act of faith that produces perseverance.

To *believe* sounds like a mental choice to exercise willpower, as if we think reality into existence. But which comes first: the belief that one can accomplish something, or the actions that lead to our accomplishment? And how do we agree upon language to describe what it means to believe?

Biblical Hebrew has only ten thousand common words, necessitating that each word carries with it many nuanced meanings. This is case for the Hebrew word believe, *aman* אמן, commonly used to communicate belief, assurance, and faithfulness, with connotations of trustworthiness, steadfastness, continuance, and much more. As a word picture, it means to *support*, like a tent peg. An example of this is in Isaiah 22:23: "And I will thrust him like a tent peg in a place of support [*aman*]." Belief is pictured in terms of supporting something, holding it firmly in place.

God could snap his fingers and make anything he desires happen in an instant. But instead, throughout the Bible, he invites us to partner with him to accomplish his will. Abram supported (believed) God, as evidenced by all the actions leading up to Genesis 15 that demonstrated his belief in him.

Here is a list of all Abram did up to this point:

1. He left his extended family.
2. He left his worldview.
3. He risked his life by leaving the protection of his family.
4. He risked the lives of his family members, for whom he was responsible.
5. He responded to the Lord at Shechem and built an altar.
6. He called on the Lord upon his return from Egypt.
7. He did what was best for Lot, allowed him to choose the best land.
8. He fulfilled his role as leader of his family by rescuing Lot.
9. He publicly gave all credit for his blessings to God in the presence of Melchizedek, king of Salem.

At any point along the way, Abram and his family could easily have been wiped out; instead, God steadfastly demonstrated his faithfulness by taking care of Abram. It takes time to grow to trust someone. Now, at this point in their relationship, God invites Abram to join him in a formal covenant and asks him to trust him with his greatest need: a son. Their relationship has grown enough to handle the weight of God's request.

This covenant will require Abram to exercise just as much faith, trust, and belief to follow God now as he did before Genesis 15. In both Hebrew and English, *belief* and *trust* are synonyms. They're intertwined, relational words, lived out through *righteous* actions. Genesis 15:6 contains the first appearance of the word *righteousness* צְדָקָה in Scripture, which can be defined as actively valuing our relationship with God by responding (with words and deeds) to *keep, honor, guard, protect,* and *preserve* our relationship with him. To be *righteous* means to be in a right relationship with someone. Abram's belief in God's promises leads him to act in a way that honors and preserves their relationship.

As with Abram, God interrupts our lives and demonstrates our value and worth to him. And like Abram, we respond by leaving our old ways of life behind to follow God. He may not move us physically to a completely different environment and culture, but the culture we're familiar with slowly becomes foreign as we begin to live in God's reality of who he says we are, who he is, and his love of others who don't know him. Just as it took time for Abram to travel to Canaan, it will take time for us to learn to trust God and take him at his word. But he will get us to where he desires us to be in our relationship with him, which requires us experiencing God's faithfulness for ourselves.

One Small Step for Man…
One Giant Leap for the Kingdom of God

After we decide to trust God, we will be tempted to go back to our old ways of living. God never promised following him would be easy nor comfortable (I can all but hear Abraham in heaven saying "Amen!"). Change is hard. Calling Abram physically out of Ur didn't erase his past— nor did God want to. I wonder if Abraham looked back at his old life in Ur and compared it to his new life following the God Most High. At what point might he have said, "I never want to go back"? Abram had to learn how to trust God, step by step, by experiencing God's faithfulness.

Our journey with God begins likewise, with small steps of faithfulness. As we follow him, we experience his trustworthiness, which gives us perspective. Eventually, we're able to see how far we've come, acknowledging that we, too, would not want to go back to our previous life. Walking with the Good Shepherd allows us to see ourselves and the world through his eyes. We have a choice to make every day: to keep walking forward with God, to turn around and go back, or to sit down and refuse to move. No matter which we choose, challenging days are sure to come.

Belief is more than just a mental choice we make; it's a relationship built upon trust. Those Patriot football players trusted in their training, preparation, and coaches, which gave them reasons to play as if the seemingly impossible were possible. God is not asking us to take a "leap" of faith; he is asking us to trust him and take small steps of faith, believing he is who he says he is—and actively participate in his mission.

Believing in Jesus is so much more than just knowing we will go to heaven when we die. Instead, our belief supports God's goal for all of creation: for everyone to know him and to trust him completely. In doing so, we bless God by pointing others to him. Our actions fulfill the promises made to our spiritual ancestor, Abram, in Genesis 12, to bless the whole world. We get to be active members in God's generational line, linking people to the promised Messiah in our present moment.

This life sounds amazing, but what does our journey with God look like today? In our last chapter together, let's discuss the next steps.

Questions

- How do you relate to Abram's story?
- Based on what you learned in this chapter, how do you define biblical belief and trust?
- Do you ever struggle with your belief in God? What helps?
- Take some time to think about your story. How have you experienced God's work in your life? How has your belief in God changed you?
- How does it feel to know you are part of the same story God has been writing since Abram?
- Can you identify a moment when you responded to God?
- Belief drives our actions. What is one thing you know God has asked you to do that you can start doing to demonstrate your belief and trust in him?

Additional Resources

Eng, Milton, and Lee M. Fields, eds. *Devotions on the Hebrew Bible: 54 Reflections to Inspire and Instruct*

17. Choose the Red Pill

You take the blue pill—the story ends, you wake up
in your bed and believe whatever you want to believe.
You take the red pill—you stay in Wonderland
and I show you how deep the rabbit hole goes.

—MORPHEUS IN *THE MATRIX*

I knew when I met you,
adventure was about to happen.

—PARAPHRASED FROM *WINNIE THE POOH*

Whoever claims to live in him, must walk as Jesus walks.

—1 JOHN 2:6

The groundbreaking 1999 movie *The Matrix* explores how we understand reality and who is in control of framing it. Philosophically, it's spot on. The main character, Neo, is visited by a man named Morpheus, who explains to him that everything he sees and experiences is a computer-programmed illusion. Morpheus offers him a choice: If he takes a red pill, then he will leave the artificially constructed reality, the "matrix," and discover what is real. Or if Neo takes a blue pill, he will return to his illusionary life as if the conversation never happened. Neo chooses to know reality. But without Morpheus' entrance into the story, Neo would have remained oblivious to what is real.

Similarly, the Bible tells how the God of the universe, Jesus, literally inserts himself into his creation—God's matrix—our reality, to explain who he is and our reason for existing. The Bible is God's revelation, providing us with the background story and leading us to the Creator's appearance in human history. Without Jesus and the Bible, our understanding of the world would be subject to our individual interpretations, influenced by the "media matrix" (professional news agencies and social media) to define reality for us, telling us what to think and how we should feel. But who are they? What is their agenda?

God's agenda is clear—he wants to be in relationship with us. He asks us to opt into his perfect perception of reality, the ultimate red pill. Yet some people prefer to take the blue pill and remain unchanged, even when presented with the opportunity to know God's true reality instead of our biased personal perceptions. Why? Because the personal matrixes we've created or accepted seem easier, or more comfortable, or more beneficial. Ignoring God's reality seems less threatening than facing the misperceptions of our matrix. Some prefer to remain blissfully unaware.

After being freed from the matrix, Neo reevaluates the world he knew based on new information. Similarly, the disciples are red-pilled in their Jewish first-century context. Jesus challenges them to reinterpret their understanding of God, his plan to redeem all of humanity, and the role of the Messiah. The red-pilling happens over a three-year period of following Jesus together. The disciples struggle to grasp what Jesus teaches them, especially regarding his upcoming death and resurrection. Not fully comprehending, they boldly proclaim their willingness to die with Jesus as they make their way to Jerusalem. (John 11:16) But when the time comes for Jesus' arrest, they all scatter. Judas is not the only one to betray Jesus that Passover night; all the disciples abandon him in their own ways. In this chapter, we'll look at three people—Peter, Judas, and the Prodigal Son—each confronted with the reality of their need for forgiveness and reconciliation with a loving Father. I think we'll see ourselves represented in each of their stories.

Confronting Reality

When Jesus is taken into custody by the Sadducean authorities, Peter follows the guards' processional but stays in the shadows. Probably torn between loyalty and fear, he trails them into the courtyard of Ananias and Caiaphas, the high-priestly family who ordered Jesus' arrest. (John 18) Peter, one of the first to follow Jesus, is now one of the last to stay close to Jesus until what he thought was the end.[1] Following his rabbi has led him here: timidly warming himself by a fire, shivering within eyeshot of where Jesus stands on trial for his life. To his horror, various individuals identify him as having been with Jesus, the accused, which casts suspicion on him, too. As he speaks, his Galilean accent suggests that he was most likely associated with Jesus from Nazareth, and those around him are quick to judge him based on that fact alone. (Luke 22:54-62) Peter denies all their accusations; in an act of supreme (but all-too-understandable) cowardice, he states emphatically: "I don't know the man!" (Matthew 26:72) Just then, a crowing rooster refreshes Peter's memory of Jesus' words, spoken hours before: "Truly, I tell you, this very night, before the rooster crows, you will deny me three times." (Matthew 26:34)

Realizing what he's done, Peter weeps bitterly. (Luke 22:62) Not only has Peter betrayed his rabbi relationally, but his three denials act as a public declaration that he no longer wants to follow Jesus as a disciple.[2]

Community Keeps Us

Days later, the painful events of Jesus' crucifixion are over, and the Sabbath has concluded. Now, some of the women who followed Jesus go on Sunday morning to the tomb to finish anointing his body for a burial. Finding the tomb empty, they rush to John's house to share the shocking news. (John 20:2) When they arrive there, the reader discovers that Peter has been staying with John and his family. Imagine his three days of processing his grief and shame! But he doesn't do it alone: he stays in community with those who love and care for him. As hard and embarrassing as it may have been for Peter to be in their presence, his response is healthy and reflects our need for community, especially when we feel our lowest.

Peter provides a stark contrast to Judas, who chooses to isolate himself. Scholars, theologians, and laypeople have tried to provide a plausible explanation for Judas' actions. What motivated him to betray Jesus? How could he commit the ultimate treachery against the Son of God? Was it just for money? Such questions are understandable. It's easy for us to denigrate Judas and cast him in a villain's role. However, none of us are that simple. We are all deeply broken people, and we all have mixed motives.

Matthew's account gives us a glimpse into Judas' heart and mind:

> When Judas, who had betrayed him, saw that Jesus was condemned, he was seized with remorse and returned the thirty pieces of silver to the chief priests and the elders. (Matthew 27:3)

This verse complicates a simple interpretation of Judas' motives. If he was just out to make money, and he knew that the Sadducees harbored ill will towards Jesus, why would he feel remorse? Didn't he suspect they intended to direct some kind of harm towards Jesus? Matthew's narrative suggests something more nuanced might be going on.

I believe Judas never expected Jesus to fall into the hands of the Sadducees. Several theories exist to explain his motives, and what makes the most sense to me is to identify Judas as a former member of the Zealots, one of several factions of Jews in the first-century. Believing they were keeping *Torah* by fighting the Romans, along with anyone who compromised with Rome, they saw themselves as fighting against idolatry.3 One of Jesus' disciples was Simon the Zealot, so it is possible that Judas was a Zealot as well. Based on their reading of Zechariah 14, the Zealots expected the Messiah to announce himself, enter Jerusalem, and immediately begin fighting the Romans to establish his kingdom. According to this view, Judas believes Jesus is the Messiah and takes it upon himself to orchestrate a confrontation, using the Sadducees' hatred of Jesus for his desired effect. If this is true, he's hoping that the arrival of armed soldiers in the Garden of Gethsemane will prompt Jesus to begin to fight for his kingdom (which, theogeographically, is in the Valley of Jehoshaphat—see How Will the Messiah Come? in Chapter 15). Judas is like the third servant in the parable of the talents in Luke 19; his misperceptions of Jesus led him to wrong conclusions about how God's kingdom will come on the earth. He isn't alone: The crowds shouting at Jesus' triumphal entry also expect him to be the conquering king.

Judas' expectations go horribly wrong. Jesus never fights. Worse, he is condemned to death and dies at the hands of his enemies. Judas thought God's kingdom would come through force, but he discovers the hard way that it comes through sacrifice and a willingness to die for one's enemies. That's a bitter red pill for Judas to swallow.

As the realization of all that is happening under the cover of darkness begins to fully sink in, Judas falls into despair. He admits: "I have sinned," most horribly, "for I have betrayed innocent blood." (Matthew 27:4)

He knows Jesus is the Messiah and that he is responsible for handing Jesus over to his enemies. Overcome with emotions, where could he go? His fellow disciples are scattered and will probably hide from him if they see him coming, fearing that Judas might seek to hand them over, too. He probably feels truly alone in the world, and he seeks to isolate himself further. Finally, overwhelmed with shame, Judas sees no way to restore what he has broken, and he hangs himself. (Matthew 27:5)

We, too, can experience deep feelings of shame when we've hurt someone we care about. Our natural inclination is to isolate ourselves in what I call our self-imposed "spiritual penalty box," remaining for however long we feel like we need to punish ourselves. Rehearsing our shame in isolation can lead to more unhealthy choices, attempting to blunt our feelings by burying our faces in a gallon of ice cream, binging on a Netflix series, going for a long run... or worse: we can imagine indulging much more harmful choices as well. In moments like these, we can feel like Judas, stuck in despair, believing forgiveness is not possible. Instead of going as far as ending our own lives like Judas did, we may instead kill and bury our broken relationships, believing they are beyond restoration and repair.

Both Peter and Judas spent the last three years following Jesus as his disciples, and both deny him. Even so, they process their shame differently. Both know they need relational restoration and forgiveness by Jesus, but Judas chooses to isolate himself, while Peter stays in fellowship with other followers of Jesus. I hold that Judas' greatest sin was not betraying Jesus, but rather not believing that he could be forgiven. Both men feel immense shame, leading one to hang himself while the other goes back to his old life of fishing. Neither of them is fully capable of grasping the reality of Jesus' predicted resurrection. That potential simply exists outside of their matrixes.

Reconciliation

Judas' life tragically ends with unresolved shame, and Peter believes his life as a disciple of Jesus has also died. However, his story is not over. The Good Shepherd is going to search for his lost sheep, and Peter is about to have an encounter with the resurrected Jesus. An angel meets Mary at the tomb and says: "Go, tell his disciples and Peter, 'He is going ahead of you into Galilee. There you will see him, just as he told you.'" (Mark 16:7)

Why single out Peter from the rest? He's one of the disciples, so why say "his disciples and Peter"? I think it is because Peter no longer sees himself as part of the group. He's already returned to what he knows best—fishing.

Take a moment to read John 21. In this story, Peter and several of the disciples have fished all night and caught nothing. A stranger from the beach calls out: "Friends, haven't you any fish?" (John 21:5)[4] Then he directs them to throw their nets on the right side of the boat; they do so and catch an amazing haul of fish.[5] Realizing it is the Lord, Peter doesn't wait: He dives in the water, fully clothed, and heads to shore.

The next line reads like a movie script describing an opening scene: "When they landed, they saw a fire of burning coals there with fish on it, and some bread." (John 21:9) By now, you know these details are given to us for a reason. The image of burning coals is found throughout *Tanakh*. They're first mentioned indirectly in Genesis 15 as coals contained inside the "smoking fire pot," personifying God in the covenant ceremony. Burning coals are also present in God's throne room, where Isaiah's lips are cleansed by coals taken from the altar of God. (Isaiah 6) Ezekiel describes the creatures in God's throne room as being like burning coals. (Ezekiel 1:13) Burning coals, then, symbolize God's presence. The identical phrase is also found in John 18:18, taking us back to the scene of Peter's denials.

The most common reference to burning coals, however, is associated with God's judgment. For example, Proverbs 25:21-22 speaks of pouring burning coals on our enemy's head: "If your enemy is hungry, give him food to eat; if he is thirsty, give him water to drink. In doing this, you will heap burning coals on his head, and the Lord will reward you." Reading this proverb in the fuller context of *Tanakh* as a whole, we can see it says that when we act in kindness, as God does, it's as if we're bringing them into God's presence—not as punishment, but rather under conviction in the face of experiencing undeserved kindness. We do this when we simply live like Jesus in a hurting world. Without using words, we can cause people to question their worldview by our actions—small red pills.

Combining all these concepts, burning coals can symbolize God's presence, either in judgment, cleansing, calling, or conviction. With the mention of burning coals in John 21, John desires to draw our attention to the fact that God is here. This opens the potential for restoration or (like in Isaiah) cleansing and calling. Maybe Jesus' fire on this morning harkens back to the night Peter denied Jesus, warming himself by a fire—only this time in reverse.

Three Repeating Questions

Can you imagine the awkward silence around the fire? Sitting there, amazed by what they are experiencing, nobody wants to say anything. Jesus breaks the silence: "Come and have breakfast." (John 21:12)

When they had finished eating, Jesus said to Simon Peter, "Simon son of John, do you truly love me more than these?" "Yes, Lord," he said, "you know that I love you." Jesus said, "Feed my lambs." Again Jesus said, "Simon son of John, do you truly love me?" He answered, "Yes, Lord, you know that I love you." Jesus said, "Take care of my sheep." The third time he said to him, "Simon son of John, do you love me?" Peter was hurt because Jesus asked him the third time, "Do you love me?" He said, "Lord, you know all things; you know that I love you." Jesus said, "Feed my sheep." (John 21:15-17)

Many commentators agree that this conversation is undoing Peter's three denials: Jesus asks him the question three times, as if each one cancels out a denial. Peter also gets a new job description: A fisherman becomes a shepherd. Deeper still, something is literally lost in translation. English only has one word for *love*, while Greek has at least three.

Jesus asks Peter twice, "Do you love [*agape*] me?" The Greek word carries the connotation of deep affection, an intimate, all-encompassing type of love. Peter responds: "Lord, you know I love [*phileo*] you"—this is a brotherly kind of love (as in *Philadelphia*, "city of brotherly love"). The love of God is even greater than what Peter can receive at this moment. Jesus asks Peter one last time, but the word Jesus uses for love in this last round changes from *agape* to *phileo*. Peter's ability to receive from the Lord is at a level of *phileo*, while the God of the universe is telling him to his face, "I love you completely." This subtle shift in wording is profound. In it, God meets Peter where he is. Jesus, in a sense, is saying, "That's okay; let's start with *phileo*, and we can journey towards *agape* together." God does the same for you and me: He meets us where we are now.[6]

Where to Begin—the Path of Righteousness

The journey of reconciliation, restoration, and joy with God and others begins when we stop running, allowing ourselves to be found. Whether we left the Good Shepherd because we were frightened, willfully headstrong, or simply confused, being found begins when we cry out to him, indicating a desire and willingness to be found. When we stop running, it is a sign of our willingness to yield our will, trusting in the love God has for us that we somehow previously misunderstood. Now we can begin to walk with God on his path.

God's heart-felt desire is to make known to us the path of life, filling us with the joy of his presence. (Psalms 16:11) To be in God's presence means we are accepted, and can begin to form bonds of trust and belonging. This is part of what's called attachment theory: when we attach to someone who loves us unconditionally, accepting us where we are, we find a place to belong.[7] All these elements combine to create our sense of identity. Who I am is based on who my people are; feeling safe and secure, I naturally want to be like them. Without being told what to do, I start modeling their behaviors like a *talmid*, as we discussed in Chapter 13. More deeply, I internalize their character and values. Experiencing a sense of belonging with God begins this process of transformation to become like him.[8] My ability to trust him and live a life that is "blameless, perfect, devoted, pure of heart" is a natural response to joyfully attaching myself to God.

Obeying God is not burdensome; in fact, it enables us to enjoy his presence and to experience his rest. 1 John 2:6 says, "Whoever claims to live in him must walk as Jesus walked." By now, you are clued into the importance of language and the metaphor of walking, meaning to "act like." Jesus perfectly obeys the Father (John 6:38), and that is our mission, too. The word that can throw us off in that verse is *must*, as if we have an obligation. The word is an exhortation for believers, for sure. The Greek word here carries a connotation of obligation with an upside, and can be translated as "it is to your benefit."9 We are blessed when we walk as Jesus did, living connected to the Father. We're also blessed because we live more deeply connected with others, while experiencing the joy of the Holy Spirit fully alive within us. As crazy as this sounds, obeying God is the most selfish thing we can do.

Some people might imagine that following God is like walking on a tightrope—one wrong step, and it's all over. It's true that the path the shepherd takes can at times become very narrow, requiring precise steps; however, at other times the path widens, allowing options. Imagine a herd of sheep following a shepherd: They don't walk single file, or march in columns like an army. They each navigate the terrain immediately in front of them, using the shepherd's visibility and calling voice to keep themselves oriented and moving in the right direction. From the sheep's perspective, they're all on their own paths, even while they all follow one shepherd.10 Not everyone's path will look the same, but we all follow the same Good Shepherd.

Returning Home

The Bible describes a God who came down from heaven to seek us and restore our relationship back to the fullness of what was once enjoyed in the Garden of Eden. It is a relational book, disguised as a theological book, which names us God's treasured possession. He will never stop pursuing us, per the terms of his covenantal promise. He will remain faithful to us even if we fail to be faithful towards him, even when we choose to intentionally walk away from him. When we find ourselves lost, we may be tempted to believe he will lose patience with our constant wanderings. But God's covenant says otherwise. Do we believe in God's reality?

Understanding the father's lavish love is the point of the well-known parable about the prodigal son. (Luke 15) This young man struggled to understand and accept living life under his father's authority, willfully choosing to leave his wisdom, security, and protection in order to live as he saw fit. Why? Somehow, the son lost trust and confidence in his father's intentions and motivations. Deciding he knew best, he set out to a far country. I used to think that this meant he traveled a great distance. Actually, the location of the far country was just across the lake from where Jesus tells this story, in the area called the Decapolis. [11] The distance the prodigal travels is not physical but cultural; he chooses to go to a pagan Gentile place, metaphorically far from those who observed *Torah*. While living his best life, he runs out of resources, attempts to ingratiate himself with the local population, and eventually ends up herding pigs. Hungry and desperate, he wonders how he can return home. His solution is to offer himself to his father as a servant and work off his debt.

The first time I taught this story to a group of young people in Israel, we were in the area where the father would have lived. Looking across the lake, I described how the father could wake every morning, gaze in the direction of the Decapolis, and wonder if his son was alive. At the time, my own five-year-old son sat upon my shoulder, and I started to cry, imagining: what if my own son someday makes a similar choice?

My own emotions reveal that the "Parable of the Prodigal Son" is mislabeled. The emphasis of the story is on the loving father, who is actively looking towards the horizon, longing for his son to return. When he does see the familiar silhouette of his son walking towards their village, he runs to meet him. As you've learned, running is shameful for a dignified man. However, his love compels him to run. But his son is still lost. His need to survive brought him home, not a desire to reconcile with the father. He is not repentant; he's hungry.

How can we tell? Because of context and allusions from the *Tanakh*. Jesus tells this parable, along with the two preceding ones in Luke 15, in response to the Pharisees criticizing him for "welcoming sinners and eating with them." (Luke 15:2) The Pharisees lived a very stringent lifestyle of obedience, and their criteria for repentance was also very rigid. All three parables seek to explore Jesus' understanding of what true repentance looks like. In the first parable, a shepherd pursues a sheep that is lost; it cries out and accepts being found, restoring the honor of the shepherd who could have been accused of either neglect or theft. The second parable tells the story of a woman who loses a coin, which represents the family's wealth she is responsible for keeping. Like the shepherd who exerts great effort to restore his honor, the woman expends time and money (burning oil) to find the coin, an inanimate object that can't cry out. When she finds the coin, her honor is restored. In both situations, the lost objects, the sheep and coin, accept being found. The sheep does not run away from the shepherd, and the coin, as an inanimate object, has no choice. Jesus defines repentance as accepting being found.

Now the son returns home and says, "Father, I have sinned against heaven and against you." (Luke 15:21) But he is still lost. Really? Well, if we know our *Tanakh*, we'd be clued in. After the plague of locusts, Pharaoh says to Moses, "I have sinned against the Lord your God and against you." (Exodus 10:16-17) We know that Pharaoh is not repentant, because he still refuses to let all the people go to worship God. More plagues follow. The Prodigal Son says the same thing, and the allusion makes Jesus' audience compare him to the unrepentant Pharaoh.[12] But the father in this story ushers in a different ending when he says: "Quick! Bring the best robe and put it on him. Put a ring on his finger and sandals on his feet." (Luke 15:22) The son accepts being found when he receives a robe, ring, and shoes—all status symbols of being the father's son rather than his servant.[13] The father convinces the son that he belongs with him, and at last the son accepts back his identity as being the son of the father.

Love red-pills us, encouraging us to return home. So, when you put this book down, what are you going to do? There are no set formulas; you are uniquely you, and God meets you where you are to walk with you.

Here are some practices to ponder and adopt:

1. Know (*yada*) that you are immensely loved. Ask God to help you experience and understand what this means to you.
2. Acknowledge that God desires you to experience his presence.
3. Remember you are never alone.
4. Accept that you can't disappoint God; understanding this truth keeps shame from robbing you of your energy and focus.

5. Start *believing* by faithfully living out what you already know to be true—one small step of active obedience at a time. Obeying God is the gift you give yourself.
6. Understand that learning to trust God fully will be a messy process—even if you wander off the path, God will pursue you.
7. Pray for the Lord to lead you to a healthy community of imperfect Jesus-followers.

Let's Get Cookin'

We are collectively God's treasured possession, a wealth of divine joy made up of individuals like you. As in a family, church, sports team, or business, all the individual members make up the whole. Each is valuable and necessary, contributing to the success of the group. How could we assign individual value to each of the people who make up the whole? That's impossible to calculate.

Paul's words in 1 Corinthians 3:16-17 capture well our present reality:

> Don't you know that you yourselves are God's temple and that God's Spirit lives in you? If anyone destroys God's temple, God will destroy him; for God's temple is sacred, and you are that temple.

The *you* here is plural in the Greek; maybe it could be better translated as *y'all*. You and I, then, are not individual temples; we're each just one stone in God's temple. We—and all other believers, both now and throughout history—make up God's temple together. Each stone needs the others for the whole building to stand firm. If we neglect to accept our place in God's temple, then the whole body of Christ is the lesser for it. Something will be painfully missing.

You matter. Your life matters. Your walk with God matters. Be alert, because our enemy will want to convince you otherwise. My prayer is that you'll be able to read God's word well, seeing how you belong as God's chosen and beloved child, his treasured possession. Living in the joy of this one ingredient (that you are God's treasured possession) will flavor your whole life—allowing others to "taste and see that the Lord is good" (Psalms 34:8) when you walk like him.

Questions

- How has stepping into the theological kitchen and studying the ingredients of God's story helped expand your understanding of God and his kingdom?
- What is your greatest takeaway from our study of the "ingredients" and how to use them?
- What you believe about God matters. Write down 5 things you believe about him. Do they line up with who Scripture says He is?
- Where do you go when you feel like you've really blown it? Throughout this chapter, we explored the stories of two disciples who betrayed Jesus:
  - In his shame, Judas chose isolation. Have you ever chosen isolation over help from others? What were the results?
  - On the other hand, Peter sought the care of trusted community and eventually experienced redemption. How have healthy relationships with fellow believers supported you? How have you supported others?
- In John 21, Jesus meets Peter where he's at emotionally. Do you need to allow yourself to be found by God? How do you need him to meet you in this season of your life?
- How has Scripture come alive as you've explored the historical, cultural, and structural context of the Bible? How will this impact the way you read the Bible going forward?

Additional Resources

Bailey, Kenneth E. *The Cross and the Prodigal: Luke 15 Through the Eyes of Middle Eastern Peasants (Revised Edition)*

Brown, Michael L. *Has God Failed You? Finding Faith When You're Not Even Sure God Is Real*

Chan, Francis. *Crazy Love: Overwhelmed by a Relentless God (Revised and Updated Edition)*

Groves, J. Alasdair, and Winston T. Smith. *Untangling Emotions (Illustrated Edition)*

"The Ride: A Christmas Parable"
https://www.youtube.com/watch?v=Xa3QphqeFyo

Warner, Marcus, and Stephanie Warner. "On the Trail" Deeper Walk International https://deeperwalk.com/podcast/

Wilder, E. James, Anna Kang, John Loppnow, and Sungshim Loppnow. *Joyful Journey: Listening to Immanuel*

The End

About the Author

John Farwell is the founder of Walk the Story, an organization focused on understanding the cultural background of the Bible. A graduate of Jerusalem University College with a master's degree in Biblical History & Geography, John has led hundreds of people through the Holy Land since 2005. He currently serves as a director for a sports development organization in the Middle East as well as an adjunct professor for Jerusalem Seminary.

John and his family have been traveling to and living culturally immersed in Israel for extended periods of time over the last 20 years. When at home in the United States, he and his family live in Raleigh, North Carolina.

Glossary

Agape (ἀγάπη)—One of five Greek words for love, *Agape* refers to the selfless, unconditional, and sacrificial love of a family or spouse without a romantic or sexual connotation.

Aman (אָמַן)—Hebrew word meaning to trust, to believe, to build up or support, be firm or faithful. As a word picture it means to be set in place like a tent peg.

Barukh (ברך)—Hebrew word for bless, to bless, or blessed. As a word picture it means to kneel to make someone else appear bigger, while the person who is doing the blessing appears smaller.

Bet av (בית אב)—Hebrew phrase meaning *the father's house*. It references the importance of the belonging, protection, identity, and worldview provided by one's immediate and ancestral family.

Boethusians—one of 26-29 identifiable groups of Jewish sects that flourished in the first century. They did not believe in the immortality of the soul nor a bodily resurrection. Some scholars believe they were an offshoot of the Sadducees, who held similar beliefs.

Chiasm—a literary device using inverted parallelism, in which concepts are repeated in reverse order.

Covenant (בְּרִית)—literally means *to cut*, referring to ancient sacrificial rites that formed part of traditional formal ceremonies that formalized binding agreements between two parties.

Deconstruction—a term used popularly today to describe the process of critically examining one's beliefs.

Derek (דרך)—Hebrew for path, way, or road. *Derek* can be used to describe a literal path or a metaphorical manner of living.

Essenes—Jewish sect which began in the 2nd century BC when a group of priests left Jerusalem, due to the corruption they perceived in the priesthood, to live a life devoted to faithfully preparing for the Messiah's arrival. They are held to be the writers or copyists of the Dead Sea Scrolls.

Ethnarch—ruler of an identifiable ethnic group who is not necessarily seen as a king or governor. In Biblical times, this role would often fall to the High Priests to represent the Jewish people in the absence of a king.

Exegesis—method of interpretation that explains how to understand a particular Bible section and how that section fits into a larger coherent narrative.

Gezerah shavah—literally means 'equal category' or 'similar decree' and is one seven principles of interpretation developed by Rabbi Hillel. A related phrase meaning *to cut from the same block* describes comparing similar words or phrases used in different verses.

Halak (הלך)—Hebrew for *to walk*, but also has the connotation of *to obey* as in to walk with, alongside, in agreement and partnership.

Hasidim—thought to be a subsect of the Pharisee movement known for their piety and practice of Torah.

Hebraism—a Hebrew idiom or expression.

Hellenism—refers to character and nature of Greek culture. Within the Biblical context, Hellenism is in contrast to Jewish way of life.

Hermeneutics—specific methodological principles of interpretation, especially the Bible.

Herodians—Jewish political group who supported Herod the Great and the Roman Empire.

Higher Textual Criticism—branch of literary studies examining the origins of author, date, location, and original audience. Higher criticism can also look at how subsequent generations read and understood the same material.

Khata (חטא)—Hebrew for *sin* in a general sense, as in to miss the mark or fail to reach one's goal.

Law of First Use—hermeneutical principle stating that when a word first appears in the Bible, its context and use provide the most fundamental and clearest presentation for understanding and interpretation.

Levant—French word meaning 'to rise'; when used in a geographic context it refers to the land that connects Egypt and Mesopotamia (Israel).

Lower Textual Criticism—branch of literary analysis seeking to recover the exact words and contemporary meaning of an original text.

Mishnah—means to 'study by repetition' in Hebrew and is also called the Oral Torah, a collection of rabbinic literature dating from the before the 2nd century BC to the end of the 2nd century AD. This six-part book compiled by Judah ha-Nasi collects Rabbinical debates on how to live out the *Torah*.

Mitzvah (מִצְוָה)—often translated into English as *command* or *commandments* in the plural, but its literal meaning, *direction to walk*, has an indispensable relational connotation.

Navi('im) (נְבִיא)—means prophet(s) in Hebrew.

Oral Law—considered by Orthodox Jews to be part of Mosaic Law, which was given to Moses at Mt. Sinai along with *Torah*. The Oral Law explains how to live out the *Torah*.

Ossuaries—'bone box' used for second burials in Jewish tradition, starting in the middle of the 2nd century BC and continuing through the 1st century AD.

Peretz (פרץ)—Hebrew meaning to 'breach', 'breakthrough', or 'burst forth'.

Pharisee—a Jewish religious group that emerged in the 2nd Temple Period who became experts in *Torah* and helped define what it meant to be Jewish.

Phileo (φιλέω)—a Greek word meaning 'to love' or 'to be a friend'.

Poleis/Polis (πόλις)—a Greek word meaning city, citadel, or community. Alexander the Great built *polis* all over the lands he conquered to spread Greek culture. The city structure and its amenities, which usually included temples, arenas, theaters, and gymnasiums, promoted a Hellenistic philosophy of life.

Prophet—Biblical prophets knew God's word and often had an encounter with God, during which God commissioned them to go to the people and recall to them their covenant partnership with God.

Protestant—is a term developed during the Reformation to describe the non-Catholic or Eastern Orthodox church.

Rasha (רָשָׁע)—Hebrew for *wickedness*; when said of a person, can be understood to mean someone who turns from God to walk their own path.

Rabbi—Hebrew for *teacher*. The Pharisees were called *rabbis* because they taught *Torah* to the people.

Remez—post-Biblical Hebrew word which means to 'hint' or 'suggest'. The word itself originates in the Middle Ages, but the teaching technique it refers to is practiced throughout the Bible, especially the New Testament. When a rabbi would quote a phrase of the Old Testament, the assumption would be their audience knew the rest of the phrase and context in which it was used, much like how we quote movie lines today.

Sadducee—high priestly class who controlled the Temple Mount and were responsible for all cultic activities of the Temple. Sadducees made money from religious pilgrims who traveled to Jerusalem and aligned themselves politically with Herod the Great and the Romans to maintain their positions of power.

Sanhedrin—derivative of the Greek word *synedrion,* meaning *council*. The Sanhedrin provided guidance and leadership locally as well as for the Jewish nation. Each town had its own council of elders, but in Jerusalem some scholars speculate there may have been as many as three different Sanhedrim. The one mentioned in the New Testament is the Great Sanhedrin and was comprised mostly of Sadducees. The number of members varied between 70 and 72 and was comprised of 65 Sadducees, 6 Pharisees, and the high priest.

Septuagint—Greek translation of the Hebrew Bible (*Tanakh*) dating from around the 3rd century BC. The academic abbreviation is LXX.

Skopos—Greek word meaning to look at, to observe, or to consider. Used in academics to examine the higher textual criticism of an author.

Stela/Stele—Vertical slab of stone, usually carved with inscriptions, erected to commemorate a notable event or the reign of a king.

Talmud—body of Jewish literature comprising the *Mishnah* and the *Germara* (a collection of rabbinical commentaries on the *Mishnah* from the 2nd century AD to the 5th century AD). We have two versions of the *Talmud*: the *Palestinian* or *Jerusalem Talmud*, and the later *Babylonian Talmud*.

Tanakh—Hebrew acronym or portmanteau from the three different sections of what Christians call the Old Testament: *Torah* (instructions or guide), *Nevi'im* (prophets), and *Ketuvim* (writings).

Torah (תּוֹרָה)—the first five books of the Old Testament. Jewish tradition holds these five books were given to Moses directly from God, which elevates them slight above other books in the *Tanakh*. Often translated into English as *law*, a fuller expression of the name *Torah*'s meaning is *direction* or *guide*.

Yada (יָדַע)—Hebrew for *to know*, which goes beyond mere intellectual understanding of facts to include first-hand, experiential knowledge.

Yarah (יָרָה)—Hebrew verb meaning to throw, to shoot, to teach, or to point out. It is the root word for *Torah*.

Yahweh (יהוה)—sacred name of the God of the Hebrews. Also called the *tetragrammaton*, a Greek word referring to the four Hebrew letters used to indicate the name in writing.

Zealots—a broad term for Jews who fought against the Romans and anyone who cooperated with them, including their fellow Jews.

Notes & References

Introduction

[1] Lois Tverberg and Bruce Okkema, *Listening to the Language of the Bible* (Holland, MI: En-Gedi Resource Center, 2004), 5.

Section One: The Ingredients

[1] Krister Stendahl, "Implications of Form-Criticism and Tradition-Criticism for Biblical Interpretation," *Journal of Biblical Literature* 77, no. 1 (1958): 38, https://doi.org/10.2307/3264328.

The Ingredient of Time

[1] William Smith, "Prophet," in *Smith's Bible Dictionary*, 1901, https://www.biblestudytools.com/dictionaries/smiths-bible-dictionary/prophet.html.
[2] Yevamot 49b; alluded to in Hebrews 11:37.
[3] Examples found in 1 Kings 13; 1 Kings 22:11; Jeremiah 28.
[4] We see this in the story of Joseph and how God sent him to Egypt to save his family. They all traveled down to Egypt to survive a famine. Joseph helped Egypt prepare for the famine, and everyone came to buy food from the Egyptians. Pharaoh ended up owning everything after seven years. (Genesis 37-46) This story is an exception rather than the rule.

The Ingredient of First-Century Context

[1] Marvin R. Wilson, *Our Father Abraham: Jewish Roots of the Christian Faith* (Grand Rapids, MI: Eerdmans, 1990), 112.
[2] 2 Shmuel Safrai, "Synagogue and Sabbath," *Jerusalem Perspective* (blog), November 1, 1989, https://www.jerusalemperspective.com/2424/.
[3] Athas, George, *Bridging the Testaments* (Grand Rapids, MI: Zondervan Academic, 2023), 230.
[4] Jordan J. Ryan, *The Role of the Synagogue in the Aims of Jesus* (Minneapolis, MN: Fortress Press, 2017), 1-20.
[5] Nathan Steinmeyer, "Archaeologists Discover New First-Century Synagogue in Magdala, Israel," Biblical Archaeology Society, December 15, 2021, https://www.biblicalarchaeology.org/daily/new-first-century-synagogue/.
[6] Shmuel Safrai et al., *The Jewish People in the First Century: Historical Geography, Political History, Social, Cultural and Religious Life and Institutions,*

vol. 1, Compendia Rerum Iudaicarum Ad Novum Testamentum. Section 1 (Assen: Van Gorcum, 1974), 968-69.

[7] This is based on Ezra 7:8, which records that Ezra arrived in Jerusalem in the seventh year of king Artaxerxes, while Nehemiah 2:1 has Nehemiah arriving in Jerusalem during Artaxerxes' twentieth year. If this king was Artaxerxes I (465-424 BC), then Ezra arrived in 458 and Nehemiah in 445 BC.

[8] Depending on your understanding of Biblical chronology, the book of Daniel and its story could have been written after Ezra and Nehemiah. Either way, Daniel's story takes place outside the land of Israel. Many scholars suggest the books of First and Second Chronicles were written post-exilically, along with the prophets Malichai, Zechariah, portions of Isaiah, and Daniel. Potential composition timelines have been suggested that extend into the late 3rd century BC.

[9] Irina Frasin, "Greeks, Barbarians and Alexander the Great: The Formula for an Empire," *Athens Journal of History* 5, no. 3 (May 22, 2019): 209-24, https://doi.org/10.30958/ajhis.5-3-4.

[10] Cyndi Parker, *Encountering Jesus in the Real World of the Gospels* (Peabody, MA: Hendrickson Publishers, 2021), 49.

[11] John H. Hayes and Sara R. Mandell, *The Jewish People in Classical Antiquity: From Alexander to Bar Kochba*, First Edition (Louisville, KY: Westminster John Knox Press, 1998), 25.

[12] Parker, *Encountering Jesus*, 49-50.

[13] See Ron Moseley, *Yeshua: A Guide to the Real Jesus and the Original Church* (Baltimore, MD: Messianic Jewish Publishers, 1998).

[14] Moseley, 104-5.

[15] Nehemia Gordon, *The Hebrew Yeshua vs. the Greek Jesus: New Light on the Seat of Moses from Shem-Tov's Hebrew Matthew*, 3rd edition (Chicago, IL: Hilkiah Press, 2005), xii.

[16] See Ann Spangler and Lois Tverberg, *Sitting at the Feet of Rabbi Jesus: How the Jewishness of Jesus Can Transform Your Faith*, Unabridged Edition (Grand Rapids, MI: Zondervan, 2018).

[17] Brad H. Young, *Meet the Rabbis: Rabbinic Thought and the Teachings of Jesus*, Illustrated edition (Grand Rapids, MI: Baker Academic, 2007) Read thoroughly Young's descriptions of both Shammai and Hillel, 190-94.

[18] Young, 190-94.

[19] Young cites Sanhedrin 88b and Hagigah 2:2, which are from the William Davidson translation of the Talmud called the *Sefaria*. This section outlines the significance of the different sections of the Talmud (the Mishnah and Gemara). He compares the rulings of the rabbis mentioned to Jesus's own interpretations.

[20] "Ethics of the Fathers," 1:1—Moses received the Torah on Sinai and delivered it over to Joshua. Joshua delivered it over to the elders, the elders to the prophets, and the prophets delivered it to the men of the great gathering together. They said three things: "Be deliberate in judgment, raise up many

disciples, and make a fence around Torah."

21 Brad Gray, "Rabbis and Disciples Pt 3: Being Like Jesus," Walking the Text, accessed July 23, 2024, https://walkingthetext.com/episode-119-rabbis-and-disciples-pt-3-being-like-jesus/.

22 Young, *Meet the Rabbis*, 12.

23 This belief is a "rabbinical tradition"—which is a polite way of saying we don't know when exactly this thought became mainstream. See Schwartz, Howard. *Tree of Souls: The Mythology of Judaism*. Oxford UP, 2007, 55. Also see One for Israel Ministry. "Did God Really Give an 'Oral Law' at Sinai? (Rabbinic Oral Law Debunked)," May 30, 2016. https://www.oneforisrael.org/bible-based-teaching-from-israel/did-god-also-give-moses-an-oral-law/.

24 Moseley, *Yeshua*, 129.

25 Young, *Meet the Rabbis*, 37.

26 "Healing on the Sabbath," First Fruits of Zion, accessed July 30, 2024, https://ffoz.org/torahportions/commentary/healing-on-the-sabbath.

The Ingredient of Responsibility

1 See Neil R. Lightfoot, *How We Got the Bible*, 3rd Edition, Revised and Expanded (Baker Books, 2010), 21.

2 Rendel Harris, "Hadrian's Decree of Expulsion of the Jews from Jerusalem," *Harvard Theological Review* 19, no. 2 (April 1926): 199-206, https://doi.org/10.1017/S0017816000007689.

3 Pamphili Eusebius, *The History of the Church*, trans. Arthur Cushman McGiffert, vol. 1, Nicene and Post-Nicene Fathers 2 (Buffalo, NY: Christian Literature Publishing, 1890), https://www.newadvent.org/fathers/2501.htm;

see also John F. Fink, "The Early Christian Church in Jerusalem," Franciscan Foundation for the Holy Land, January 13, 2014, https://ffhl.org/early-christian-church-jerusalem/;

and Richard Baukham, "The Relatives of Jesus," *Themlios*, January 1996, https://www.thegospelcoalition.org/themelios/article/therelatives-of-jesus/.

4 Kenneth Scott Latourette, *A History of Christianity, Vol. 1: Beginnings to 1500*, First Edition (Prince Press, 1997).

5 See John Dominic Crossan, *The Historical Jesus: The Life of a Mediterranean Jewish Peasant*, Reprint Edition (NY: HarperOne, 2010), in which Crossan presents the same research discussed in his documentary.

6 Kate Murphy, *You're Not Listening: What You're Missing and Why It Matters*, Reprint Edition (NY: Celadon Books, 2021), 78-88.

7 Kim Phillips, "Following the Footnotes: The Masoretic Text," Tyndale House, Cambridge, April 11, 2023, https://tyndalehouse.com/explore/articles/the-masoretic-text/.

8 Hayes and Mandell, *The Jewish People in Classical Antiquity*, 85-93; also see Flavius Josephus, *The Wars of the Jews or History of the Destruction of*

Jerusalem, trans. William Whiston (Project Gutenberg), Chapter 8, accessed August 6, 2024, https://www.gutenberg.org/files/2850/2850-h/2850-h.htm.

[9] Israel Knohl, *The Messiah before Jesus: The Suffering Servant of the Dead Sea Scrolls*, trans. David Maisel, First Edition (Berkeley, CA: U California P, 2002), 56-62.

[10] "Learn About the Scrolls," The Leon Levy Dead Sea Scrolls Digital Library, accessed July 25, 2024, https://www.deadseascrolls.org.il/learn-about-the-scrolls/introduction.

[11] Sidnie White Crawford, "Has Every Book of the Bible Been Found Among the Dead Sea Scrolls?," *Bible Review* 12, no. 5 (October 1996), https://library.biblicalarchaeology.org/article/has-every-book-of-the-bible-been-found-amongthe-dead-sea-scrolls/.

[12] Lightfoot, *How We Got the Bible*, 136.

[13] Jewish refugees fleeing the chaos of the Roman destruction of Jerusalem at the conclusion of the Bar Kokhba revolt (AD 132-35) hid in these caves. *See* Joan E. Taylor, "Secrets of the Copper Scroll," *Biblical Archeology Review* 45, no. 4 (October 2019), https://library.biblicalarchaeology.org/article/secrets-of-the-copper-scroll/.

[14] Bart D. Ehrman, *Misquoting Jesus: The Story Behind Who Changed the Bible and Why*, Reprint edition (NY: HarperOne, 2007), 1.

[15] Ehrman, 89.

[16] Ehrman, 5.

[17] Wayne Grudem, *Systematic Theology: An Introduction to Biblical Doctrine* (Grand Rapids, MI: Zondervan Academic, 2004), 90.

The Ingredient of Reading Like the Original Audience

[1] Ehrman, 11

[2] Luke 18:12. *See* Anthony J. J. Saldarini, *Pharisees, Scribes, and Sadducees in Palestinian Society: A Sociological Approach*, New Edition (Grand Rapids, MI: Eerdmans, 2001); Jacob and Neusner and Bruce D. Chilton, eds., *In Quest of the Historical Pharisees* (Waco, TX: Baylor UP, 2007), 128; Safrai et al., *The Jewish People in the First Century*, 1:816.

[3] Even today, Israel shuts down from Friday afternoon until Saturday evening.

[4] Shabbat 53b.

[5] My personal background prompts me to ask this question. I grew up on a farm with apple trees near the road. It was commonplace to see cars pull over so their passengers could take an apple or two off our trees. That's called "stealing." My initial reaction is to think the disciples are stealing the farmer's grain.

[6] W Ewing, "Bible Map: Nob," in *Bible Atlas* (Bible Hub, 2024 2004), https://bibleatlas.org/nob.htm.

[7] We have no record of what happened to Kileab, David's second-born.

[8] In Jewish law, the principle of *pikuach nefesh* (פיקוח נפש) states that saving a life takes precedence over almost any other religious rule, including the Ten Commandments of the *Torah*.

[9] David N. Bivin, "Medieval Jargon on First-Century Lips," *Jerusalem Perspective* (blog), July 1, 1999, https://www.jerusalemperspective.com/1898/.

The Ingredient of Knowing Yourself

[1] "Five gospels record the life of Jesus. Four you will find in books, and one you will find in the land they call Holy. Read the fifth gospel and the world of the four will opened to you." This quote is attributed to St. Jerome, who lived in the 4th century AD, but the quote's exact origins remain unknown.

[2] Professor Jim Monson's quote is often repeated throughout the halls of Jerusalem University College.

[3] quoted in Plato, *Theaetetus*, trans. Benjamin Jowett (Project Gutenberg), https://www.gutenberg.org/files/1726/1726-h/1726-h.htm.

[4] Marsha L. Dutton and Patrick T. Gray, *One Lord, One Faith, One Baptism: Studies in Christian Ecclesiality and Ecumenism in Honor of J. Robert Wright* (Grand Rapids, MI: Eerdmans, 2006), 32.

[5] We can get ourselves stuck in a narrative. The stories we tell ourselves run on a loop in our heads, but do our stories reflect reality? Chris Bruno, CEO of ReStory Institute, addresses this issue when he says: "Children are great recorders of our history, but terrible interpreters of it." The stories we tell ourselves can determine how we feel about the present as well as shape our future. Our narratives can limit what we think is possible by misinterpreting our past and labeling ourselves and others. We are dynamic human beings, capable of incredible resilience, able to adapt, heal, forgive, and live connected to God, ourselves, and others. An outsider's perspective is often helpful to provide another perspective on how to interpret our stories. *See* ReStory Counseling. "ReStory Institute." Accessed October 16, 2024. https://www.restory.life/restory-institute.

[6] E. Randolph Richards and Brandon J. O'Brien, *Misreading Scripture with Western Eyes: Removing Cultural Blinders to Better Understand the Bible* (Downers Grove, IL: InterVarsity Press, 2012), 12.

[7] Johnson, Susan M. *Hold Me Tight: Seven Conversations for a Lifetime of Love* (New York: Little, Brown & Co, 2008), 26.

[8] Ben Witherington III, *The Problem with Evangelical Theology: Testing the Exegetical Foundations of Calvinism, Dispensationalism, and Wesleyanism* (Waco, TX: Baylor UP, 2005), 1-18.

[9] Jayson Georges, *The 3D Gospel: Ministry in Guilt, Shame, and Fear Cultures* (Timē Press, 2023).

[10] Young, *Meet the Rabbis*, 34.

[11] Alfred Edersheim, *The Temple: Its Ministry and Services as They Were at the Time of Jesus Christ* (Chicago, IL: Arcadia Press, 2019), 58-62.
[12] Edersheim, 19-36.
[13] Edersheim, 113.

The Ingredient of How We Understand History

[1] "Paul Revere's Engraving of the Boston Massacre, 1770," Gilder Lehrman Institute of American History, accessed July 9, 2024, https://www.gilderlehrman.org/historyresources/spotlight-primary-source/paul-reveres-engraving-boston-massacre-1770.
[2] David McCullough, *John Adams* (NY: Simon & Schuster, 2004), 66-68.
[3] I recommend essays on the philosophy of history by Jordan J. Ryan in the appendix to his book *The Role of the Synagogue*.
[4] A discovery by British diplomat Henry Austin Layard in the 1830s sent shock waves around the world. He found the palace of the Assyrian King Sennacherib located in Nineveh (present-day Mosul, Iraq). Layard unearthed wall reliefs in Sennacherib's palace depict his conquering of Lachish, one of the forty-six cities he destroyed on his way to deal with King Hezekiah (2 Kings 18 & 19). This discovery matched the history chronicled extensively in the Bible about a campaign to invade Judah around 700 BC, which ended in a failed siege of Jerusalem. The wall reliefs give the impression of a military success. However, the Bible tells us that the military campaign ended in a stunning defeat for Assyria. Sennacherib's account indirectly admits but smoothly glosses over his failure to take Jerusalem. Public relations might be the second-oldest profession! *See* Hoerth, Alfred J. *Archaeology and the Old Testament*. Grand Rapids, MI: Baker Academic, 2003, 347-53.
[5] Robert W. Funk, *The Gospel of Jesus According to the Jesus Seminar* (Santa Rosa, CA: Polebridge Press Westar Institute, 1999).
[6] Again, a quote from Paul Wright.
[7] In the 1830s Edward Robinson, a linguistic scholar, traveled to Palestine with the goal of identifying biblical locations. The Bible as a historical document served him well as he successfully located many biblical sites. *See* Edward Robinson and Eli Smith, *Biblical Researches in Palestine and the Adjacent Regions: A Journal of Travels in the Years 1838 and 1852*, Reprint edition, vol. 1 (Cambridge UP, 2015).
[8] Gordon Govier, "Biblical Archaeology's Top 10 Discoveries of 2018," Christianity Today, December 27, 2018, https://www.christianitytoday.com/news/2018/december/biblicalarchaeology-top-10-discoveries-2018-israel.html.
[9] Hazael, king of the Arameans revolted against Jehoram king of Israel (as predicted by the prophet Elisha in 2 Kings 8:12). Joram convinces his nephew Ahaziah, king of Judah, to form an alliance to defeat Hazael. They met on the

battlefield at Ramoth-Gilead, where Joram was wounded (2 Kings 8:28-29). He fled to Jezreel to recover only to be killed by his rival Jehu (2 Kings 9:14-37) who also wounded Ahaziah who later died as well.

[10] *The Lost Tomb of Jesus*, Documentary (Eggplant Picture & Sound, 2007). See also: James D. Tabor and Simcha Jacobovici, *The Jesus Discovery: The Resurrection Tomb That Reveals the Birth of Christianity* (NY: Simon & Schuster, 2012); Simcha Jacobovici and Charles Pellegrino, *The Jesus Family Tomb: The Discovery, the Investigation, and the Evidence That Could Change History* (NY: HarperOne, 2007).

[11] Fiction author James A. Michener astutely highlights the potential for confusing information to confound archaeologists' interpretations in his novel *The Source*. The story follows an archaeological team digging in Israel, and each chapter represents a stratum of history. In one chapter, a family heirloom that had been kept for hundreds of years was buried in the Tel, only to be discovered later by archaeologists in a stratum that did not match its timeline. Many factors can make interpreting archaeological finds confoundingly difficult.

[12] Tel-Aviv University, "A Glimpse into the Wardrobe of King David and King Solomon, 3000 Years Ago," phys.org, accessed July 9, 2024, https://phys.org/news/2021-01-glimpsewardrobe-king-david-solomon.html.

[13] "El Araj Excavation Project," *The Center for the Study of Ancient Judaism & Christian Origins* (blog), August 14, 2023, https://www.elarajexcavations.com.

[14] You can find several lectures by Dr. Notley providing more details on YouTube.

The Ingredient of How We Communicate

[1] This is a composite definition put together by Google's AI overview, drawing from archived pages of the *Oxford English Dictionary* and other sources.

[2] Gene Edward Veith, *Postmodern Times: A Christian Guide to Contemporary Thought and Culture* (Wheaton, IL: Crossway, 1994).

[3] Paul Smith, "The Wonder and Weirdness of Postmodernism," Integral Christian Network, June 4, 2022, https://www.integralchristiannetwork.org/writings/2022/6/4/the-wonder-andweirdness-of-postmodernism.

[4] I realize that the revelations of Mr. Zacharias' hurtful and abusive actions can cause a visceral reaction simply to reading his name. His sins were egregious. At the same time, God gave him an amazing mind. His sinful actions, even though they taint our memory of the man, do not diminish his intellect or the profound truths about God that he shared. I'm not acting as an apologist for him, certainly not defending his actions. But I have to acknowledge that his work helped me grow intellectually and spiritually. I was upset and deeply disappointed when the news broke about his failures. I apologize if reading his name is triggering or offensive for you.

[5] Ronald Reagan, "Address to the National Association of Evangelicals" (Sheraton Twin Towers Hotel, Orlando, FL, March 8, 1983), https://www.youtube.com/watch?v=FcSm-KAEFFA.

Section Two: Reading with Different Eyes

Speed Bumps

[1] Michael S. Heiser, *Brief Insights on Mastering Bible Study: 80 Expert Insights, Explained in a Single Minute* (Grand Rapids, MI: Zondervan, 2018), 96.

[2] John had challenged the tetrarch of Galilee on the legitimacy of his marriage to Herodias, his brother Philip's ex-wife (Matthew 14:3). Notley, in a JUC lecture in spring 2024, explained the issue here is not divorce, but that in Jewish law you can't marry someone with whom you had an affair. Divorce and remarriage were permissible; they just could not be premeditated. See also Young, *Meet the Rabbis*, 55-56.

[3] R. Steven Notley, "ONLINE HIST 6/469 Jesus and His Jewish World," Jerusalem University College, n.d., https://juc.edu/academics/course-descriptions/course/jesus-jewish-world/.

[4] Brad H. Young, *Jesus the Jewish Theologian*, Reissue edition (Grand Rapids, MI: Baker Academic, 1993), 49-74. Young dedicates a whole chapter to this one passage. Both he and Notley were students of David Flusser at Hebrew University in Jerusalem.

[5] Young, 54.

[6] Notley explains at length the differing view of when the kingdom of heaven would come. Some believed in a two-stage coming of the kingdom: The Messiah's arrival followed by judgment. This perspective can be found in the writings of the Qumran Community. A traditional rabbinic view involved a three-stage process, with the middle part being the Messianic age. Notley, 306-7.

[7] A concurrent belief was that this figure could also be Moses. Notley explained in a lecture that this interpretation is based on Genesis 20:23.

[8] Visit the Jerusalem Perspective website if you would like to do a deep dive on this: David N. Bivin and Joshua N. Tilton, "The Kingdom of Heaven Is Increasing," *Jerusalem Perspective* (blog), October 25, 2018, https://www.jerusalemperspective.com/17478/.

[9] Notley, "The Kingdom of Heaven," 292-93.

[10] Notley, 293.

[11] Young, *Jesus the Jewish Theologian*, 52.

[12] Both Notley and Young make this point.

[13] Kenneth Bailey, *Jesus Through Middle Eastern Eyes: Cultural Studies in the Gospels* (Downers Grove, IL: IVP Academic, 2008), 397.